MILITANT
NORMALS

MILITANT
NORMALS

How Regular Americans
Are Rebelling Against the Elite
to Reclaim Our Democracy

KURT SCHLICHTER

**CENTER
STREET**

NEW YORK NASHVILLE

Center Street
Hachette Book Group
1290 Avenue of the Americas, New York, NY 10104

centerstreet.com

twitter.com/centerstreet

First Edition: October 2018

Center Street is a division of Hachette Book Group, Inc. The Center Street name and logo are trademarks of Hachette Book Group, Inc.

The publisher is not responsible for websites (or their content) that are not owned by the publisher.

The Hachette Speakers Bureau provides a wide range of authors for speaking events. To find out more, go to www.HachetteSpeakersBureau.com or call (866) 376-6591.

Library of Congress Cataloging-in-Publication Data has been applied for.

ISBNs: 978-1-5460-8195-1 (hardcover), 978-1-5460-8194-4 (ebook)

Printed in the United States of America

LSC-C

10 9 8 7 6 5 4 3 2 1

To my wife, Irina, American and Normal by choice

Contents

Introduction

The whole idea behind this book is to give the reader a simple and coherent explanation for why American society has become so polarized over the last few decades, and during the last few years in particular. It is not meant to be a dreary slog. It is not a political science treatise. You will not find academic theories or a lot of citations and footnotes. That is just one of several reasons that no college student will ever see this book show up on his syllabus.

The primary reason is that it is entirely sympathetic to Normal Americans and their struggle to reclaim what belongs to them—the United States of America.

So, this book is not strewn with the kind of jargon I learned as a poli sci major. I hate jargon. It is one of the many tools that experts tend to use to make their areas of expertise seem more complex and difficult than they really are, thereby making themselves indispensable. What's happened and is happening now in our country is not that difficult to understand. My purpose is to provide a clear, uncomplicated way of thinking about what is going on so the reader can more effectively exercise his or her birthright—sovereignty. I hope I have done that.

This book was written for Normal Americans. Note the capitalization—the term *Normal* appears throughout the book, and the concept is important. One way to understand American society today is to see it divided into two general classes, an Elite and the Normals. The Elite are those people, the experts, who run the day-to-day operations of society's institutions—like the government, the media, academia, and Hollywood. But today, America's Elite also includes those who merely identify with the values and ideology of the Elite. You don't actually have to be elite to be Elite, and the consequences of that low bar to entry explain a lot about why the Elites are so upset that the Normals elected a guy like Donald Trump.

The only real qualification for joining America's modern Elite is to choose to affiliate with the Elite. The guy who runs Goldman Sachs? He's Elite. But so is the twenty-three-year old dude with the goatee and knit cap spending all afternoon in the Starbucks tapping away on his iPad Pro, sipping a cruelty-free green tea as he tweets "TRUMP RUSSIA TREASON!" at conservatives on Twitter.

Let me reiterate something. Being in the American Elite has nothing to do with actually being elite, as we typically understand that word. You don't have to be special to affiliate with the Elite. To the extent our Elite is a meritocracy, it is a meritocracy without merit—and without a willingness to accept accountability when it fails to perform adequately. If the last thirty years have taught us anything, it is that.

To be Elite today, you just have to decide that you aren't like regular people.

The Normals are everyone else.

The Normals cede day-to-day control of the operations of society's institutions to the experts. Those experts and those who identify with them are the Elite. The Normals would happily let the Elite do what the Elite does and focus on living their own lives if the Elite would both perform competently and not subject those it is supposed to be serving to an escalating series of petty oppressions—and some not so petty oppressions.

Now, those are very broad generalizations, but generalizations are useful. Not every member of the Elite will precisely conform to the general characteristics of the Elite, nor every Normal precisely conform to the general characteristics of the Normals. But in general, these generalizations are generally sound.

Within each broad caste you will find further divisions. While most of the Elite holds to a center-left political ideology—enough so that sometimes as you read this book you will see that it is almost identical—there are members of the Elite who lean to the right. It gets interesting when class loyalty clashes with ideology, and you often see people prioritize the premises and assumptions of their class over their alleged political ideology.

That's where the tiresome Never Trump contingent comes in. When you see alleged conservative and noted cruise shiller Bill Kristol tweet about how he hopes the mandarins in the bureaucracy will step in to neutralize the policy choices of our elected president, you see someone ditching his putative conservatism in favor of class solidarity. And it probably does not hurt that if his fellow Elites were to succeed, Captain Kristol and his crew would stand to return to the positions of relative prestige they held before the Normals tired of Conservative, Inc.'s inability (or unwillingness) to win and elected Donald Trump.

Normals is not a synonym for *conservative*. The Normals tend to be center right, if you have to place them on the political spectrum, but that's mostly because traditional American values like faith, family, and patriotism have become identified with center-right politics as liberals have either stopped defending them or abandoned them altogether. However, Normals do embrace some concepts that ideological conservatives (like me) consider heresies, such as doubts about "free trade." Further, some Normals are on the left—there were Normals who supported Bernie Sanders. They feel the high and mighty are giving them a raw deal, and many of them chose Trump over Hillary Clinton for just that reason.

The Normals embrace traditional Main Street values—faith, family, and patriotism—and a sense that America and Americans must be the priority. This puts Normals in conflict with an Elite that has eschewed traditional patriotism for at best a kind of ironic detachment from outright manifestations of it—the "flag waving" they find so *déclassé*—and at worst, an idea that they are "citizens of the world," immune from the crude nationalism you will find should you be forced to venture west of I-95. When your central image of yourself is not as an "American," then why would you put either America's or Americans' interest before anywhere or anyone else's?

The tension between the Elite and the Normals arose largely because today's Elite no longer shares such core values (even if, like the Kennedys, they merely pretended to do so for public consumption), and because the Elite no longer respects the Normals as the reservoir of those values. Back in the forties, Hollywood made movies extolling the Normals as the source of those values— *It's a Wonderful Life* (1946), anyone?—but no longer. Starting in the sixties, the young members of the Elite began to reject these traditional values. This sparked a conflict both with the older Elite *and* with the Normals, who struck back in the guise of Nixon's "Silent Majority."

The Elite today are the heirs of those Elite rebels from the sixties. But unlike previous generations of the Elite, this generation is imbued with the anti-Western, Marxist poison they learned in academia thanks to the faculty acolytes of the Frankfurt School. (For a closer look at those monsters, see Michael Walsh's essential books *The Devil's Pleasure Palace: The Cult of Critical Theory and the Subversion of the West* [New York: Encounter Books, 2017] and *The Fiery Angel: Art, Culture, Sex, Politics, and the Struggle for the Soul of the West* [New York: Encounter Books, 2018].)

And because of this, combined with their own class prejudices and the temptation to preserve and enhance the privilege and power that comes with their status, the Elite has allowed itself to believe that the Normals are mindless, racist bigots bewitched with religious nonsense and an irrational love of firearms. Class membership has thereby become a moral test, and the Normals fail.

Today's Elite hates the Normals—*hates them*—and it acts accordingly.

Except the Normals have noticed. And they are starting to hate the Elite right back.

MILITANT
NORMALS

CHAPTER ONE

The Sleeping Giant Awakens, and Boy, Is He Pissed Off

I did not start out as a Donald Trump fan. That actually puts it mildly—I started out as a hardcore Trump opponent, though I was never Never Trump. I would have voted for pretty much anyone else before checking the box for that monstrous harridan Hillary Clinton. I had proved that in the past—I voted for John McCain and Mitt Romney, though they were each unsatisfactory in their own way. I drew the line at Jeb! Bush, though—I would have refused to vote for either Sr. Please Clap or Felonia Milhous von Pantsuit. Instead, I would have spent election night consoling myself with a full-bodied California cabernet while I watched Fox report on what America did when faced with the political equivalent of choosing between a cold sore and leprosy.

You see, I was an ideological conservative. I dug the ideas, the wonderful mix of individual freedom and ordered liberty envisioned by the Founders. I had for as long as I could remember. I was deep in the conservative movement, and joined up in the mid-eighties when I fought Marx-loving ex-hippie professors among the eucalyptus trees at the University of California, San Diego, while writing for its conservative campus paper, *California Review*. I read *National Review* and the *American Spectator*, because if you were a conservative back in the day, you had nowhere else to score your conserva-fix but *National Review* and the *American Spectator*.

So, when Donald Trump came down that escalator with his latest wife and announced he was running, I wasn't paying attention because the whole idea was ridiculous. Hell, I had been laughing at Trump since reading *Spy* magazine thirty years ago. I even remembered the whole tiny hands thing from back then. I was vaguely aware he had a television show in the 2000s, but I never took him seriously. Why would any conservative? Trump was a novelty act, a joke distracting from the seriousness of the mission to stop the progressive onslaught.

We were losing, and our country was at stake. And some people were putting their money on the host of *The Apprentice*?

Nope. Count me out.

————

So, like most hardcore cons, I ignored Donald Trump and focused on the real candidates. You know, the ones who could actually win.

Those would be the ones Trump eventually mopped the floor with.

Those guys.

Pretty soon Trump was running at the top of the polls, besting sixteen other candidates, and I was shaking my head. It baffled me, and many like me. We Republicans were running a bunch of accomplished, intelligent, truly conservative candidates, as well as Jeb!, and they were all losing to . . . this guy?

Really?

Who the hell was supporting Trump anyway? Where were these people? I sure didn't know any of them. By then I had recently retired as an Army reservist, and I was mostly hanging around other Los Angeles lawyer types on the western edge of Los Angeles. The rest of my time was spent with doctrinaire conservative activists. Not a lot of diversity. The upshot was that I wasn't around many normal Americans.

And like my conservative comrades, I had forgotten about them.

That was the problem, and I didn't even know it. I had forgotten about the very people who fueled our movement, who fueled our country, figuratively and literally.

Who are they anyway?

These are the normal Americans, the Normals, the people who made America into what we think of when we think of America. They built this country, and they defended it. They grow the food and truck it to our Trader Joe's. They don't unfriend people on Facebook for having wrong thoughts, and they aren't focused on perfecting their neighbors through the power of social justice. They just want to live their lives in a stable society, meaning they don't want to be robbed walking down the sidewalk, and they want to be shown a little respect.

What they are not defined by are color, sex, religion, or even sexual orientation. They don't inform you of their preferred pronouns when they meet you and shake your hand. They don't obsess on those things, like their alleged betters do.

They don't read policy papers, and they find politics a necessary evil. Most don't live in big cities on the coasts. Most don't drive Priuses or bike to work. And most don't eat kale, to their credit—if you need a reason to doubt the eliteness of the Elite, you need only cite its inexplicable fondness for salads made with that noxious weed.

Normals don't think about their carbon footprint, mostly because they think that if Channel 7 Eyewitness News Action Weather's weatherman Sunwood "Sunny" Blueskies is hit and miss about the chance of rain next Monday, nobody has an actual clue about what the weather will be in the year 2118. They'll roll the climate dice and keep driving their Ford Explorer with the third row of seats that holds most of their kid's soccer team, thank you very much.

They just want to live their lives freely, while having a say in their government and culture. They do not want to do politics 24/7 like I do, and maybe you do. They would prefer to leave that to the Elite to do, the self-appointed caretakers of the duties of running the country at the macro level.

But what they are done tolerating is an uppity Elite that has screwed up its macro task of running society's institutions yet has taken unto itself the job of micro-regulation of Normals' lives. You see, the Elite finds the Normals morally deficient and thinks it has to correct them.

The Elite is wrong.

Normals want to be able to support their families without being disrespected by Elitist snobs and without being exploited by the ruling class. They prefer their kids not get killed fighting wars the politicians who send them do not consider important enough to win.

And in 2016, Donald Trump was the only candidate really talking to them.

Hell, he was the only one who acknowledged the Normals even existed.

But I didn't see that.

Nor did the vast majority of my fellow ideological conservatives. Most of us had signed on with the Elite—yes, conservatives can be part of that caste, though they are not the majority—and we had adopted many of their tribal prejudices and preconceptions. But we forgot about the people whose hard work and, sometimes, blood let us be Elite.

Because he had no respect for the things I thought he should have respect for, like ideology, Trump set off my charlatan detector big time. His embrace of conservative heresies, like protectionism and not bombing the shit out of anyone who looked at us sideways, did not impress me. This guy wasn't a Republican, not like the ones I knew, not like the kind I was. He was certainly not like Saint Ronald—one of my greatest memories was seeing Reagan's last campaign appearance ever in 1984 at a shopping center in San Diego just before he pummeled that hapless sap Walter Mondale in the first presidential election in which I ever voted. But while Trump may not have had the conservative ideological rigor Reagan had, he did have something else.

He connected with people. Just not with people like me.

In fact, he did the opposite. By going all in on the Normals, Trump drew the wrath of the Elite, this time including both the majority on the left and the minority on the right. Except instead of being crushed by the Elite, like Mitt Romney was or Jeb! would have been, Trump reveled in the Elite's hatred. He fed on it. He wore it like a medal.

My primary season *Townhall.com* columns about Trump were scathing, and pretty soon CNN was calling me in as a coherent conservative who would reliably trash Trump. I didn't mind—I was simply saying what I sincerely felt, and I thought it was my sacred duty to talk my fellow Republicans out of their growing insanity. The day of the debate in Las Vegas on December 15, 2015, I sat on an outside set with CNN's Brooke Baldwin, cracking her up with my latest column about how Trump was the GOP's crazy girlfriend—sure, she's fun for now, but one morning you're going to wake up alone with the bed on fire plus your credit cards and the keys to your Porsche gone, if not your kidneys.

We laughed. Then that night, onstage, Trump slaughtered the opposition.

Trump's message was resonating. Not yet with me, but with others. And he was saying some good things, too, things I liked. While other candidates were dancing around the idea of cracking down on illegal immigration, if not embracing all-out amnesty, Trump was all in for enforcing the law. And I had to admit, the idea of not getting into any more wars where we were not willing to do what was necessary to win was starting to appeal to me. Killing bad guys is one thing, and I'm all for it. Killing our own guys because we are playing footsie with our enemies and tying our boys' hands with rules of engagement that put them in danger? I had deployed twice, and there was a lot to be said for win or go home.

It all came together for me a week later on December 22, 2015. A CNN producer contacted me at the last minute to come on and do a segment about Trump, of course, because CNN never talked about anything else except Trump. It would be a short Skype hit from my office instead of up in Hollywood at the Sunset Boulevard studio, which was fine. I hated that drive through Los Angeles traffic—everywhere is over an hour away from everywhere else in Los Angeles. I did not ask the specific topic because I didn't really care. Whatever they pitched me, I'd hit.

So, I threw on a jacket and tie and sat down, hooked up on Skype, and there was Don Lemon guest hosting. I never liked the little weasel much, but whatever. He was just another light-weight host to joust with on a Tuesday morning. There was also a Trump supporter on the panel, a nice lady who would barely have a chance to speak, and then me, the designated Trump hitter.

Lemon then started up with the Trump atrocity du jour. Every day, something was The Worst Thing Ever. That tradition continues to the present.

That fateful day, The Worst Thing Ever was that Trump had characterized Hillary's loss to Barack Obama in the 2008 primary as her having been "schlonged." Yeah, Trump uttered a minor Yiddish vulgarity. Colorful and evocative, sure, but from Lemon's demeanor and breathless outrage, this was apparently the greatest crime any man had ever committed in the history of ever. Lemon fulminated for a bit, and then he threw it to me to comment.

But something snapped.

"Schlonged?"

I just didn't care.

I *couldn't* care.

And I told Don Lemon so. I explained to him that Trump uttering the word "schlonged" could not stir within me even the most rudimentary concern. I believe I suggested that only Dr. Stephen Hawking could calculate the inconceivably vast figure quantifying my lack of caring.

I simply refused to give a damn.

Lemon was stunned.

I was off narrative, and he struggled to wrangle me back into the herd. But I felt ornery, and I went further astray.

I mentioned that I especially couldn't care about Trump saying "schlonged" when Hillary Clinton was herself a notorious sex abuser enabler.

Oh, and I pointed out that Bill had used his intern as a walking humidor.

I think I pointed that out twice.

Lemon went nuts. Failing to deliver the Trump thumping I was so good at was bad, but to disrespect Her Majesty in such a colorful and memorable manner? Well, that was unforgiveable.

Lemon told me I couldn't talk about Hillary's history of covering up for her perv hubby. It was *verboten*.

Oh, really?

Now, I didn't go to war to come home to seek permission from the likes of Don Lemon to speak my mind, so I repeated my point because *the hell with Don Lemon.*

Things got a bit heated.

Suddenly, my Skype screen went blank.

Hmmm.

I thought it was a technical glitch—Skype television appearances are always hit and miss. But then a monotone voice came up from my speakers.

"You're clear." Then nothing. The connection closed.

CNN had hung up.

Hmmm again.

Usually the producer would tell me how awesome I was before clearing me. I figured she was probably just busy. I thought no more about it and started back to work on some legal brief when my iPhone went crazy.

Texts. Twitter direct messages. Emails.

It seemed Don Lemon had cut me off on-air. And the conservative world loved it.

I have never been back on CNN since, which saves me the nightmare drive. And getting cut off got me a bunch of media hits and a couple thousand new Twitter followers, so advantage Schlichter.

Yet, it seemed . . . odd. Why the overreaction? Things had gotten testy on the air before, but it was never a thing. Sure, I was hinting pretty graphically about Bill's Cohiba peccadillos, but if you've ever seen Lemon looking like he's half in the bag pawing at his co-hosts on CNN's New Year's Eve shows, you know he's no prude.

But this time I had, at least for a moment, disrupted the network's attempt to derail Trump, and its flunkies had freaked out. Then I realized why.

They were afraid of him.

———

But that was not the specific moment that I knew Trump could win. That was just one of many moments that were slowly opening me up to the possibility that *perhaps* Trump could win, that something was happening with the Trump movement that posed a profound threat to the status quo. To the Elite.

The moment I first knew Trump could win, that it was not just a theoretical possibility, occurred when my wife and I were talking to another couple in our Los Angeles beach-adjacent town. I'll mask their identities a bit to try and keep the identity of the gentleman who convinced me secret—if he were unmasked he might end up un-masculated. Literally.

It was in the midst of the primaries. We were out somewhere in town and met this other couple, your typical upper-middle-class SoCal people with good jobs, a nice but hugely overpriced house, and some kids they treat like royalty. The wife is a nice lady, but let's just say she was not a Trump fan. She was getting wound up. You know the drill. "Trump's a racist and sexist and a misogynist and hates women and Mexicans and blah blah blah."

I expect that even today, somewhere in her walk-in designer custom closet, she's got a gyno sombrero just waiting for the next ridiculous march of the unoppressed.

Anyway, I decided to let Irina deal with her—I preferred drinking my cabernet to being bombarded with her basic opinions. These were the same ill-formed, simplistic, and condescending bits of consensus leftist group-think that the establishment and its poodle media were dumping on all Americans every single day. Pure Elite drivel.

I took a sip and I pitied her husband. The poor guy. If she nattered and ranted like this to random people, I could only imagine the bombardment of grating Trump whining he endured day in and day out. I looked over at him standing silent out of her line of sight.

Then it happened. He did something, and I just knew.

He rolled his eyes.

Not hugely, not theatrically, but subtly.

She was droning on about Trump's myriad failings, and he rolled his eyes.

He was not yet completely broken.

He was rebelling.

He wasn't going to scream or shout, or get in her face. He wasn't going to say a word. No, he was just going to march into that voting booth, pull the curtain shut, and mark his secret ballot for whoever he damned well pleased regardless of what she thought.

He was just a Normal guy, and he wanted Trump.

Maybe he truly liked Trump, living vicariously through him as the candidate told off all of the kinds of people who sought to squash this average suburbanite dad. Maybe he hated Hillary, since he had to deal with the progeny of the movement that had turned The Smartest Woman Ever Was from a nice, repressed Goldwater Gal into a spiteful, repressed commie-lite crone. Or maybe he just wanted to flip his wife the bird without getting a shit-ton of grief and being cut off from the suburban booty.

Maybe it was all of them.

Regardless, he was going to tell her he voted for Hillary, but he was really going to pull that lever for Donald J. Trump because *the hell with you for telling me I can't.*

I knew then that Trump could win.

Could win. I wasn't certain of it, not even early on Election Day, that most glorious of days when Frau von Pantsuit's dreams died in such a public and humiliating way. I thought Trump *might* pull it out, with some luck and some divine intervention, but I was pretty certain we would be inaugurating another President Clinton. With her unique combination of malice, stupidity, and absolute certainty of her superior moral and intellectual standing, I gave that dizzy diva a fifty-fifty shot at pushing our country into a civil war.

But when it came to Hillary, the American people had other ideas.

Trump's voters, the Normals, were a lot like that husband. For a long time, they have been disrespected, taken for granted, and bossed around by their purported betters. Now they are done with it. Openly or covertly, they're down for a fight.

Typically, Normals aren't political, except when they have to be. They have better things to do, like their jobs and barbecues and anything else besides obsessing about other people using their proscribed pronoun. They just want to support their families, and be with them. They want to be able to count on a stable society where their families are safe on the streets, and they want a stable economy where their talent and hard work can get them ahead. And, instead of being needled by social justice warriors and smug late-night hosts about the faults liberals always seem to find in them, they want a modicum of respect.

But for so long, America's ruling caste—the Elite and its adherents in the media and academia—have failed to provide any of that. There was once an unspoken agreement with the Elite: You can be the Elite and do your Elite things and we won't pay much attention, but you have to do it well and let us live relatively undisturbed. If you do that, we're cool.

But the Elite didn't keep its end of the bargain, so we're not cool.

The Elite did not just fail to do its job running our institutions and providing us a stable society and economy, though it has failed to do those things. The Elite has decided to declare war on the people who make up the backbone of this country because it just cannot live knowing the Normals are out there living free and uncontrolled. And in doing so, the Elite ignited the conflict we are living through today.

The Elite decided they had to burn down the country to save it.

There was an economic war on the Normals. You saw it on your bank statement when you diligently saved for a rainy day, like responsible people do, and you scored a big 0.5 percent interest because the Fed is holding down the rates. The Elite loves low rates. But if you are saving for retirement, you can't tolerate that, so where do you have to put your money? In the market, which means you are giving your money to Wall Street, which means... the Elite.

Weird how that works out for the Elite and not for the Normals. But then, everything always works out for the Elite and not for the Normals.

How about illegal aliens? The Elite is unified on that, though for different reasons. The Democrat Elite like illegal immigration because they hope that these trespassers will import the same foolish leftist voting patterns that made their homelands into the shitholes they fled from. The Republican Elite loves the idea of a docile workforce that won't complain or get uppity because their big corporate donors love that idea. Heck, *everyone* loves illegal immigration—except Normals.

Normals are the ones who get hit-and-run by illegals driving without insurance and see the cop shrug as the laughing intruder drives away from the scene in his rickety Corolla. Normals are the ones who find that the jobs Americans won't do are really jobs Americans aren't allowed to do because someone who snuck up here from Guatemala will sweep floors for four dollars an hour under the table instead of demanding minimum wage plus employer payroll taxes. Normals are the ones who bury their kids when some MS-13 Dreamer caps them as part of his gang initiation.

Ted Cruz ran a brilliant campaign ad[1] created by the Madison

McQueen firm that pointed out how, if illegal aliens were taking jobs as trial lawyers, stockbrokers, and newspaper editorial writers, there would totally be an illegal alien crisis.

Oh, there would so totally be a crisis.

And then there is the condescension and contempt Normals endure at the hands of their betters, something made even more galling because our betters rarely turn out to actually be better. Barack Obama summed up the Elite's attitude toward Normals pretty well with his "bitter clingers" comment. But Hillary Clinton did it even better. Leveraging the political savvy and smarts for which she is known by those lacking both political savvy and smarts, in the midst of an election she felt compelled to call half of America "deplorables" for opposing her.

The punchline is that she still has no idea why she lost.

Maybe someone can interrupt her nightly Chardonnay guzzle and email her the 411 via her private server. She lost because Normals are tired of this crap.

They are tired of being treated as if they are stupid.

They are tired of being treated as if they are moral illiterates.

They are tired of being disrespected.

And they are especially tired of it being done to them by an Elite that has no foundation for considering itself elite other than its members consider themselves elite. What, exactly, is so damn elite about today's American ruling class? Does it have some sort of unbroken track record of success that we just haven't heard about?

Let's review some of the Elite's greatest hits from recent years.

Let's see . . . Iraq. The establishment begged us to trust them and, well, that went poorly.

How about the financial crisis of 2008? Normals didn't have

a lot to do with the levers of the economy, so that kind of leaves only one class to blame, doesn't it? But hey, don't worry. The Elite that caused the disaster got the bailouts. The Normals who didn't? Well, they got to fund the bailouts of the people who did.

Stagnant wages. Opioid crisis. Obamacare. Is it too much to ask that this meritocracy demonstrate a little merit once in a while?

If our Elite had achievements commensurate with its level of self-regard, there would be no Trump because we would already be living in Eden.

This is not the first time this kind of uprising has happened. There have been revolts by the Normals in the past. Most of the time, the Normals rise up, make their point, and go back to watching their kids play soccer or whatever they did in the past before America's youth was infected with foot-and-ball disease. In the late sixties, Richard Nixon called on the "Silent Majority" to help him (and the older Elite) beat back the hippies and the New Left when the cowed Democrat Party nominated George McGovern. The Normals answered, kicked ass, and then went back to bed.

The Normals roused themselves again at the end of the seventies with the tax revolt and the election of Ronald Reagan. Then they went back to sleep.

Ross Perot helped stir them a little, mostly unsuccessfully. Bill Clinton, for all his faults, is a master political operator, and he had grown up around Normals. He knew how to keep them if not happy at least from not getting particularly riled up. Remember, it was conservative activists who led the charge to impeach him, not Normals. Most Normal Americans knew he was a creep, but things were going okay, so "Meh."

Normals don't expect the Elite to be perfect. If the Elite delivers, it gets a lot more leeway when it misbehaves.

Then came the Tea Party in 2009, a direct response to the bailouts and Obamacare. The bipartisan establishment went all in to strangle the movement in its crib, and to some extent the Elite succeeded in temporarily driving the movement underground. But what was different this time was, unlike with Nixon or Reagan or even Bill Clinton, the Normals did not get what they wanted. And because they were never satisfied, and because they remained under constant attack, they never went back to sleep.

Instead, they came back again in 2016 demanding change, this time less politely, with red Donald Trump ball caps reading MAKE AMERICA GREAT AGAIN instead of pitchforks and torches.

The axis of American politics used to be really simple—"Left/ Right," with most folks clustered in the center. If you were a Democrat, you were generally left. If Republican, generally right. There was some overlap, but that one axis was a pretty effective metric for American politics.

Not anymore.

There's a new axis in town, and it's shaking things up. The new axis is best understood as "Elite/Normal." You could also call it "Establishment/Anti-Establishment," or maybe "Insider/ Outsider," and it crosses right over the old "Left/Right" axis to give a much more complex, but accurate, picture of American politics today.

It's about class.

It didn't used to be, because the Elite and the Normals both generally accepted and respected the same traditions and values.

They no longer do, and the distinguishing feature of our current situation is the permanent war of the Elite against the

Normals based on that schism. Throw in the failure of the Elite's institutions to meet the demands of the angry Normals, stir in social media tools that did not exist before, and you have a corresponding permanent mobilization by the Normals. The Elite backlash against the Normals' demands for relief was vicious, and therefore the Normals have grown more vicious in response—witness the widespread cheering when Trump bludgeons some establishment hack on Twitter.

The Elite started playing by new rules, and it should not have been a surprise to anyone that the Normals got behind someone who was a master of those new rules.

This battle of the castes explains some of what we have seen in the wake of Trump's success, especially some of the strange bedfellows we've observed. A number of Trump voters did not come to Trump from some other Republican—it's pretty hard to imagine someone digging Jeb! then thinking, "Well, no one clapped when he said please, so I guess I need another candidate...gee, Trump looks pretty similar." Some of Trump's voters came from Bernie Sanders, a socialist running as a Democrat Party member, a party which today itself seems to consist mostly of socialists.

Bernie was as much an outsider as Trump—the Democrats were just nicer to him when they lied, cheated, and stole the nomination away from him. Many of his voters cared much less about "Left/Right" than "More of the Same/Change." They figured Trump might deal the pain to the Elite, while Hillary would just bring down upon them more of the same misery they had been experiencing. They voted for Trump.

On the Republican side, you have pols much, much more interested in keeping business as usual as opposed to implementing the policies they paid lip service to back home in the sticks at election time. That's why their enemy often seems not to be the liberals across the aisle but the conservatives expecting them to vote like they promised, which tends to be how the Normals prefer. But at a certain point, establishment Democrats and Republicans—all members of the Elite—have more in common with each other than with their frustrated voters who are at the point where they just want to burn the whole mother down.

This can't continue. The sleeping giant is awake again, and it is really pissed off and is showing no signs of drowsiness. There's a fight going on between the bipartisan establishment committed to the status quo and the Militant Normals who want change. The stakes are enormous. There will be a resolution. Somebody has got to win. Which means somebody has got to lose.

The only question is, "Who?"

CHAPTER TWO

Who Are the Normals?

C all them the Normals.

Normals are the people who make America America, the ones who feed it and fuel it and drive it around, and who get up every day to take care of their families. They are the suckers who show up for jury duty without a sure-fire plan for getting kicked off the panel. They pay their taxes but get bitter about the deadbeats they see ahead of them in line at the Safeway buying cases of Dr Pepper with EBT cards. Yet, nonetheless, every year they faithfully and timely write their checks to Uncle Sam.

They are the ones who sign on the dotted line and end up in Third World hellholes with M4s shooting it out with the local religious fanatic/pederasts in wars they didn't ask for and that their leaders often have no plan for winning.

What do the Normals do for America? They merely offer their sweat, their money, and their blood. Most of the time, they do so without complaint. Yet, their alleged betters, that bipartisan meritocracy without merit that is America's Elite, still hates them.

Not merely has disdain for them.

Not only disrespects them.

Hates them.

That is the crux of the problem, and the genesis of this chaotic moment in history. America's Elite has morphed from a caretaker caste granted access to the levers of power to run things while everyone else goes about their lives into a self-serving guild that despises the very people whose interests it should be serving.

In the past, the Elite at least paid lip service to the centrality of the Common Man in the American political scheme of things. The Democrat Party was, at one time, proudly the Party of the Working Man. But today, it is proudly the Party of the Silicon Valley Zillionaire, the Brooklyn Hipster, the Bitter Middle-Aged Divorcee Who Teaches English in a Unionized Public School, the Hollywood Pervert, the *Vox* contributor, and the LGBTQKLHU&%! Activist Whose Pronouns Are "Xip" and "Xork."

The sliver of the Normals that the Elite approve of is the underclass—reliable votes and obedient serfs of the Elite. The Elite happily keeps them in line with bread and circuses. When it mentions them at all, it is to use them as a bludgeon—the underclass is, of course, the fault of the Normals. But so is everything.

The Republicans fetishized the Normals, too, in the sense that they at one time represented Main Street merchants, the yeoman farmers, and the upper middle class who were the backbone of the nation. The town Buick dealer, the local lawyer, the manager at Bethlehem Steel—these were the classic bourgeois Normals of the Republican base. But the Republicans also lost sight of their own constituents. Instead of Normals, the Republican Party began catering exclusively to the big-money donor types and to the puny know-it-alls of Conservative, Inc., that tiresome network of DC/NY-centered think tanks and publications that pushed a bunch of utopian ideas generated by a bunch of people who had done nothing in their life except go to college and write unread position papers while completing a fellowship at the Liberty Forum Coalition for Freedom.

This alienation between the parties and their core Normal constituencies increased as the bipartisan Elite not only cut the Normals out of their calculations and positioning but grew to hold the Normals in contempt. For the Democrats, Normals represented a hateful legacy of bigotry and reaction. For the Republicans, the Normals' parochial concerns interfered with business as usual. Both parties were happy to have Normals' votes and their tax dollars, but neither had any intention of actually letting the Normals have any kind of influence on what the Elite did with the power entrusted to it.

So it came to pass that by the 2016 campaign, both major parties were heading toward Election Day utterly oblivious to the fact that the Normals were seething. And the consequences of that oversight changed American history.

Today, at long last, the Normals are making themselves heard again, loudly and vigorously. It's not the first time. The Normals have gone by several names over the years, but at their core they have always been the same. They are nationalist and patriotic, with a hint of populism, and periodically infused with anger at an Elite that has totally failed to do its job. The Silent Majority of the Nixon years faded into the background well before Gerald Ford was sworn in. It arose again in the Tax Revolt of the late 1970s and in the election of Ronald Reagan. We saw it briefly stir itself on behalf of Ross Perot in 1992, but it was not until the Tea Party movement of the first term of Barack Obama that the Normals roared back to the forefront of American politics. That movement waned, but it did not go into hibernation. The Tea Party failed to change the Elite—or, rather, the Elite failed to change itself in response to the Tea Party—and the Normals rose again in 2016 in the most improbable election in the history of the United States.

The natural resting state of the Normals is a kind of rational apathy. They do not *want* to be focused on politics. They want to focus on family and faith and earning a living. Normals view politics as a marginally necessary evil, and prefer to cede that dirty job to the Elite. The Elite likes the power and prestige, and the ability to take a cut of the spoils, which come from overseeing the operations of our society's institutions. It is an arrangement that works—when the Elite does its job and minds its place.

But when necessary—when the Elite has failed to satisfy its part of the unspoken bargain—the Normals will revoke their political and cultural power of attorney, step back into the arena, and make their displeasure known.

That's what happened on November 8, 2016.

The Normals have risen again, but having made their point they are not withdrawing back into their private lives the way they did in the past. This rising is different. This time they *can't* go back to sleep again. The 24/7 news cycle and the presence of social media, along with the changed nature of the Elite, make that impossible. There is no down time; there is no longer any empty political space where nothing much happens and things just sort of flow along like a lazy river. Every day is a crisis, mostly because politicians and the media believe they benefit from crises. To sleep is to die, and the Normals know it. Like Michael Corleone in the abysmal *Godfather Part III* (1990), just when they think they're out, they get pulled back in.

So the Normals keep fighting. And now their complaints are being funneled through the bully pulpit that is the Oval Office—often via its occupant's Twitter account.

If you want to understand how you got President Donald Trump, you have to look at the people who chose President Donald Trump over sixteen other Republicans of various levels of establishment respectability, and over The Most Qualified Woman in the World.

The Normals elected President Donald Trump—or, arguably, they rejected everyone else. It is a distinction without a difference. They chose him, willingly. Here was a man with manifest personal failings, many ridiculously overblown—as we have seen, everything Trump is or does is, and must be, The Worst Thing Ever. Here was a man of uncentered ideology—a Republican sometimes, and Democrat others, and an Independent occasionally. Here was the least likely of presidents, a concept so ridiculous before it happened that it was famously a punchline in an episode of *The Simpsons*.

Yet, that's who the Normals picked. And that's the most graphic evidence of their displeasure with the current state of their country. Sometimes, it seems, you do have to burn down a village to save it, and sometimes you have to elect a Donald Trump president.

What would ever possess the Normals to do that?

———

To understand their motivations, you have to understand who the Normals are and what they have gone through in the last half-century of American history. You have to understand how empowering the Common Man went from being the solution to the problem. The focus on securing the freedom and prosperity of the Normals went from being the rationale for the United States to being an obstacle to the glory the Elite believes America can only achieve if it is fundamentally changed into a cosmopolitan, soft-socialist nanny state run by a transnational ruling class. Those short-sighted Normals, determined to assert their own interests and preferences, are a real problem for an Elite fixated on its own interests.

The Normals gave their everything to their country, and over time found their country with an increasingly detached and alien Elite at the helm, charting a course that ended up with Normal America crashing into the rocks. This is not a purely American phenomenon either, though its manifestation in the United States is different than elsewhere. You can see it in the "Little Englanders" who defied their betters to demand Brexit, and in the frustrated Frenchmen and Germans who look to outsider parties to make their voice heard over the blare of the Elite consensus.

Who is a Normal anyway? It is someone who does not choose to identify with the Elite.

It is important to understand that not all Normals are identical, nor are all members of the Elite. These are generalizations, and like all general rules there are exceptions. The exceptions do not disprove the basic point.

Normal Americans generally leave the day-to-day management of America's institutions to those with the expertise and the affinity to run them. These are the Elite, though membership in the Elite is broader than simply those people with actual power and includes those who choose to affiliate themselves with the beliefs and norms of the Elite. You can be Elite if you are a GS-14 making trade policy in the Department of Commerce. But you can also be Elite by being a marketing consultant married to that bureaucrat because you subscribe to the same worldview, which often (but not always) includes liberal politics.

Elitists tend to value credentials, particularly academic ones. They also tend to trust institutions, and why wouldn't they? They are the class responsible for running them, and they tend to value the prerogatives of institutions over the personal interests of individuals. That's how you get the FBI essentially using manufactured evidence to pry a FISA warrant out of a judge, and then, when exposed, the Elite closes ranks to cry out that our federal law enforcement institutions are under attack. What about the guy who got spied on in violation of the law? Meh. It's the Elite institution that matters, not some uppity rando insisting on his constitutional rights.

The Elite tends not only to revere and respect institutions and those with the expertise to manage them, but expects others to revere and respect them, too. Reverence and respect are, after all, part of the consideration for being Elite.

A Normal is simply someone who does not identify with the Elite and its core values. The Normals generally know who is one of them, largely because if someone chooses to identify with the Elite he will rarely let you forget it. While the Normals probably won't use the term "Normal," they will certainly use a term that evokes something similar.

"Middle class."

"Working class."

"Red stater."

"Regular Joe."

"American."

That last is one of the key discriminators—Normals tend to

eagerly and proudly identify themselves as "Americans." It's central to their identity, and they are deeply patriotic. They aren't blind to the flaws of their country, but they love it—deeply and without the kind of mealymouthed reservations their Elite betters always seem to have to offer as a disclaimer before reluctantly displaying any kind of patriotic sentiment.

A Normal is never a "citizen of the world," and Normals do not shift uncomfortably in their seats, as the Elitists tend to, when someone correctly observes that the United States of America is the greatest country on Earth. Their patriotism comes asterisk-free.

Normal status is not completely geographically dependent, though that can be a pretty good indicator. According to the *New York Times*, Washington, DC, one of America's premier pustules of Elitism, voted 90.9 percent for Hillary Clinton.[1] In contrast, in West Virginia, where you don't utter the word *elite* in the presence of children or respectable ladies, the *Times* reported that the voters went 67.9 percent for the thrice-married New York billionaire.[2]

The big coastal cities of Boston, New York, Seattle, and Los Angeles all fly the blue flag. You get to the outskirts of those urban centers and, in general, things change. Where the buildings are typically under three stories, you find Normals. Find the high-rises, and you find the Elite.

Nor is Normal status conferred by race or ethnicity. The media likes to talk about the unruly masses as "white," but that term is losing its meaning. Race seems to be a subject young people never tire of yapping about even as the point of origin of their distant relatives prior to coming to North America becomes less and less of an issue in selecting their mates. To the extent a lot of Normals are "white" reflects the fact that a lot of America outside the cities is still "white." But Normals come in every color and creed.

The Elite are certainly confused about the Normals—who they are and what they want. Much of that comes from a lack of familiarity. That's not to say that a portion of the Elite is not made up of lapsed Normals—as with atheists, the angriest ones are often the ex-believers. But as Charles Murray documented in his book *Coming Apart: The State of White America, 1960–2010* (New York: Crown Forum, 2012), the world of the Elite and the world the rest of America dwells in are becoming more and more segregated. Many in the Elite have never done a brake job, carried a rifle, or gotten smacked in the face in a bar fight. Nor have many outside the Elite seen a Michael Moore movie, drank kombucha on purpose, or worn a felt vagina-pun on their head to protest the election of an alleged sexual abuser over the enabler of an admitted sexual abuser whom they supported.

A Normal is fairly likely to have gone to church in the last month. A Harvard grad living in Georgetown is unlikely to have gone into a church in the last four weeks unless someone died— and even then it would probably be a church the family hired for the occasion with a rent-a-pastor who carefully curates the homily to avoid any awkwardly specific references to the Savior that the decedent didn't actually believe in.

Those different experiences lead to very different worldviews and to an Elite that does not understand the Normals it presumes to lead—and that hates what it believes it understands about them.

The Elite's media is supposed to help gather that information to inform its fellow Elitists, including those with actual decision-making power, but it has itself become packed with Elitists who lack any life experience outside college and grad school. Most mainstream media members do not know any Normals, or they have long since moved on from those with whom they grew up.

They share the bigotry and prejudices of their class. Except for a few intrepid reporters like Salena Zito of the *New York Post*, none of the people in the media charged with going and finding out what was happening bothered to. When they did, it was more like a Margaret Mead anthropological expedition where, instead of trekking off to Samoa, some *Washington Post* reporter with a French poetry bachelor's from Princeton and a J-school diploma from Columbia who cut his teeth writing for *Daily Kos* would fly into Tupelo for an afternoon to marvel at the locals, then call back to his editor with a story pitch along the lines of:

After church on Sunday—they totally believe in Jesus, if you can believe that!—the congregation gets together under a tent for a potluck and talks politics. It's not really very sophisticated—they blame undocumented workers for problems, which is totally racist. In fact, while they never actually come out and say it, they are all super racist. Cutting regulations? Racist. Being afraid of terrorists? Racist. Not wanting men pretending to be women whipping it out in the restroom next to their teen daughters? Transphobic, and probably racist, too. Somehow. Because, I've learned, that the farther you get from the coasts, the more racist America becomes. Oh, and do not, whatever you do, go canoeing out in red America because you know what they'll do to you. Haven't you seen that red state documentary, *Deliverance*?

This is pretty much what our Elite thinks. It's probably too kind.

Yet these Normals are the people who put Donald Trump in

the White House, beating the full court press of the press and the rest of the ruling class. You might think they would get some credit for pulling off that feat, but if you listen to the loudest voices in our culture, the Normals are the worst people in the world.

Muslim extremist butchers? Bad, in theory, but you know who the real Taliban is? Catholics who prefer not to chip in for abortions.

Drug gangs who terrorize the ghettos? Well, the Normals are the ones who elected Ronald Reagan and his CIA, who—before the CIA became brave heroes speaking truth to power on or about January 20, 2017—invented crack and forced the local youths to sell it.

Freeloaders who free-ride on the welfare system? Victims of the Normals' selfishness. The real problem, for some reason, is people who support themselves and their own families.

The modern Elite needs and wants an enemy, and the Normals make for a great villain. The Normals don't fit in the grand scheme of things their betters envision. Normals just want to live their lives and raise their families in peace. Unforgivably, they seem to want hope and change without fundamentally transforming America.

They are branded racist, sexist, homophobic, and all the other countless *-ists* and *-phobics* that their alleged betters have invented.

Many believe in God, which today is the greatest of heresies. They don't believe in science, especially such "science" as a frigid winter proving global warming exists or that someone can transform his/her sex by merely feeling like it.

The Normals are square, bourgeois, and totally uncool. Having contempt for them flatters the Elite hater, allowing the hater to revel in his or her own edginess. Or xir's edginess—we would not want to risk misgendering a hater.

Even worse, the Normals refuse to acknowledge the manifest superiority of their betters. The fact that the Normals do not sufficiently respect or revere the Elite, or honor its myriad weird taboos and shibboleths, is infuriating. The barbarians! They even refuse to confess and do penance for the privilege inherited from their great-great-great-great-great-granddad who came from outside of Düsseldorf!

The Normals were, for a long time, reluctant to fight back. Lucky for the Elite—that's the best kind of enemy, one too busy supporting his family to jump into the ring and start punching. But then, you can only push people so far. Like a little drunk in a bar who keeps poking, poking, poking at the big guy who just wants to finish his pint of unironic Pabst, eventually the pest is going to get a fist in his face.

The Elite poked and prodded and pestered. Eventually, the Normals were going to find their Donald Trump, whether his name was "Donald Trump" or something else. And can you really blame them?

Many are angry. They want change. And they are not about to back down.

Call them the Militant Normals.

CHAPTER THREE

The Making of a Militant Normal

Not everyone wants to be Elite. Normal people just want to be normal.

You wouldn't think so if you pay any attention to popular culture and politics. Americans grow up in the shadow of celebrity, one of the public faces of Eliteness. Whether that status comes from making movies, making music, from being in the media, or even from politics (which is the pathway of choice for ugly and boring people to get famous), it sometimes seems that being in the public eye is the natural American state of nature, the goal all good citizens should seek to attain. But that is silly.

Most people are not and never will be famous, even in the loosest definition of "famous," like "Twitter famous" ("Whoa, I just met @StarWarsSuperfan69 in real life, and he's just like he is online! Squeeeee!"). Moreover, most people are sane and do not want to be famous. And most people don't care if they are Elite.

They just want to live a good life. They want to raise their family and to see their kids succeed. They want to spend time with their friends. Many want to have a deep religious life, having an actual relationship with God instead of possessing a vague, unfocused pseudo-spirituality that offers no judgment, requires no sacrifice, and involves twigs and/or magic crystals.

They want to be prosperous, not because they are greedy, but because they simply want to have the material things that make them comfortable and give them options. Those in the Elite are often quick to judge the alleged materialism of others, often from the high ground of material comfort. Hence, the phenomenon of Upper West Side dwellers wondering aloud why those rural rednecks in Montandakota are allowed to have huge, carbon-spewing pickup trucks, and then promptly jetting off for a week to a village in Tuscany to revel in authentic Italian rural peasant life at a five-star villa before flying back home to Manhattan.

Normals want to be safe and secure, not having to worry about criminals wandering the streets or Wall Street collapsing and taking everything they have saved down the drain with it.

They want to be proud of their country, to see it strong and free, and when it is in danger, they want to serve themselves or at least support those who do.

But they also want a modicum of respect, and they want a level playing field in the economy and in the culture. They want a say in the governance of their own country. They are citizens, not subjects. That's why they have guns—because subjects don't have the means to object if it comes to that. Citizens? Citizens pack a 12-gauge solution to tyranny.

This is not much to ask. But for decades they have been asking for it, and they have not been getting it.

So how does a Normal morph into a Militant Normal? What does it take to get a regular person who isn't loud, isn't outrageous, and isn't particularly political to go pull the lever for a New York City billionaire who is all of that and more?

The answer lies outside of the Elite bubble, both geographically and experientially.

Say you grew up in Fontana, California. Fontana is an industrial town in the Inland Empire east of Los Angeles, out in the ugliest of terrain—urbanized desert. The desert was never meant to be bulldozed. Whatever is not landscaped is brown dirt and gnarled brush. The winds off the Pacific Ocean push the polluted air from the commuters gridlocked in the Los Angeles basin back over Fontana, where it sits trapped by the San Bernardino Mountains to the north, and San Jacinto Mountains to the south. The brown haze compounds the misery of the searing summer heat. You don't buy a car with a black interior in Fontana.

There are no McMansions there, no overdone townhouses with BMWs parked out front. The houses are decades out of fashion, smallish ranch-style dwellings for a postwar middle class intent on booming out babies and making up for lost time spent trudging through the jungle in the Philippines with the 40th Infantry Division or on the bridge of a destroyer hunting U-boats in the North Atlantic.

Strip malls follow strip malls as you drive down the surface streets. Lots of chain stores, chain restaurants, and chain hotels. Interstate 10 runs east-west through the south edge of town, and it lets you pass right by it without even noticing the city if you don't know what you are looking for. Fontana is not as flashy as—and doesn't have an amusing name like its neighbor to the west—Rancho Cucamonga.

You won't catch much of our Elite in Fontana or, for that matter, in Donora, Pennsylvania, or in Lawton, Oklahoma, or in a thousand other similar towns dotting the country. It is unhip, uncool, and unimportant to our best and our brightest, some of whom harbor a special hate for the Fontanas because they escaped from one themselves by managing to obtain the credentials that allowed them to leave their shameful Normal past behind.

Yet there are those who love America's Fontanas.

Fontana is not perfect, but it is home. It's a community, with people who have known each other for decades, often growing up together and mixing and mingling in schools and churches and the bowling leagues and soccer leagues and Little League. They have their favorite restaurants, some local, some chains, but all theirs. And their jobs are often there, including the businesses they created—garages, medical practices, pet shops, whatever. They made Fontana what it is, a hometown. That may not mean much to swells in Washington or Beverly Hills, but it means everything to the people who call it home.

Sure, Fontana has its problems. There are bad parts of town where the meth heads gather and where the police keep their eyes open. In towns like Fontana, often the big factories have closed, moving the manufacturing work overseas or south of the border, making it hard to find the kind of solid, long-term, nine-to-five jobs that many of their parents held.

But there's still pride. In these towns, as you drive down the main street, you'll often see red, white, and blue banners hanging from the light posts with the serious faces of young men and women in their country's uniform.

Army Private Jones.

Air Force Captain Smith.

Marine Lance Corporal Salazar.

And sometimes there is a gold star on the banner, representing the town's blood sacrifice for our country.

So, say you grew up in Fontana. You went to Fontana High School. Maybe you were a defensive tackle on the football team, the Steelers, whose mascot is a jut-jawed steelworker in a hard hat. Except the Kaiser Steel plant that created modern Fontana shut down back in 1983.

You graduated, though school was not your thing. You liked working with your hands, doing things instead of talking about them. Some of the other kids were enrolling in community college. Others were going away to school. But more years of books and studying? Not for you. You wanted to do something, to be something, and you wanted to do it now.

Plus, those goat-banging bastards needed to pay for what they did on 9/11. You had never been to New York, or Washington, or Pennsylvania, but that didn't matter. Those were Americans. You watched it happen, stunned, on the classroom television in Mr. Calhoun's English class, the first month of your senior year.

So as graduation approached, you went down to the recruiter—there is always a recruiter in America's Fontanas—and signed up with the squared-away Marine staff sergeant who eyeballed you up and down and, after thinking about it, decided to let you see if you had what it takes to be a part of his beloved Corps.

If you had what it takes. No one ever gave you anything before, and you didn't expect to be given that, either.

The night before you left, you and your friends had a party at Jeff's house, and you were hungover as hell when you kissed your girlfriend good-bye and shipped out to the Marine Corps Recruit Depot in San Diego. Your dad walked you out to the car when the staff sergeant came by to pick you up ("Don't you make me chase you down, recruit," he had growled over the phone the night before). Dad was beaming with pride. He still had a scar from where some NVA sniper popped him with a Russian-made SKS rifle at Khe Sanh. The military tradition ran in the family. Grandpa had been a Devil Dog at Guadalcanal, though he never talked about it, or about his brother Phil, who didn't come back from Tarawa.

At the MCRD, you got thrown into a training platoon and met a bunch of guys who were totally different from you and would soon become exactly the same. It was tough, but so were you. Sure, the Marine drill instructor was a hard-ass, and you didn't like anyone being in your face screaming, but you could take it. You'd thrown some punches and taken a few in high school, and the harder the training got, the harder you got.

Was that a tear in your dad's eye when, a couple of months later, you stood out in formation in your dress uniform, and received your Eagle, Globe, and Anchor?

Now it's April 2004, and you are a lance corporal going into the meat grinder of Fallujah with the 1st Battalion 5th Marine Regiment, moving with your company through the dull gray wreckage of that Iraqi city under withering enemy fire. But you don't complain. Fighting is what Marines do.

Your team leader, a country boy from Alabama with a taste for Copenhagen, peeked around a corner and a 7.62 mm round blew out most of the teeth on the right side of his jaw, ripping a ragged hole as it exited through his cheek. You shouted for the corpsman, a young sailor whose parents fled Saigon after the Democrats in Congress betrayed South Vietnam and cut off the aid America had promised. Then you pressed a pressure bandage on the gaping wound, trying desperately to keep your friend from choking to death on his own blood.

Your lieutenant, a black guy who had played football at the Academy, ran across an open space between buildings to get to his wounded man, little volcanos of dust erupting where the sniper rounds hit. He made sure your buddy was evacuated, then he told you that you were the new team leader and to move your Marines out.

After all, those *jihadi* bastards weren't going to kill themselves.

You got sprayed with shrapnel from an exploding rocket-propelled grenade while clearing a school the terrorists were using as a command post and torture chamber. Your team got the duty of helping bag the bodies of the victims. It was not much of a wound, not compared to the others you had seen, though it hurt like hell. You felt bad bothering the corpsman over a few frags of shrapnel in your chest, but First Sergeant made you get it checked—he wasn't losing a team leader to infection because of sheer stubbornness. As soon as Doc finished picking out the readily accessible bits of metal and slathering the holes with antibiotics, you put your gear back on and ran back to your Marines. There was another push coming, and you needed to be there with them even if you were still bleeding.

After the fight, you were a little surprised, and maybe a little ashamed, that you got the same Purple Heart as the guys who really got hurt. That's why you keep the medal in a drawer to this day and never take it out. But you finally understood why Grandpa always changed the subject when you pestered him about what he did in World War II.

Back home, out of the Corps, you needed a job, and you decided again that you wanted to follow in your dad's footsteps and become a roofer. Sure, you knew from watching him that it was hard work, but you liked to work with your hands, and you remembered how he would drive you around Fontana, pointing out buildings and telling you, "I helped build that."

Your dad, now retired, still knew some contractors and gave you some leads, but everywhere the answer was the same—"No thanks." What was the deal? If your tour in the Corps showed anything, it was that you could perform—you would show up on time, drug-free, and ready to hammer. But it seemed that the crews were all immigrants. And maybe not all legal ones.

You expected a fair day's wages for a fair day's work, and not to be paid under the table. But that was disqualifying. "I'm sorry," one contractor said. "I have to hire them. Everyone else does. I can't compete using American labor." You had nothing against immigrants—they were good guys, just trying to make it themselves—but that seemed…wrong.

So, instead, you found a job through a veterans' program at a Walmart on East Foothill Boulevard, stocking shelves for nine dollars an hour with no benefits.

Welcome home.

But you did your job and moved up. The half-steppers quit or kept stocking, but you got promoted. Soon, you were in the management program. You even started interviewing job candidates. But an awful lot of them frowned when you told them about the pay, and about how you expected them to get there on time and be sober and ready to work. They would get up and tell you, "Forget it. I can make almost as much with food stamps and Section 8, and I don't have to do shit."

You married your girlfriend at St. Joseph's Church. The priest got a little tipsy at the reception. It was a real good time.

After a while, your wound started hurting from the hunks of shrapnel still buried in your muscle, and you had a cough you couldn't shake that you would swear had to be related to all that nasty Iraqi dust and the fumes from the burning diesel and shit at the forward operating base. So you called up the Department of Veterans Affairs for some help. Your first appointment was the next slot available, four months later.

When you got there, the waiting room was crowded with vets young and old, and the staff treated your presence as an imposition. You sat down next to a young guy who had been in the Army in Afghanistan and was there for post-traumatic stress disorder counseling. You had had some nightmares, and every April you got so quiet and withdrawn that your wife became concerned. Maybe the VA could help you, too, you wondered. But your new friend shook his head. "They just give you a bunch of meds," he said. "They don't fix you. They just drug you up until you stop complaining."

After three hours, you were about ready to leave when they finally called your name. The doctor, a contract employee with a nearly unintelligible accent, seemed to think you were exaggerating the pain from your wound—"Look, removing the remaining pieces is a non-essential procedure; so you'll have to wait." And though he couldn't identify a cause of your cough, he was absolutely sure it wasn't service related. He prescribed some Advil and a codeine cough syrup. "You'll like the codeine," he said, grinning. You threw it away when you got home.

Time passed. Even as a manager you were not making the money that your dad had made, the kind of money that let you get a house and maybe take a vacation once in a while. You now had kids, and that was great, but now you also had more expenses.

You could never seem to get ahead, but every day you still got dressed and went in to work. And every couple weeks you knew when the welfare money got deposited because the store swelled with customers.

Fontana was changing—there were more and more illegals, and one hit your wife's Honda in the supermarket parking lot. He had no insurance, and the police officer just shrugged. "Nothing I can do," he said. The illegal went on his way, and you got stuck paying nine hundred dollars to pull out the dent, nine hundred dollars you didn't have. But you were lucky compared to your buddy from the football team. He got shot coming out of a 7-Eleven with a cup of coffee one night by a gang member who was here illegally. You found out from his widow that the killer had been deported twice before and the cops had picked up and released him just a month earlier for drunk driving. But nobody mentioned that in the paper or on the news.

You largely gave up on television after one too many shows depicted American troops in the Sandbox as psycho murderers. You didn't need that bullshit because you knew the truth. You carried the truth under your skin.

Someone tried to peel off the yellow ribbon on your wife's Honda—who the hell would be against supporting the troops? And you walked out of a family Thanksgiving dinner when a cousin home from Berkeley informed you that you were a sucker who was complicit in war crimes by participating in a bogus war for oil that was based on Bush's lies. He thought he had won some sort of victory by driving you out; you, and the rest of the adults, understood that the sophomore was lucky you chose to leave rather than introduce his goateed mug to a wall face-first.

You never liked politics. You never really paid attention to them. And you hated politicians—liars and crooks, the bunch of them. Sure, you voted, but it wasn't the animating force in your life. You certainly didn't watch the Sunday morning shows and you'd chew glass before opening a Twitter account. Politics was not the center of your being. No, it was more like . . . a duty. You did it, to the extent you had to, only because that's what Americans did.

You voted for Barack Obama in 2008 because he seemed like a cool guy and the whole Wall Street bailout thing just seemed like a scam designed to get people like you to pay for the greed of the people who were supposed to be running things and who had screwed up. Hell, you'd suffered more consequences from the first sergeant for being late to formation once than these Wall Street punks had for almost wrecking the economy. The bailout thing really chapped your ass; when you couldn't pay a hundred-dollar bill, you got a dunning letter and a ding on your credit. But when the bankers and brokers couldn't pay their billion-dollar tab, they got your money.

More and more, it looked like the system was rigged for the big guy and against the little guy.

Plus, you were still angry that George W. Bush had got us into a war then dithered around for years before deciding to actually win it at the end of his presidency. You had chafed under rules of engagement that tied your hands and put your friends at risk. You knew where the enemy was. Why weren't we going to get him? And why weren't the politicians insisting the Iraqis pull their weight? You were proud of your service in Iraq, even if you didn't talk about it much, but you also questioned whether all that blood and all those lives were worth it. If the Iraq War wasn't worth winning by doing what it took to win, why was it worth your buddies' lives?

But then under Obama, all your hope for change vanished. Where was the recovery he promised? It looked like he was just about divvying up tax money among his allies—the tax money you sweated to earn. And Obama never seemed to take the right side. He picked fights with the cops. You liked cops. Your cousin was a cop, and at dinner he would talk about how it was getting so the police were afraid to bust criminals.

Obamacare was supposed to make things better, but you still had to pay for your family's insurance, and those bills didn't come down. They went up, a lot, and when you got the first one around New Year's Day, you knew this was going to be another summer without a vacation.

The roads seemed to get worse all the time; driving on I-10, the bumps and ruts shook your Taurus so hard you thought it might shake those little shards of RPG warhead right out of your body without surgery. When you had to take a flight out of LAX, you were stunned at how decrepit the place looked; the rest of Los Angeles didn't look much better. America was falling apart— where did that trillion dollars for shovel-ready jobs go?

Not to Fontana, that was for sure.

Whenever you encountered the government, it was like you were an afterthought. Your kids' teachers seemed disinterested, and you spent a lot of time reading to your kids to keep them developing. The district seemed to have trouble finding funds for phys ed and art classes, but they somehow always seemed to have the funds for another program for the illegal alien kids who spoke no English but were filling the rolls. It was clear who the priority was, and it wasn't you.

You tried to avoid politics, but politics didn't seem to want to avoid you. There was always some fight between the politicians in the news, some government shutdown, something. There was always an excuse for why things weren't getting any better. Democrats, Republicans—they were both useless.

And then there was the growing sense that you were the one the smart set off in the cities blamed for the things that were going wrong. It was as if they hated people like you. More and more, you heard how you wielded some sort of privilege based on where your great-great-great-grandfather came from. Privilege? You worked for every single thing you had. Privilege? The privilege of getting blown up in some Arab shithole fighting people who, a couple years before, you hadn't even known existed, but who a bunch of guys in Washington with fancy degrees had decided were important enough to conquer that they would risk your life to do it?

And when you complained, you were "racist." Racist? Even before the Corps, in high school, on the team, you had friends of all flavors. Your platoon had looked like the United Nations. Nobody cared about color. These guys were all OD green, olive drab, and they would all die for you, and you for them. You didn't hate people because of their race or heritage, and you'd think anyone who did was a fool.

But illegal immigration was a real problem in Fontana, and no one cared. The issue wasn't that they were Latinos—half your friends were Latinos (and you never understood why saying "Some of my best friends are whatever" was supposed to be a tip-off to being a racist when having friends of different races seemed like pretty damn good evidence that someone is not racist). The issue was that they were here, and that was against the law, and that caused problems for American citizens.

Why were the government and the media more concerned

with the problems of people who weren't supposed to be here than with the problems of their own fellow citizens?

This is our country, you figured. We should get to choose who comes in and who doesn't, and we should decide that based on what's good for America. That's not crazy or unreasonable. Mexico chooses who comes over its borders. Every other country does, too. Why not us?

There were laws—illegals are illegal—but the government was choosing not to enforce them. *Choosing* not to. You didn't pay all that much attention in civics class, but you knew that wasn't how things were supposed to work in a democracy. You were a citizen, and your representatives had passed a law, but now the government was choosing not to enforce it. Wait, aren't you supposed to have a voice? Aren't you supposed to have a say in your own governance? Instead, some liberal politicians—you weren't much on politics, but you noticed that a lot of this stuff was traceable back to liberals—just decided on their own that what you want doesn't matter.

Every day you experienced the real-life consequences of illegal immigration, the strain on the schools and hospitals, the crime, and the hassles like the dent to your wife's Honda, and these were important to you. They had a real impact on your life. But the politicians didn't care. They never talked about your concerns. Your concerns didn't matter to them. The money men behind them were more interested in shipping in more and more immigrants, legal or not, because there was money in it for them. The Democrats wanted more to make more Democrat voters. But your problems?

Not important.

You don't matter. That was becoming crystal clear.

You were having trouble matching the lifestyle your parents had, and you worried about your kids. But it didn't matter to the big shots who for decades were sending so many great jobs making stuff overseas or down south of the border. Well, the rich people who owned the companies made more money, but you?

You made do.

So, who was your voice? Who would speak for you? Who would fight for you? The politicians were always *talking* about fighting for you, and they were always *saying* all the right things at election time, but then they got into Washington and they did nothing at all—if they didn't do the exact opposite of what they had promised.

You were genuinely torn between voting for Mitt Romney and voting for Obama again in 2012. But not because they were good choices.

You looked at Mitt, and you were happy that conservatives like him at least seemed to like America. When you saw a liberal with a flag on his lapel, you got the impression he was wearing it as a joke. But Romney seemed just as eager to fight more wars in weird countries no one ever heard of before—why again were we going to fight in Libya?—and, like the liberals, it was going to be someone else's kids doing the fighting.

Kids like yours.

Plus, Mitt looked like That Guy From Corporate who showed up every few months to tour the store, and then a week later a bunch of people got laid off "to promote efficiency." Mitt made his career outsourcing American jobs. Was he going to stand up for the guys here at home who wanted to work, or for the guys in the back of the limo signing the papers moving the air conditioner assembly plant to Juarez?

That was not hard to guess.

Mitt as your voice? Mitt fighting for you? Was that a joke? Mitt, with his perfect hair and perfect suits and twenty-five perfect kids, all of whom grew up rich and comfortable and none of whom could be bothered to serve a hitch for their country? No. There weren't a lot of Tigg or Tugg or Scoot or Boot Romneys in the Corps.

Mitt was at home at parties you'd never get invited to and on golf courses that would never let you on the green.

But Obama wasn't any better, and in some ways, he was even worse. At least with Mitt, you only got the idea that he merely didn't care about you. With Obama, you got the impression that he and his liberal cohorts actively hated you.

In those cultural fights the liberals always picked, Obama was siding more and more with the wealthy snobs in the cities, with his Hollywood pals whose movies and television shows made fun of you when they weren't calling you a racist thug. You would see on Channel 7 News every couple of weeks that the president had flown into Los Angeles (and gridlocked traffic for his fans on the Westside) to do a Beverly Hills fundraising dinner with David Geffen, whoever that was. But he never seemed to find time to make it out the sixty-eight miles to Fontana to see how normal Americans were doing.

Obama talked a lot about climate change, which you remembered used to be called "global warming" until one too many "global warming" conventions had been snowed in. Now it was "climate change," and any kind of weather proved it existed. Heat wave? Climate change. Hurricane? Climate change. Cold weather and no hurricanes? Also climate change. You may have gotten a C in science, but you were still pretty sure that this wasn't science.

The thing is, the solution they always offered seemed to be

some new tax—on carbon, on gas, on breathing, whatever—and more regulations. How come the solution to every problem was always to give the people running things more money and more power? You weren't a coal miner, but you felt for those coal miners because the Obama administration seemed determined to put them all out of work. *How would they feed their families?* you wondered, and then you realized that was something the administration and its supporters did not seem to care about at all.

Those coal miners were expendable. How long until you became expendable, too?

You had waved off his clinging to your guns and religion crack back in 2008—you clung to both—but now it seemed more and more that it represented what he really thought. Obama seemed to want nothing more than to strip you of your .45 M1911A1, though you had only ever used a gun in defense of your country and now needed one to protect your family. Why were you the bad guy for just wanting to protect what was yours? Wasn't it in the Constitution? Sure it was. Abortion wasn't, but they still found that in there somewhere.

And Obama and his liberal cronies seemed to hate your religion, and for no good reason. You just wanted to go to church. You didn't care what other people did. That was between them and God. But the liberals seemed determined to make a bunch of nuns pay money for abortions. Why? Why did they have to do that? Why pick that fight?

And for that matter, what was this thing about gay wedding cakes? Okay, so if gay people want to get married, fine, but why do you have to bankrupt people just because they don't want to be a part of it? Can't people just live and let live? Aren't there a dozen other cake bakers people can go to get their cake?

That's not tolerance. That's a threat. Agree with us, think how we want you to think, or else.

You know, threatening an American, telling an American that he's going to do what you say, is a dangerous business. If you're smart, you don't want to walk into a bar in Fontana or Donora or Lawton or in a thousand other towns and announce, "Hey you redneck shitkickers, here's how it's going to be."

Americans, at least the ones outside the blue coastal cities, are an ornery bunch.

You sat out the election. When the president was reelected, you shrugged. Maybe this time he'd keep his word, you thought. But you didn't really believe it would happen.

And it didn't. The second Obama term continued the same trends, and even amplified them. The economy didn't get better, not for regular folks like you. At work, you had to deal with more and more regulations; from your friends who had their own businesses, you knew that these regulations hit small companies— which did not maintain an army of lobbyists and make giant contributions to the politicians like Walmart did—even harder. The infrastructure continued to deteriorate. The VA continued to be useless. The wars dragged on; dirt your buddies had bled over got handed back to the fanatics of the Islamic State in Iraq.

ISIS. You know, the guys Obama called the "JV team."

The liberals doubled down on their contempt for you. From what you heard, today's colleges were less devoted to learning than to fueling racial feuds. Maybe that wasn't all bad—you had little savings, and, anyway, you had no idea how you would pay for college if your kids wanted to go.

Obama was also siding even more openly with crooks against cops. You watched the video of that punk in Ferguson robbing the store minutes before he picked his last fight with that cop, and yet the media and politicians were making the thug a hero. It was clear whose lives mattered to them and whose didn't.

Then there was the weird transsexual thing—for some reason, it was now suddenly vital that grown men must share restrooms with little girls. You had no problem with transsexuals—you didn't know any, but if someone felt that way, he/she had enough problems and you had no reason to add to them. But men coming into girls' restrooms? That was worse than crazy—it was dangerous.

It was like they were just trying to do it to show you that they could, that you had no say, that they could do anything they wanted to you.

They were picking a fight.

And Hillary Clinton would have only made it worse. She radiated contempt for the little guy, the forgotten men and women. But then there were the Republicans. Jeb Bush? Really? There were 330 million Americans and the Republicans can't find someone who isn't another Bush?

And the rest—all the same, none of them ready to fight for you.

That's when you realized that is what you wanted. After taking punch after punch, you wanted a fighter. Someone who would stand up and give it back as hard as he got it. As hard as *you* got it.

And then you noticed Donald Trump.

———

The story of our guy from Fontana does not simply check off a bunch of boxes representing a list of characteristics necessary for admission into Normalcy. Rather, our guy represents the values and experiences that typically distinguish the Normals from the members of our self-appointed moral and intellectual superiors.

Normals are—if you will pardon the expression—diverse. Our guy from Fontana doesn't live in a big coastal city, though some Normals do. You can find Normals everywhere. It's just that in some places—Manhattan, West Los Angeles, any place that calls itself a "campus"—they might be keeping their heads down. After all, being a Normal is often a magnet for hassles.

He doesn't have a bunch of paper credentials issued by the conformity assembly line that is academia, though some Normals do.

He doesn't have a fancy job, and he isn't going to be famous, though some Normals do and are.

He's focused on faith and family, and for him, patriotism isn't a punchline.

He supports himself and is willing to lend a hand to those in need, but at the same time, he expects everyone to carry his own rucksack and resents those trying to stick their rocks inside his.

A Normal is not necessarily some rural rustic out of J. D. Vance's *Hillbilly Elegy: A Memoir of a Family and Culture in Crisis* (New York: Harper, 2016), but he can be. A Normal might be driving a car that cost more than his parents' first house. He or she could have been the owner of a small business, or a manager at an auto plant, or a cop, or a guy who did twenty years in the Air Force and now teaches school. He can be black, white, Asian, or Hispanic; gay or straight; young or old. But in general, the general qualifications apply.

A Normal's faith and family are his focus.

A Normal's patriotism is not ironic.

A Normal's self-sufficiency is a choice.

A Normal's attitude gets bad when you start pushing him too far.

Today, a Normal is someone the Elite would prefer to sit down and shut up, if not die or be enslaved. The Elite wants the Normals to get out of the way of progress toward the liberal utopia of peace and prosperity that is just out of reach, blocked by the intransigence and selfishness of the people who created and maintain America's peace and prosperity.

Being a Normal is a state of mind. But more and more today, that Normal state of mind is "militant."

CHAPTER FOUR

A Meritocracy without Merit

That there are Normals implies that there are Abnormals. But the term *Abnormals* is not really a useful formulation. Instead, let's call them the Elite, for lack of a better term, though very few of them are actually "elite" in any meaningful sense. Rather, many in the Elite are aspiring to be elite, but most just end up as people who base their own self-image upon their certainty in their moral and intellectual superiority to the Normals. These are the affiliate Elite. They are the run-of-the-mill smug liberal diversity trainers, government bureaucrats, and internet loudmouths who spend their time safely #resisting people who would never actually hurt them.

Are they liberal? Most are—the Elite embraces Frankfurt School–derived modern American liberalism because the feel-good nostrums of liberalism flatter the Elite's sense of moral superiority. Liberalism in the Elite is like an intellectual bedbug infestation—contagious, difficult to cure, and gross all at once. That's why even those who enter the Elite as conservatives risk infection. Look at the allegedly "conservative" representatives like Jeff Flake who arrive in Washington, DC, and promptly "grow" in office into illegal alien–loving, gun-grabbing big spenders. One bite of the bug can be fatal to your conservative principles.

Liberalism informs and defines their lifestyles and values, and it is through the taboos they respect and the shibboleths they honor that the members of the Elite seek to define themselves as not being members of the Normal caste. Exclusivity is part of the appeal, though it's the simplest thing in the world to join the Elite. You just have to believe. You don't actually have to do anything. America's Elite is a meritocracy that has abandoned the notion of merit.

Few institutions demonstrate this better than our colleges. The key to the value of college is not mastering the curriculum. It is gaining admission. Once you get in, the hard work is done.

Let's take the example of Harvard, which is America's greatest institution of higher learning, according to everyone who ever attended Harvard and won't shut up about it. It has certified its own students as prodigies. The *Harvard Crimson* reported on December 3, 2013, that the median grade at Harvard was an A–, while the most common grade was an A.[1]

Well.

Now, this is not to say that Harvard graduates are unskilled—for example, they are remarkably adept at infiltrating the fact that they went to Harvard into every conversation they participate in. That has to count for something. But this near-horizontal grading curve does raise the question of how the grade of A, which generally signifies "outstanding," is so readily available? If most Harvard students are "outstanding," or at least "outstanding minus," you have to wonder, "Compared to whom?" It can't be to other Harvard students.

Either Harvard has rejected the idea of competition, which

grades used to measure, or Harvard is comparing its students to everyone else in the world and simply assuming its students have prevailed. It might well be both, and neither should come as a surprise.

Obviously, Harvard has not completely rejected the concept of competition—it prides itself on how competitive it is to be admitted. But four years of high school grinding and trying to perfect an enrichment activity–packed résumé that will make the admissions officers drool is the last really hard work a student has to do to get this coveted credential. The diploma is what matters, not what you studied. And you get the diploma if you get in. Whether you major in computer engineering or create your own Gender Identity Issues in Belgian Literature of the Seventeenth Century major, you're essentially done before you start.

You get into Harvard or another Elite college, and you've got your invitation to the Elite—as well as an opportunity for training in the correct attitudes and behaviors of an Elitist, courtesy of the faculty and an army of helpful social justice warriors who wander the campus with verbal cattle prods to enforce their version of order.

Unlike the affiliate members of the Elite, these students have the ability to eventually rule because academia offers them the promise of power, both political and cultural. Membership in the Elite is a basic prerequisite to obtain an Elite position where you can actually wield some authority—usually in the pursuit of Elite goals and objectives.

Washington, DC, and every state capital are packed with aspiring entrants into the Elite. They all want to someday be the one who makes the rules and issues the commands, to use government or an institution to impose their will. And, as members of the Elite, they are steadfast in their confidence that they are capable of doing so—nay, that they are *called* to do so, to shepherd the poor begotten souls who live outside of the weekend driving distance of a beach and cannot guide their own lives. Liberal or conservative, Republican or Democrat, if you are within the Elite, the impulse to control is the same.

I am called upon to rule. Heed my commands, little men and women, for I know best.

And in the cultural meccas of Hollywood and Manhattan, the homes of the entertainment industry and the media, the impulse is the same. It is influence and even control, to decide what is right and what is wrong on behalf of that dreary lump of humanity that has never walked a red carpet or been a talking head on Jake Tapper's show.

Now, of course, the vast majority of the Elite never reaches the lofty heights of influence or fame. Most members of the Elite live lives of quiet presumption, identifying with those who wield real power and thereby claiming a sliver of it for themselves. They aren't personally powerful, but if they subscribe to the Elite's dogma, then they can feel a tiny thrill when they observe some more potent member of the Elite exercise his power.

That explains the joy of some associate adjunct professor of Marxist poetry whose toes are peeking out of the socks he wears with his Birkenstocks when he watches a strapping frat boy brought low by a faculty kangaroo court for not getting a notarized videotaped statement of consent from the buzzed sophomore Chi Delt who accused him of assault after she got woke in her Gender Studies seminar seventeen months after he stopped returning her texts the morning after he got to second base.

That explains the giddy high that a sour, divorced middle-aged marketing consultant from Chicago gets when she learns that Congress has imposed another restriction on the rights of people far away to buy AR-15s, which apparently shoot automatic clip bullets or something.

That explains the pure delight the ironic pork pie hat set in Brooklyn feels when learning that some Christian cook will be bankrupted because he felt his religion compelled him not to spell out "Steve + Frank Together 4ever" on their devil's food wedding cake.

For most members of the Elite, there is not much actual eliteness involved in being members of the Elite. Elite status is just a placeholder for actually achieving something—maybe you can't actually *be* better than others, but damn it, you can sure *feel* like you are. For the majority of those within the Elite, there is merely the vicarious thrill of being part of something bigger than themselves—something bigger than themselves that takes as its reason for existence bullying everybody else.

After all, what's the fun of being Elite if you can't rub the Normals' nose in their own subordination?

————

But usually, it is a voluntary subordination. The Elite does serve a role—the Elite does the necessary jobs within society that Normal people don't want. It provides experts to operate the institutions. The Elite gets power in order to do so. A Normal generally does not want to wield power. It's not attractive. It's not what matters to him. Instead, the Normals want to focus on faith, family, and work. Political power? Politicians are hacks at best, and most of the time simply a pack of crooks. Cultural power? Rock stars and movie idols are drug-addled losers with personal lives of Mogadishu-levels of chaos.

Normals don't want to do this stuff. Not if they don't have to. Enter the Elite.

Now, the Elite is eager to do the job of running the country and the culture. And a bit of attitude about doing so—having some pride in doing so—is a natural human reaction. "People like us guide the rest of the people of this country," the Elite tells itself, and that is true, to a point. The problem arises when the Elite doesn't do it very well.

After all, if you are going to announce that you are "the best and the brightest," you kind of need to demonstrate some basic competence. Otherwise, it gets awkward.

But what happens when the Elite not only screws up the job it was given to do—and for which it is paid in power and status—but when it simultaneously decides it actively hates the people who hired it in the first place and whose interest the Elite has been entrusted to represent?

––––––––––

Every society has a class that distinguishes itself by not being common, by not being like the dreary regular people. Every society's elite naturally succumbs to some level of elitism. Smugness, of some level, is a natural characteristic of any elite. That's part of the payoff for being elite. You get to be smug. But sometimes the focus of a society's elite becomes enjoying the privileges of being elite, rather than doing the job of an elite. The problem arises when being elite becomes an end in and of itself.

In recent decades, America's Elite has more and more fixated on distinguishing itself from the Normals. But what it pursues is much more than mere differentiation. It is unvarnished domination.

What our Elite today feels is not duty to the Normals but, rather, contempt for them and a desire to break the Normals to the Elite's will. Politically, this manifests in the Elite pursuing policies that at best ignore the needs of the Normals and, at worst, seek to punish them. Transgender bathrooms aren't about boys pretending to be girls feeling better about their delusions. It's about letting the Normals know that the Elite can violate their most sensitive and private moments if it feels like it—and that the Normals can't do a damn thing about it.

Culturally, this takes the form of a nonstop barrage of hatred and invective aimed at everything the Normals hold sacred. The Elite claps like trained seals for overpaid morons in tights and helmets kneeling during the national anthem because—well, no one has ever provided a coherent reason why. There isn't one. It began as a poke in the Normals' collective eye by a millionaire of questionable quarterbacking skills and ended up a poke in the Normals' collective eye by the entire Elite.

Take that, people who had absolutely nothing to do with whatever the hell pissed off Colin Kaepernick. And the Elite nodded along, an idiot chorus singing along with the mindless tune.

It felt good. It felt *better* than good—it felt positively wonderful to spit in those rubes' faces.

Would-be rebels trying to safely scandalize the bourgeois by transgressing the Normals' old, tired mores—always the society's traditional mores—are as old as history. Young Romans and Athenians did it. Alcibiades got out of town ahead of the headsman after being blamed for castrating some holy statues, exactly the kind of thing one does to freak out the squares. Look at the bohemian artists and the hippies, both experimenting with free love and scandalizing all decent folk. While not necessarily wielding political power, they certainly wielded cultural power in their respective times and places. Other members of the Elite might not consider these ruffians "elite," and they certainly did not approve of such shenanigans—no need to antagonize the masses. The Elite largely shared the same morals and values, even if paying tribute to them only in their breach. The difference today is that now our Elites cheer as one for whatever transgression any other member of the Elite launches. They are united in their transgressive conformity.

Thus, today we have hip, young Elite rebels like Lena Dunham rejecting conformity while announcing "I'm with her!" regarding an elderly, warmongering corporate collaborator.

Edgy.

The Elite has become much more unified across its various factions because almost every sector of it embraces Frankfurt School American liberalism. While there are conservative Elites, many of them members in good standing in Conservative, Inc., liberalism is still the common tongue of those who think they are destined to rule, a language based on hack clichés and faulty premises, but whose intricate grammar is mercilessly enforced by a not-so-secret police consisting of angry feminists working out their daddy issues, perpetually outraged sophomores who think dissenting opinions are violence, and middle-aged diversity consultants who warn that holiday parties are horribly exclusionary unless they are a celebration of the solstice. Can't have any Wiccans upset on their watch.

You have the political Elite, the cultural Elite, and a social Elite (like hipsters, with their rarified tastes for things like undrinkable pumpkin-infused IPAs and their inexplicable fetish for primitive vinyl albums). Then there is the affiliate Elite, like the suburban mommies who clenched their perfectly manicured fists as they watched foul-mouthed has-been Madonna talk about blowing up the White House at the Women's March following Trump's inauguration.[2] They aren't edgy and they aren't exercising any power themselves, but damn it, they are showing solidarity like a boss.

But these are unofficial labels. Elite status can also be formal, or at least so rigidly engrained in a society that it might as well be written in the statute books. Look at England. They actually have a codified elite, the royals. The English take their monarchy a lot more seriously than in other European monarchies, where you might find yourself in the checkout line at the market buying muesli next to His Royal Highness King Olaf the Haphazard. The Brits actually hold to the notion (or at least, embrace the effect of the notion) that some people are "noble" by the grace of God or, in wacky Prince Charles's case, Gaia. Princes, dukes, barons, queens—there is a whole ridiculous hierarchy of carefully stratified individuals who are, somehow, better than everyone else because of who they were born to, even if their formal political power has long been circumscribed by the commoners.

Note that the truly powerful half of the bicameral Parliament is the House of Commons, with the House of Lords having had its members' powers limited to the point that they now seem more of a gaggle of eccentric old men (and a few women) than a real power center. Of course, the House of Commons is made up mostly of very uncommon commoners, and long has been. Any deliberative body that includes the likes of Winston Churchill—a scion of privilege and the image of a member of the Elite at its best—should hardly reference "Commons" in its name.

The nobility is relatively rare in real life, but it is ubiquitous on the front pages of the Fleet Street tabloids displaying behavior that once scandalized English Normals until they became inured to it—"Oh, there's a snap of bonny Prince Zippy wearing an SS uniform and goose-stepping through Piccadilly Circus with his chums from Eton. Hmmm. Pass me a crumpet, luv."

What is much more common are the commoners who are hardly common at all. They are the toffs, the well bred and well born. But except for their detachment from the man in the street, or riding the Tube, they are nothing like Churchill. They are much more like Neville Chamberlain, sadly.

The informal class system of England makes pikers of Americans trying to throw shade at their presumed social inferiors—largely because American Normals don't feel particularly inferior to members of the American Elite, while a dozen Englishmen dropped at random onto a desert isle will immediately sort themselves out into a hierarchy utilizing social clues and cues only they can detect. After a couple minutes, Bennie will be calling Bertie "Sir," and Bertie will be calling Bennie "Higgins" and having him fetch his liege a coconut.

The British elite has cracked open the once tightly barred entry door just a bit. The elite granted newcomers a bit of access to the most selective schools and jobs that are the tells indicating an upper-class toff. Don't be fooled, though, into thinking that the English elite has been democratized. Your father still matters, as does your grandfather. And your race, though they'll be really nice to your face if you're from one of the wrong ones because it's now fashionable to be seen palling around with a descendant of someone whose great-great-great-great-grandfather was shot by your great-great-great-great-grandfather at the Khyber Pass.

Still, the elite and the rest shared in common both their formal religion, through the Church of England, and their informal religion, patriotism. You could be the most humble farmer, or a cab driver, or a duke, but by God, you were an Englishman, and that meant something. Today, Christianity is merely a punchline when the Anglican Church's own bishops aren't turning it into blasphemy. The elite and the truly common share their alienation from God as well. Church is for old ladies and the occasional funeral. And patriotism? If you wave the Union Jack someone is likely to report you for committing a hate crime—and worse, the bobbies are likely to show up and nick you.

While the barriers between classes were higher, in the past there was at least a sense of obligation of the big people to the little men and women. Being a gentleman didn't merely mean you got to slip past the nineteenth century version of the velvet rope at the nineteenth century's version of a nightclub. It meant you owed something to the little people and that you held yourself to a certain standard.

That's why when all hell broke loose, the captain of the RMS *Titanic* chose to go down with the ship rather than take a seat in a lifeboat from a passenger. History is replete with stories of English gentlemen in battle standing by their men when they could have run—sure, they had their batboys bring them roasted Cornish game hens and a fine Madeira at dinner the evening before while their men devoured who knows what, but when the lead flew, there they were, out front. Because that was what gentlemen did.

Perhaps the last gasp of this old elite was Margaret Thatcher, who grew up over her father's shop. She became elite, but it was her embrace of the English version of normality and its centrality to the English identity that made her a success and gained her so many enemies among the establishment. She was the one who told George H. W. Bush—a member of the American Elite if there ever was one—not to go all wobbly in the face of Saddam Hussein. When the IRA blew apart the hotel where she was to speak, killing a number of her party members, she damn well spoke anyway because the hell with those mick bastards.

Today, not so much. Contrast the steely resolve of Lady Thatcher with the goofy antics of the prime minister played by Hugh Grant in that celluloid abomination *Love Actually* (2003). "Look!" the movie seems to say. "Why, he's just a regular guy!" Leaving aside whether regular guys ditch Elizabeth Hurley to pick up genderfluid hookers off the Sunset Strip, because you can't forget that sordid anecdote when watching Grant on-screen, the film seems to be one big excuse for dropping the standards that once distinguished gentlemen and ladies from the rabble. Our elite is free—liberated!—to act like fools, it tells us. Oh, the elite doesn't have to give up any power. It's still in charge and still gets all the perks of being elite, but it just doesn't have to do any of the stuff that sometimes made being elite inconvenient, like having to act like adults.

The "Cool Britannia" nonsense of Tony Blair that sought to substitute cheesy pizzazz and empty celebrity for what remained of traditional English values accelerated the decline. Now the modern English elite is much like the modern American Elite. They certainly believe they have more in common with each other than their respective Normals. And that's bad.

As we have seen, the American Elite takes many forms, but

like Normals, there are qualifications for membership. The key one is a rejection of the idea that you are a Normal, that you are one of those regular guys, which often translates into one of those unenlightened cro-mags lurking in states the Elite usually visits by crossing over at thirty-six thousand feet.

Someone in the Elite is special, at least in his own calculation. He is *not* like others. Normals are proud of who they are, while a member of the Elite is proud of who he *isn't*.

Being Elite means being special, even if that specialness comes from merely choosing to affiliate yourself with it. Being Normal is just that—it's not a status you look to acquire. You just are. Normal status is a label, not an identity. But Elite status is an identity, one that fills a void in the psyche of one who bears the label. Elitism is, therefore, largely defined by rejecting Normality.

While it is remarkably easy to join the Elite in general, certain branches, like the political or cultural Elite, may take some effort to join. But being inside the big Elite tent is easy. You choose to be. One of the myriad mandatory beliefs of the American Elite is the bizarre notion that you can change your gender on a whim, but, in fact, you can choose to identify as Elite simply by doing so— and by signing on to the ideological baggage that comes with it.

For some, the choice to enter the Elite is made for them at about the time they come out of the womb, having survived their mother's right to choose. They are born into it, and they grow up around the Elite. No other future is possible. They compete for entry into the top preschools and, later, the top colleges—this is one of the only competitions the Elite really approves of. But the skids are greased—a child of a *New York Times*-subscribing law-yer and a freelance blogger with a pussy hat in the closet of their Brooklyn townhouse is destined to join the Elite well before he, she, or xe gets accepted into the Department of Gender Studies at Wellesley.

Others make a conscious choice, because being Elite at least appears to mean that you are, well, elite. Lots of members of the Elite grew up in Normal homes. And many of them look at their Normal parents and wince. But the cognitive dissonance is worth it. It can be very attractive to be special, to know that you are a part of a club whose membership serves to distinguish you from, well, all those Normals.

You *know* more. You *feel* more. You *are* more.

It's seductive, and that is why many millions of people identify as Elite whether they are, in fact, elite in any meaningful sense or not.

The easiest strata of the Elite to spot are the celebrities. In fact, you can't not spot them. They are everywhere. Of course, the term *celebrity* has been so stretched out and distorted over the last few decades that it pretty much constitutes anyone many other people are aware of, regardless of context. There are the usual rock stars and movie idols, but real celebrities are relatively few and far between. With a zillion bands out there, "celebrity" encompasses both the drummer for U2 and the drummer of The I Ate a Hamster Experience, which you probably never heard of but is totally on the cutting edge of the new alt-folk underground trend, and it records only on vinyl for that authentic sound those in the know demand.

The galaxy of "stars" now includes both Tom Cruise and the guy who plays the sassy co-worker on the Netflix original series *My Mom the Zombie*. Then there are the people with millions of fans because they have a YouTube channel where you can watch them narrate their Call of Duty games or watch them examine their new Harry Potter action figures. Others have a lot of Twitter followers because they tweet incessantly about their lunch entrées or their stupid dog.

But while celebrity does not exclude the possibility of Normality—Hollywood stars like Adam Baldwin and Nick Searcy are famously Normals, with solid family lives and none of the attitude that characterizes the Elite—celebrity does make it hard to be Normal. That's because a key element of Elitism, as currently manifested, is the joy Elitists derive from making other people bend to their will.

Now, the will that folks are to be bent to is not really the will of the individual bender. Rather, it is the will of the Elite caste itself that the lesser humans must be bent to. That will often manifest itself in the Elite's dogma, which is often described as "political correctness." The Catholic Church would be hard pressed to match it in complexity and inflexibility. It's all tiresome liberalism, all the time. Luckily, for those interested in mastering the minefield of problematic acts and wish to learn the catechism, you can flip on MSNBC and hear Rachel Maddow preach it.

The Elite have their rituals and their taboos, their sacred texts and their conventional wisdom. All of it is rigidly enforced, and it must be positively exhausting to try and keep up with it and avoid the scowling scolds who make it their life's work on media, both social and otherwise, to enforce it. For example, the phrase *chain migration* went from a perfectly adequate description of a troubling policy to racially insensitive (the word *chain* evokes slavery, context be damned) literally overnight. Of course, besides the tedious moral preening, this sort of thing has the added effect of putting powerful, evocative language off limits, replacing it with terms like *family reunification migration* that obscure the meaning.

Besides language, there are the Elite beliefs a member just cannot reject and remain acceptable. Imagine the aforementioned Tom Cruise coming out on a talk show again—okay, maybe that's a stretch after his couch jumping wackiness the last time. Imagine hard, then imagine him coming out on the set, with the audience hooting and slapping fins like an army of ecstatic trained seals, and telling Ellen DeGeneres, "You know, I really don't buy this global warming stuff."

Cue the record scratch noise.

This will never, ever happen. It will never, ever happen even if Tom Cruise believes that global warming is nonsense. He might. He's not a dumb guy—crazy, maybe, but not dumb—but he's never going to *say* it. You just don't do that in polite company, meaning Elite company. No Elitist is going to do it. Not Tom Cruise. Not the guy who plays the wacky neighbor on a TV Land sitcom. Not the guy who got a billion views of his self-tattooing videos. Not the hooker who got arrested with a New York governor and started her own fragrance collection called "Executive Sweat." They are all going to toe the line. Dissent just isn't done. Because when it is done, you get excommunicated from the Elite.

Remember Nick Searcy and Adam Baldwin—stars, right? But not Elite.

There are those in the Elite who hold positions of real authority—the politicians and bureaucrats. That's a relatively small group—the damage the political class does to America is far, far out of proportion to its members' actual numbers. And there is some overlap with the celebrities—a politician can be a celebrity, too, but except for the most prominent ones that usually only happens in Washington, DC, where it's possible to dazzle a young lady and get laid by trading on your gig as the Assistant Undersecretary of Agriculture for Legume Issues.

But the real role of the politicians vis-à-vis the Elite is to turn the desires and goals of the caste into reality.

They do that not just through legislation, but through infiltration into the bureaucracy. And, what's more, they consider this a sacred trust that they exercise on behalf of the American people—a trust they more and more exercise without bothering to consult with the American people, because they are the experts and they know better.

After all, they are members of the Elite.

But the Normals the Elite serves—though its definition of *serve* is largely service-free—are a cipher. Even if the Elite were to care, which it does not, the Elite has no idea what Normals truly want or need, and what the Elite *thinks* they want or need, the Normals often don't really want or need. And besides, what the Elite thinks the Normals want or need is morally wrong on every level.

Here's the really interesting part. What the Elite wants or needs is *always* morally right on every level. All the true and good and moral policies they enact and enforce? Well, those totally happen to correspond to the tenets of the Elite consensus. How about that?

It's remarkable. And super convenient.

For the Elite.

We saw a wonderful illustration of the political Elite in action when Trump was elected. Now, we should spare some pity for our poor Elite overlords in their hour of pain and confusion. All of them had been fully utterly completely totally convinced that The Smartest Woman in the World was going to mop the floor with the orange-pated provocateur from Queens. It was going to be wonderful—with a woman in the White House and at the helm of the eager bureaucracy, they were going to finish the work Barack Obama had done on beginning the fundamental transformation of the United States into a version of Venezuela with more snow and fewer *telenovelas*.

But then the Normals betrayed their benefactors and picked . . . him.

The bastards.

So what did all those hundreds of thousands of members of the Elite infesting the federal government do? Well, they lost their collective shit.

Some of it was hilarious. Doddering functionaries tendered their resignations as if this was some sort of powerful act of defiance, only to receive a "meh" in response. It's a tribute to how out of touch they are that they believe bureaucrats quitting is going to wreck the Normals' day. Then there were the internal resisters who wanted to fight a rearguard action against things like wetlands regulation reform by comparing themselves to the secret society of plucky young wizard rebels in *Harry Potter*.

Sometimes, it seems like liberals have only read one book.

Other antics were not so funny. The most dangerous manifestations of this phenomenon were the top-level hacks and slugs who had spent the last eight years disgracing the Department of Justice and the Federal Bureau of Investigation. The leadership of the DOJ and the FBI, in conjunction with the holdovers at the White House, decided that they ought to unleash the full power of the United States government's surveillance capacities on their political enemies because that was perfectly cool. It was totally different when Nixon did it, you know.

He wasn't a Democrat.

Trump was a Republican, and he wasn't even one of those reasonable, Elite Republicans who helpfully rolled onto his back and displayed his soft, vulnerable tummy whenever a liberal Elitist on television or in the *WaPo* got angry. He was defiant and vulgar, and, worst of all, he displayed none of the respect and reverence due these proud public servants. Respect and reverence are vital perks for the Elite. And this Trump fellow refused to offer them.

So these proud public servants, these experts entrusted with our most powerful institutions, harnessed the authority of America's law enforcement and intelligence communities to attack their personal political enemies and told themselves they were doing God's work.

Except none of them actually believe in God. Their god was the government, but only as long as the government was run by people like them.

So, in a way, the Elite's god is themselves. And that's the crux of the problem. The Elite is its own higher authority, and it answers only to itself.

How could that go wrong?

CHAPTER FIVE

The Making of an Elitist

Being elite does not necessarily have anything to do with being Elite.

Someone in the Elite may have some achievements, but achievements are not necessary for membership and they are certainly the exception rather than the rule. The American Elite, and other elites around the Western world, consider themselves a meritocracy, yet they never demand that any of their members actually show any merit. You can fail and fail and fail, and many in the Elite do, and yet they still remain Elite.

Being Elite is not about being elite. It's about choosing to identify as Elite.

How do the Elite think and feel? What makes them select the path to Elitism, because it is a path you have to select. You have to want to be in the Elite. You choose it, even when you are born to it.

West Los Angeles is a majority-Elite enclave just east of Santa Monica and separated from America by several parallel ten-lane freeways and a lot of attitude. It was also Obama's abused lover. The inhabitants slavishly devoted their time and money and fervor to his cause even as he treated them like one of Bill Clinton's flings. For Obama, gridlocking Westside traffic and trapping the faithful was the equivalent of telling his most slobbering fans to put some ice on it.

You see, Obama did the most evil and odious thing he could to his own people—he would land at LAX about fifteen miles to the south and then take a motorcade north up the 405 and through the side streets on his way to someplace like Jeffrey Katzenberg's pad for a soiree with the gang from DreamWorks, some other studio execs you never heard of, and a few personalities whose names you can't mention anymore because they got all handsy and grabby with young gals or younger guys who didn't get the memo that while you kept your mouth open during, afterward you kept it closed tight.

But long before #MeToo became #GeeLiberalsInHollywood-WashingtonAndTheMediaActedExactlyHowWeThoughtThey-Acted, West Los Angeles was the Los Angeles you think of when you think of Los Angeles. Robert Downey Jr. might be getting a latte ahead of you at a Starbucks in Brentwood. There are Bentleys and Aston Martins, most driven by sketchy, swarthy dudes whose business cards read "Producer." Sports legends decapitate people on the leafy residential streets and get away with it. But West Los Angeles is not the reality of Los Angeles.

There are many different Los Angeleses. East Los Angeles has a vibrant Hispanic culture. West Los Angeles has armies of forlorn Hispanic nannies for rich white families being disgorged from the scores of dirty buses that run west down Olympic and Wilshire in the morning and being picked up by those same buses heading east after six. The beach cities have the surfers and affluent white guys who usually end up with Asian women. In West Los Angeles, that lifestyle is considered a bit too on the nose. In

South Central, you have a large black community that is coming together to try to improve the lives of its residents. In West Los Angeles, or at least the swankier parts of it, when a black person appears you have a bunch of LAPD cop cars coming together to find out what he's doing there.

West Los Angeles has the money vibe and a bit of the hipster vibe, but mostly it has a huge liberal vibe. Ted Lieu is its congressman, and calling him "dumb as a post" is a harsh and unwarranted attack on the brainpower of posts. Posts are, at least, useful. Ted's entire oeuvre in Congress appears to be tweeting pics of himself with famous Hollywood perverts and issuing dire warnings that Trump is Hitler + Mussolini + Mao + Stalin + Castro.

Well, maybe not the last three—to liberals, they totally meant well, unlike Trump.

West Los Angeles is the land of "Trump is not my president," though Trump totally is their president. But the residents apparently feel that if they hold their breath long enough and resist resist resist, they will one day awaken and Trump will be gone and left at the helm in the White House will be . . . Mike Pence.

Oops.

Long-range strategic thinking is not a big thing in West Los Angeles. In fact, there's no need to think at all. You just open your mind and your heart and let the liberalism flow through you like Luke with the Force. And to further confuse the sci-fi metaphors, you must accept assimilation because resistance is futile.

This is where Kaden, our aspiring member of the Elite, was born into this world of lefty dogma and material comfort. His mom was a lawyer. He was a designer kid because she was thirty-seven when she decided a child was the next expensive accessory she simply had to have. She took time off to have him and never quite forgave him for slowing her ride down the rails of the partnership track. But she only dealt with him for a couple weeks before going back to work overseeing movie deals—she was the go-to gal for finding ways of ensuring that movies made for $10 million that gross $250 million never, ever made a profit, and thereby cut out all the folks who signed on with a promise of a piece of the back end.

Of course, thereafter, young Kaden was no trouble at all. He was Lupita's problem.

Dad was a plastic surgeon—the beaches were filled with his bouncy, bouncy handiwork. Dad was born to be a doctor like *his* dad and also a liberal like his dad—when Kaden's father was an idealistic intern he had treated Cesar Chavez for a hemorrhoid and it changed his life. From then on, Dad had been so impressed that he vigorously supported the United Farm Workers union by buying only union-picked lettuce and grapes, which was easy because that's all the local market would sell. Kaden had noticed his father's deep commitment to social issues and continued that family tradition by only buying lattes made with fair trade coffee that was picked by certified woke coffee pickers.

Every night, Dad would complain about how all civilized countries have a single-payer health care system. He spoke to a lot of citizens of those countries when they came here to America to get their medical care, so he totally knew the score. He read the *New Republic* until it turned too right wing, then switched to *The Nation* until it turned too right wing.

Now they lived in a big house north of Wilshire—it was vital that it be north of Wilshire because can you imagine not living north of Wilshire? Every four years, they did their civic duty and wrote checks to the Democratic National Committee. Every four years, they put signs for the Democrat in the front yard. It was always baffling when their guy (or gal) lost—they never saw any signs for Republicans around town. Dad still wondered what happened to Mondale Mania back in 1984—everyone he knew was feeling it!

Obviously, Ronald Reagan was the worst president imaginable, determined to get us into a war and, well, it was pretty obvious how much he hated black people. But then George H. W. Bush came along and, well, he was even worse than Reagan. He did get us into a war, which America unfortunately won. And, of course, you knew what Bush thought of black Americans—that went without saying.

Luckily Bill Clinton came along, and what a breath of fresh air. Clinton's wars in Bosnia and Kosovo were clean and antiseptic and, best of all, started by Democrats, and they totally solved all the problems in the Balkans forever. Also, he loved black people. You could tell because he said so.

Clinton made draft dodging okay again, and Dad could now openly say that his moral opposition to opposing communist tyranny in Vietnam was why he had faked being homosexual to get out of the draft. Not that being homosexual was bad—he made it clear that he would have loved to have been homosexual if that was how he was born, and he had mostly not been. It was a little sad when Bill Clinton had imposed "Don't Ask, Don't Tell," but it was really those rednecks, hicks, and racists still in the Democratic Party who made him. If only someday those people could be purged from the party—then there would be no stopping us!

The Republican attempt to impeach Bill Clinton for lying about sex was an outrage. What kind of Neanderthal would go into a moral panic about sex? And if Hillary Clinton—who seemed really awesome—was okay with it, who were we to judge?

Mom and Dad voted for Al Gore in 2000 and were devastated when he lost. It was clear, so very clear, that the Florida Supreme Court and not the United States Supreme Court should have made the final determination about those hanging chads. States' rights were so important at the moment, after all.

George W. Bush, known around West LA as Chimpy Bu$Hitler-burton, was even worse, a million times worse than Reagan and Poppa Bush. Bush W. got us into another war. Luckily, Iraq turned into a quagmire for several years until, tragically, Bush 43 began winning it again. And he obviously hated African Americans. You could just tell.

John McCain and that awful, awful Sarah Palin would have been the worst of all. They would have kept winning the wars and they obviously hated black people, who by then were black again.

But luckily, Barack Obama came along, and if any member of Kaden's family had had the capacity for religious sentiments they would have felt them then. Obama was urbane and well spoken, a stark contrast to the stuttering Texan mess of W.'s diction. He was highly educated—Harvard, everybody! Did you hear that? Harvard! And he was president of the law review. Sure, his college records never got released, and no, he didn't publish a law review article, but he got into Harvard and got onto the law review. And he didn't do anything in the Illinois Senate or the United States Senate, but he was a senator!

And that was enough. This guy talked well and a lot, and he checked all the boxes. He was the embodiment of the Elite, especially in the way that he had never actually accomplished anything before being elected president. Oh, and he was black, and in the theocratic tradition of liberalism, voting for a black candidate was a way to purchase an indulgence to cleanse you of your original sin.

Kaden was born into sin as an affluent white kid in the United States. There was a lot of guilt that he would be able to display down the road, even if he never felt guilty. Bearing liberal guilt was a lot like being an ancient sinner who changed into his oldest, rattiest clothes before he would cruise down to the temple to rend his garments while crying out in anguish about repentance.

Lupita raised Kaden with the kind of loving care you would expect from someone getting paid below minimum wage under the table. She even taught him Spanish—"Real Spanish, the authentic Spanish of the countryside of the real Mexico," Mom had beamed, pronouncing the *x* as an *h* in what she assumed was the real Spanish style. Lupita nodded politely. She was from El Salvador.

After Kaden had run up to his mommy and announced *"¡Soy un gringo pendejo!"* and Mommy had hugged him because she was so proud of her lil' citizen of the world, Lupita stopped with the Spanish. Instead, she flipped on the television and let him watch all the cartoons his mother forbade. He was sad when Mom and Dad let Lupita go the minute he was ten and could stay home alone after school. Marcela, the maid, and Juanita, the other maid, were just not the same.

Kaden and the rest of the local children would sometimes gather at the park and play. It was there Kaden began to learn about diversity as he realized that there were many different types of rich white kids. Some had red hair, some had yellow hair, some had brown hair, and all had an immigrant acting-mommy off to the side chatting in Spanish about what assholes her employers were.

It was in the competition for admission into kindergarten that Kaden first understood that some people were better than others. Obviously, there was something wrong with the kids at the public school because Mommy sure didn't want him to go there. The word *shithole* was used, but certainly not in the racist way Donald Trump would use it years later. No, Mommy used it with love.

She took time off work to drag him to audition at a succession of tony private schools. The grim administrators would size him up and down and ask about his "development" and "readiness." Luckily, when Kaden decided to eat the eraser on the principal's desk, the principal had stepped out of the room. He couldn't breathe and pointed to his throat. As she gave him the Heimlich, his mother hissed, "Don't you screw this up by choking!"

It was clear that the schools were selective and that it was a sellers' market. But still, the administrators could barely conceal their pride at their academic rigor. "This is one of the most exclusive schools in West Los Angeles, and you can be sure that Kaden, if selected, would be attending class with a truly distinguished group of fellow scholars. I'm really not supposed to reveal it, but Bea Arthur's grandchildren are both enrolled here at the Brentwood Montessori Academy for Excellence."

Mommy was sure stressed. One morning, she exploded in rage. "What are you thinking, Kaden? We have an interview in twenty minutes and you spill açai smoothie all over your romper? Don't you want to go to Yale? Well, stop crying and act like it!"

They did a lot of classroom walk-throughs at the various schools. All the kids seemed pretty much the same. One of them was eating paste, and the teacher seemed very, very upset because

Ashleighee was vegan and it was unclear whether the paste was animal product–free.

Kaden was eventually accepted into one of the fancier schools—the administration had decided they needed to add some diversity to the student body by accepting some kids whose families worked in the trades, like law and medicine. He was a good student. The first quarter he got a "Smiley ++" in "Self-Esteem."

And once he got into the school, that was it. The stress vanished. Everything that came after was an afterthought. Kaden absorbed that lesson well.

His elementary school fed into a prestigious private high school—the thought of him enrolling in the Los Angeles Unified School District never entered into any of their heads. Every year, the private high school gave a couple of kids from Inglewood a scholarship. Voilà, there was some diversity.

The curriculum focused on making them "active participants in their own citizenship," and his class learned about the threat of global warming caused by the use of fossil fuels. He typed out the last few lines of his freshman paper on the subject on his laptop while in the back seat of his Mom's Mercedes S-Class as she sat idling in the morning drop-off line.

In fourth grade, they had begun his college application preparations in earnest. He needed a language and Spanish was too— what did his admissions consultant call it?—"unexceptional." Japanese maybe? No, you didn't want to go Asian—again, too unexceptional. Catalan? *That* was the ticket. Close enough to Spanish that he already had a base, but edgy enough because who the hell spoke Catalan? Besides, Barcelona was the height of cool for some reason—the divorced, middle-aged women who sorted through the piles of applications in the Ivy League admissions offices would see he was fluent in that language and swoon, dreaming of walking streets full of Gaudí-designed buildings and being wooed by tough yet tender Catalonian men.

But it was a struggle. His Catalan tutor, Franco, grimaced when Kaden tried out his limited Spanish.

Kaden was involved in sports, too. He played soccer and had a shelf full of trophies he had won for showing up. They didn't play for points in the West Los Angeles league. "It's about teamwork and the joy of sports." His coach told him that the fact he had never scored a goal—that he had barely kicked the ball all season—did not mean he wasn't crucial to the team's success. "Sports aren't about winning. Sports are about participating!" He did not need to mention that his participation would be noted on a future college application. If it weren't for that block-check, none of the kids would be there.

In his freshman year, with his application deadline just two years away, he started a charity called "Meals for the Oppressed" where his mom would stop at a McDonald's and buy a few dozen hamburgers and then give them to the local homeless people south of Olympic. He was not allowed out of the car, not allowed around the homeless, and especially not allowed around McDonald's.

For their part, the bums loved college admission season. One kid distributed a bunch of bright red hats to the local shiftless and idle that read CARE ABOUT ME. Her charity was called Hats of Caring. She would eventually be admitted to Princeton.

Kaden received all A++'s in all his Advanced Placement classes. The SAT was key, and he had a tutor for that, too. He learned the math that would be tested, and the English that would be tested. In history, he learned about Europe's history of colonial oppression, and how the American Revolution against colonial oppression was a reactionary spasm by a bunch of slave-owning white males whose sole goal was to subjugate women, minorities, indigenous peoples, the differently-abled, and the trans community. His school did not celebrate Columbus Day or Christmas, which Kaden thought had something to do with the Christians recognizing the birth of Santa Claus under a pine tree near Rudolph's stable.

The Fourth of July holiday was no big deal, either, and his family only once ever considered flying an American flag. The thought had crossed his father's mind right after 9/11, but he discarded it when it became clear that the real tragedy was the hateful backlash against practitioners of the Religion of Peace. Plus, Bush 43 was probably in on it.

By the time he graduated, he had read the works of Maya Angelou and studied the Harry Potter saga and its scathing critique of Margaret Thatcher's Tory government—the Iron Lady was pretty much Voldemort. He could not name a Shakespeare play, a president before Bill Clinton, or a book of the Bible (there was no copy in his house or in the school library). He was pretty sure that the Civil War ended when Abe Lincoln dropped the atomic bomb on Pearl Harbor.

Kaden didn't know much about Islam except that all those bigots out there in Kansas and Texas and stuff hated Muslims, which meant they had to be okay. His teacher had also informed the class that the hijab was a symbol of female empowerment. He wrote that in his notes and, sure enough, it came up on a test. He got an A+++.

When he started noticing girls—by the mid-2000s people hung out; they didn't date—his parents had "the talk" with him about

sex. He was pretty clear on the mechanics already—his elementary school had started teaching them about it in second grade,
and he had aced the quiz on sodomy. But his parents wanted to
make sure that he understood that sex was a serious issue, and
that he needed to obtain consent before moving to the next level
of intimacy, because if he didn't some lying bitch could screw up
his whole future. Also, they said, women should be valued and
respected, and always wear a rubber so some tramp won't infect
you with a disease.

Most important of all, his parents told him, they would totally
pay if his partner needed an abortion. They would even give her
a ride to a clinic without telling her parents if that's what it took
to keep his future secure.

He got into one of his target colleges back east, Columbia. His
parents were thrilled, and so was he. Now that he was admitted,
he could relax again. Which he did, for five years.

It was at college where, for the first time, he met strange, exotic
people who were not from West Los Angeles or similar places.
Sure, he had traveled before school. He had been to Europe and
Japan, to New York City, and to Colorado to ski. And he had
driven to Lake Tahoe once, also to ski, so it was not quite accurate
to say he had never been east of I-5. He just hadn't stepped out of
the SUV except for gas until he reached the slopes.

He knew there was a town called Fontana, but he couldn't
find it on a map.

There was a guy in the dorms who was a little older and
who seemed more serious than everyone else. While Kaden grew
dreadlocks during his Bob Marley phase, the guy always kept his
hair short. The others whispered that he had been in the Army
or something before he went to college. Kaden had never met

anyone who had actually been in the military before. He never even remotely considered joining up, nor had any of his classmates. He was pretty sure that the Army was not the one with the ships, but he wasn't positive.

Kaden pitied the poor guy. Once, after some bong hits and Heinekens, he had stumbled over to the guy and apologized on behalf of America for him having been suckered into Bush's illegal war for oil.

"I was in Afghanistan," the Army guy replied, baffled.

"I know," Kaden said, nodding. "Bush's illegal war for oil."

Later, Kaden wondered how someone...like that...could have gotten into that school. He worried that if people knew that Columbia's standards were so low that even some soldier could get in, it could devalue his degree in communications.

Kaden had always considered himself a socialist, but college really helped him create an intellectual framework for what he was feeling. He read Marx and Engels and the works of Bernie Sanders, and he was excited by what he was learning. He did not bother taking any history courses, as there was no need to learn about the Soviet Union, or China under Mao, or the National Socialism of the Third Reich. After all, real socialism had never been tried, so what was the point?

Every once in a while, he would encounter an idea or opinion that challenged his own preconceptions. But not for long—as a defender of free speech, he felt he had a special responsibility to shout down and silence those who abused it by expressing ideas he disagreed with.

It was at Columbia where he decided to pursue journalism. He was bursting with opinions that he wanted to share with the world, and being a reporter seemed the best way to do that. After all, the newspapers, television, and the internet were all full of opinions. His journalism professor leveled with the class that the idea of objectivity was an outdated concept, unsuited to modern times when the audience needed the guidance of experts in the form of trained journalists to help lead them to the truth. Otherwise, they might embrace bad ideas and vote for Republicans.

That was the purpose of the institution of the press. Those in the class would take their places within this proud institution and ensure that it remained a beacon of enlightenment in the fog of parochial ignorance that engulfed so much of America.

"People are shallow and small-minded," the professor warned his students. "It is your job to help them be better. And though they will not appreciate it, you have a responsibility to guide them to the truth. After all, democracy dies in darkness."

Kaden nodded, and he accepted this great responsibility eagerly. He liked feeling that he was a part of something bigger, part of a special group of people with the training and education— the expertise—to make a difference.

Most of all, he liked not feeling like everyone else out there. After all, he was bringing the light that would keep democracy from dying. And most everyone else would spend their lives riding a tractor or loading boxes or whatever those other people did.

He would be special.

He would be Elite.

After graduation, he moved to Washington, DC, to start working for a news website covering the government. With his life experience, they scooped him right up.

Washington was very diverse, with young Elite graduates from all sorts of different colleges. He even made friends with someone who was originally from Alabama. She used to tell him how when she was a kid her parents made her go to church, and how her dad used to hunt deer. Obviously, she was disgusted by her troubled upbringing. For Kaden, it was a real education in how truly awful red America was. He knew his calling would be to fight against its ignorance and against the redneck monsters who dwelled there.

Washington under Barack Obama in the first couple years of his administration was an exciting city full of people working together to create a better tomorrow. When Obamacare was enacted, Kaden celebrated with a honey-cinnamon IPA in a bar packed with other ecstatic reporters. What a step forward! Of course, the right-wing media, including Fox—who the hell watched Fox, anyway?—was going crazy, telling lies about how you were not going to be able to keep your doctor if you liked him and how your family's bills were not going to be cut by $2,500 a year.

And then the Republicans retook the House, and then the Senate. How did that happen? Clearly, the lies from Fox and the Koch brothers and the National Rifle Association and Fox tricked those idiots in the red states into voting Republican. It was outrageous—those idiots should have been voting for Democrats!

Now it was all hands on deck—Obama and the dedicated government officials under him needed all the help they could get. Kaden loved to break the big stories about Republican malfeasance whenever he could. And he was not above helping out a Democrat friend with stepping on an embarrassing story. After all, they were all working together, and this was a life or death struggle between the forces of light and the forces of darkness.

Darkness was, after all, where democracy died.

But there was a mass of people out there who were an obstacle to progress. Kaden didn't know any of them. He had never driven out of the Beltway to find any of them, but they were out there.

Stupid.

Ignorant.

Racist.

Sexist.

Consumed with their ridiculous belief in their imaginary friend Jesus.

In love with their phallic-symbol assault rifles, although the mass shooters he and his media pals gave wall-to-wall coverage never, ever cooperated by being conservative Christian NRA members.

They were incorrigible, irredeemable, but it was Hillary Clinton who put it best. They were "deplorable."

They were everything Kaden and his friends wanted *not* to be.

They were the enemy.

And they had to be crushed once and for all.

Luckily, The Smartest Woman in the World, the pantsuited savioress of Elite America, was going to bring down the righteous thunder upon them. It was a testament to their loathsomeness that they had selected Donald Trump—arrrgh, Donald Trump!—as their nominee. Trump could not possibly win. He shared their crassness, their moral bankruptcy, their stupidity. But his defiance—their defiance—could not just be forgiven.

They were going to pay.

Obama's problem is that he had been too nice to the rabble. He hid his contempt for the Normals, sort of, and while he would mess with them, he did not make his disgust with them the centerpiece of his administration. But Hillary would. She was all about the payback for their daring to seek to interfere, for their daring to object.

Kaden and those like him were thrilled that Hillary Clinton would not pretend to be the president of all Americans. She would be the Avenger of the Elite. That's what the Elite really wanted.

Their stupid religion? Sure, the Normals could keep it—within reasonable limits. They can do whatever they want in private, mostly, until the Elite got around to dealing with that. But for now, in public, they will acknowledge and bow down to the true Almighty, the government with Hillary Clinton at the helm.

Their concerns about immigrants? Too bad. It is long past time to replace an electorate that fails to understand its place.

Their jobs in coal and fracking? Better learn coding, because those industries are gone. And if that wrecks the economies of Texas and those other states, well, then maybe they ought to vote smarter next time.

And their guns? The Constitution is a living document that was never meant to be an obstacle to the government doing what it wants. The only people who should have guns are people who report to…the Elite. Armed citizens are citizens, not subjects—which is precisely the point, and the problem.

And yeah, their little girls are going to have to watch men in dresses come into their restrooms and pee. Why? Why is that so important?

Because it teaches the Normals who's boss.

And then on November 8, 2016, the giddy anticipation Kaden felt, knowing that soon he would be helping to finally tame the rabble and put them in their place once and for all, turned to heaving, hilarious sobbing.

Hillary Clinton lost.

But Nate Silver had promised him! He was an expert on statistics, damn it! Science! And Rachel Maddow went to Oxford! Rachel, how could you let this happen?

It was the Normals.

They did this.

Those people out in states where Kaden had never been, doing jobs Kaden had never done, never even thought of, living lives Kaden could not even imagine, did it. They did it to him and every smug, spoiled, overeducated jerk who thought he had some sort of divine right to push them around.

The next morning, after obtaining explicit consent, Kaden hugged his girlfriend. Being attracted to women was a burden—he was bummed that he identified as cisgender straight, no matter how hard he tried to change that. Her eyes were red and puffy from crying, just like his.

"I so respect you for rejecting patriarchal stereotypes and for so openly expressing your feelings and for being willing to sob in public last night," she said, even though inside, his whimpering and weeping kind of disgusted her.

"Thank you," Kaden whispered. "But we have to be strong. Now we have to act to stop the worst person ever to be president."

He handed her a pink knit cap.

"He's probably going to start a war," she said.

"Yes, and he totally hates black people." Then he donned his own pussyhat. "Now we must resist."

CHAPTER SIX

The Expert Scam

The Elite's justification for its own position is its expertise, which it uses to run society's institutions on behalf of the Normals who are busy doing other things, like generating revenue for those institutions. Government, media, Hollywood—you are supposed to have skills to be a part of them. And yet all the Normals see is chaos and failure.

That's the disconnect. You have a bunch of people who want the respect and reward that comes from applying their expertise successfully without actually having done so. Some, the affiliates and hangers on who grasp at membership in the Elite simply by aping the Elite's attitude, have no expertise at all.

An expert is supposed to be someone with demonstrated skills in a certain field. In law, because lawyers hire experts to testify all the time, the word has a specific definition. The Federal Rules of Evidence, Rule 702, "Testimony by Expert Witnesses," defines an "expert" as:

> A witness who is qualified as an expert by knowledge, skill, experience, training, or education may testify in the form of an opinion or otherwise if:

(a) the expert's scientific, technical, or other specialized knowledge will help the trier of fact to understand the evidence or to determine a fact in issue;

(b) the testimony is based on sufficient facts or data;

(c) the testimony is the product of reliable principles and methods; and

(d) the expert has reliably applied the principles and methods to the facts of the case.

This means that in court, and elsewhere, an expert is supposed to be someone with knowledge that most others do not have—"scientific," "technical," or "specialized." He makes decisions based on facts and data, and his analysis is based on proven techniques applied to the situation. Expertise can be broad or narrow. There are many kinds of experts we encounter in our daily lives—doctors, lawyers, but also teachers, priests, movie producers, and even the guy who fixes your Dodge Caravan. Because they are experts, we give them certain tasks to do that we either cannot or do not want to perform ourselves. For example, you could probably ask your spouse to check you for prostate issues, but you are wiser to go with a urologist.

Many of the Elite are experts, though not every expert (like your auto mechanic) is Elite. Some are technical experts; others are experts in performing the tasks of governance. That's no surprise, and that is the way it should be. After all, the point of the Elite is to have a group of people ready to do the jobs that are essential to the job of day-to-day governing and to other societal tasks.

But some of those experts are not good at being experts, at

least not in any real sense of the word. And their results speak for themselves. Iraq. Chicago. *The Emoji Movie.*

If a purported expert is offered to testify in court by a party, and the expert does not meet those qualifications, he is excluded and barred from offering his opinion. In court, to be an expert, you actually need to be an expert. You have to demonstrate competence.

In American society, including in politics, you don't. To be an expert, too often all you have to do is repeat what the Elite wants to hear.

Expertise is one of the tools the Elite employs to exercise the power delegated to it by the Normals. It is a sword to enforce their will, and it is also a shield it deploys to protect itself from accountability.

"Shut up and listen to the experts," the Elite demands. But you never hear the Elite demand any accountability for when the experts they promote are wrong. That's not an accident. If experts are seen to be fallible, then the Elite is seen to be fallible, and the Elite can't afford to be seen as fallible.

As in any human activity where there is no accountability, the Elite's experts screw up on a regular basis. Here's a test. Look down at your toast. There might be butter on it—or maybe not. If not, it's because the experts told you that rich, creamy butter was gooey, yellow death. But now, the experts are not so sure. Maybe the Grim Reaper comes in the form of bread, that carby nightmare you spread that delicious, healthy butter upon. Which is it?

The experts are not so sure anymore, though for a while they were positive, and their hypotheses condemned generations to consume the culinary abominations that are low-fat foods. And that's a problem for an Elite that seeks to use experts to place certain questions out of bounds for input by the Normals they wish to govern.

Progressivism, a disease of the Elite, is notorious for its preference for governing through the wisdom of detached, neutral experts who will be guided solely by the best of science and philosophy. These great minds will not be subject to the passions and prejudices of lesser men and women. Their fact-based, logical rule will usher in a new age of enlightened governance.

And they've been trying to impose a regime of rule by experts, with varying levels of intensity, since the Progressive Era of the early twentieth century, and everything's gone great since then.

Wait, what?

————

When the Elite talks about expertise, it really is not talking about using experts as they should be used—as technical advisors to the decision makers. The Elite does not want that. It wants experts—*their* experts—to be the actual decision makers. The demand for rule by the experts is a demand for rule by the Elite all gussied up and tricked out so it looks bright and shiny and selfless where, in reality, it is precisely the opposite.

The Cult of the Experts is about taking the power to make *major* decisions away from the Normals. Normals readily cede the minor decisions to the experts in America's institutions; that's what experts are for. But for the *big* choices, the *policy* choices, the Normals demand a say, and today's Elite experts hate that.

In a proper representative democracy, experts provide advice and suggestions, and it is the people, the Normals, who should make the policy decisions via their elected representatives. In other words, the scientists at, say, the Department of Science, make the day-to-day decisions, but they don't make the *policy* decisions about science. They give advice to the Secretary of Science, who was appointed by the president, whom the people elected, and the Secretary of Science makes more substantial decisions, but within the bounds of the laws passed by the people's representatives in Congress. And the very biggest decisions? Those are reserved for the president or Congress—people whose names appear on a ballot.

But the Elite wants to skip all those steps where the Normals, via their representatives, might actually get a say in setting policy. They want to go to direct rule by the experts, with the confidence that the experts will always be loyal to the Elite.

And the Elite no longer makes a real effort to hide that fact. Tom Nichols, a noted Never Trumper who teaches at the Naval War College, even wrote a book titled *The Death of Expertise: The Campaign Against Established Knowledge and Why It Matters* (New York: Oxford University Press, 2017). His ultimate point boils down to the idea that Normals should defer to the experts and stop trying to influence policy based on their own interests and let the experts decide. Normals' objection is to what Nichols calls "established knowledge," because experience has taught Normals that "established knowledge" is not always "accurate knowledge." It is, instead, always the "knowledge" established by the Elite to support the Elite's preferences and agenda. This "established knowledge" is not necessarily an objective fact, and it denies human nature to argue that it always will be. After all, experts are people, too, which means they can be just as greedy, small-minded, bigoted, and selfish as they think the Normals are.

The campaign Nichols's title refers to is simply the refusal of

Normal Americans to defer to the Elite. And why should they? The hallmarks of an actual expert are neutrality and objectivity, at least in the scientific field (there are also social science experts, who are to science as electronic dance music is to music). Experts often incorporate the scientific method into reaching their conclusions. They carefully gather data and test it against a hypothesis. If the data supports the hypothesis, so be it. If the data does not support the hypothesis, they go get themselves a new hypothesis. The data proves what the data proves—if you really are an expert and not a hack.

Science, after all, is a way of gathering and systematizing knowledge, not some sort of pseudoreligion. When the Elite preens about "believing in science," they really are not talking about accepting the conclusions that the data compel regardless of whose apple cart they overturn. If they did, Facebook would not be offering you 7,684 choices for your gender identity. You'd have two choices, because there is no combination of chromosomes that creates a "two-spirit nonbinary femme butch otherkin who identifies as a corgi."

That is not science, and science is not a cafeteria where you get to pick and choose the things science applies to and the things it does not. When a member of the Elite starts flapping his talk hole about "believing in science," what he, she, or xe means is that he, she, or xe firmly believes in the approved tenets of Elite dogma. But instead of leveling and admitting it is dogma, it gets labeled as "science" in order to allow anyone who dares question the sacred tenets to be dismissed as some sort of slack-jawed kook who eschews fancy book learnin'.

The mind-numbing tweets of Neil deGrasse Tyson, the director of the Hayden Planetarium at the Rose Center for Earth and

Space in New York, demonstrate the problem. He's an icon for the kind of guy who wears a T-shirt that reads I FUCKING LOVE SCIENCE on his way to the alternative healing bookstore where he works. Tyson's specialty is dumbing down science for people who wish to seem smart, offering them unimaginative observations phrased as epiphanies designed to blow his cultists' collective minds. For example, on January 1, 2017, he welcomed his awestruck Twitter followers to AD 2017 with this shocking insight: "To all on the Gregorian Calendar, Happy New Year! A day that's not astronomically significant…in any way…at all…whatsoever."[1]

Whoa.

Heavy.

All over America…nay, all over the planet…people were swallowing the red pill and awakening to the shocking secret that dates on the Western calendar are not based on any particular astronomical occurrence.

Ta da!

You know, if you want to be regarded as elite, and not merely a member of the Elite, you ought to raise your game. And it's all a game. It's not the pursuit of knowledge. It's wearing pedestrian knowledge like a funny hat and walking around a cocktail party just waiting for people to ask you about it.

The idea of "science" has become just another means by which the Elite attempts to disempower the Normals it should be working for while flattering itself. You will often see a Christian fish symbol stuck on the back of an SUV—well, you often do in the parts of America beyond the flight range of seagulls. There's a similar symbol of a fish with little legs you will often see on Priuses covered with seagull droppings—and in case you don't get the joke, the word *Darwin* is there inside the fish. Take that, people who do not believe the unutterably complex interplay of physical laws within the universe and the mind-bogglingly complex collection of organic structures and processes that constitutes life just sprung into being from nothing for some reason.

Where the original fish identified persecuted Christians for their brothers in Christ, the Darwin fish is a cult identifier for the least persecuted people in human history, the American Elite. They *want* you to know who they are, and they want your deference. So do the experts among them. The Elite's experts want to be treated with the respect and reverence due those who dedicate themselves to nonpartisan, disinterested service.

Except, like our media, they don't actually want to be disinterested public servants. They want to be partisan players pursuing an agenda—while still getting the same kind of deference that might be appropriate for those who are not.

The notion that Normals somehow have an unreasoning hatred for experts is ridiculous. Many of the Normals themselves are experts in their own fields—let's see a patent lawyer from Manhattan track a deer. The problem is the exploitation and perversion of Elite expertise to conduct a power grab that disenfranchises Normal Americans.

Expertise is good, and it is necessary. The notion of the Elite itself is based on the idea of expertise—by training, experience, and inclination, the people in the Elite are prepared to operate the levers of power in our society on behalf of the Normals who are off doing something else. The "on behalf of the Normals" is the key part of that sentence—expertise is properly understood as a resource designed to fulfill the Normal citizen's ability to exercise self-governance. It is not designed to *replace* that ability to self-govern.

But what happens when the servant—and the Elite and experts are properly understood as servants—decides he's smarter than the master and wants to actually be the master?

The disenfranchisement of the Normals by the Elite and their pet experts is not a side effect; it is the goal. They are the Keepers of the Secret Flame of Science. Cede them your autonomy and despair!

To hide the truth, the Elite reacts to criticism of experts who swerve outside of their proper lane by trying to frame any objection to their overreach as one to expertise itself. This is worse than dumb—it's a lie, and not a very convincing one. No one would prefer to do his own C-section on his wife. You want doctors with years of training wielding the scalpels. And you want them to be experienced. In fact, you want the doctors to walk into the operating room bored nearly to tears and chatting about their 401(k)s as they scrub up and stride over to the patient. You want them talking about anything but the surgery as they slice through the abdominal wall, pull out the kid, and flop the uterus, which looks like a raw flank steak, onto the patient's stomach.

The husband can peer over the curtain and gape at this tableau with confidence. For the docs you want, this is nothing special because they have done a couple thousand of these. They've seen it all. This is no big deal. You don't want the shaky new resident to start cutting and suddenly exclaim, "Holy crap, that uterus totally looks like a flank steak!"

Hell, you want those doctors to go out for a flank steak afterward.

You want them to be technically proficient. But it's your (or your wife's) body, and that's where you get a say. Because before they start slicing and dicing, these specialists, these experts, must come to you. They must come to you and explain what they think you should do, and why, and what the risks are. And then...

And then, *you* make the decision. Not them. You.

They may think you are making the wrong decision. Maybe wifey wants to keep pushing. Maybe she had a friend involved in one of those rare circumstances where a simple caesarean section procedure went to shit, and she doesn't want to roll the dice. Maybe she just doesn't trust doctors.

It doesn't matter.

In the end, it doesn't matter what the expert surgeons think. It's not for them to make that decision. They are the technical specialists. They give their best advice, and they sit back and let the proper decision maker make the decision.

That can be frustrating for an expert. After all, an expert gives the advice he thinks is right. He's trying to identify the best option available. And sometimes, that stubborn patient makes the wrong decision.

Why not skip the middleman? Why not let the doctor choose and the hell with what the patient wants?

Two reasons, one utilitarian and one philosophical.

The utilitarian reason involves information and priorities. The doctor actually has only a narrow range of information at hand—the objective technical information regarding the procedure. He knows that cold, if you have an experienced surgeon. But he doesn't have all the information that is relevant. What else is relevant? Well, the patient's objective and subjective priorities and the patient's concerns.

The patient may have objective objections to the procedure. There may be an issue with insurance and money, or a concern about the scarring. The hospitalization and recovery time might matter in terms of employment or caring for other kids. These are all objective issues the doctor must brief the patient on before getting consent, and therefore it's not unreasonable for issues to perhaps form the basis of granting or withholding consent.

And there is another objective issue, rarer but significant. The surgeon could be wrong. This patient might not be a proper candidate for a caesarean section, and the patient (who might have a second opinion or even be a doctor herself) might know it. Tens of thousands of patients die every year from medical malpractice. Experts' advice is not always sound. Sometimes the data is incorrect or incomplete. Sometimes the expert draws the wrong conclusion. Sometimes the expert is just flat-out incompetent. And there is also the natural tendency of an expert toward an opinion that he is personally comfortable with. If you ask a surgeon if surgery is necessary, you might find that a surgeon is more likely to go for the scalpel than an obstetrician who does not do any cutting. That's not a flaw—that's natural, which is the point. Experts are human beings, and they operate within the bounds of human nature.

But sometimes experts are wrong. The mere status of an expert is not, in and of itself, a guarantee that the opinion you are being offered is sound. Look at the Federal Rules of Evidence rule—it is premised on the notion that *both* sides will appoint an expert. This implies that those experts will disagree, meaning that at least one of them is wrong.

At least one is always *wrong.*

And there's more—since they are both being paid, there is the chance that their monetary compensation will influence their opinions. It should come as no surprise that every single time a trial lawyer cross-examines an expert witness on the stand, he begins with a question along the lines of, "How much is my opponent paying you to testify here today?"

Every single time.

After all, human beings are human beings, and experts are not necessarily without self-interest and, occasionally, greed. While this is not likely a consideration in a surgeon recommending not to go with a vaginal childbirth, it's not entirely irrelevant that a surgeon does not get paid unless he operates.

But there are also subjective issues at play, issues that revolve around the patient's priorities. The patient is the one who puts a value on having a vaginal birth—some women don't care and just want that baby out of them right freaking now, while others find it very important to have a natural childbirth for whatever reason. Maybe she just really wants to have a baby that way because her sister did, and a caesarian would make her feel less "womanly." Maybe the doctor thinks that's silly. Maybe you do, too. But she doesn't, and what everyone else thinks does not matter.

The patient's preferences are important even if you can't quantify them in terms of percentages, or at least they should be important in a culture that recognizes the inherent liberty due all human beings. That's the philosophical part—you don't have to have an objective reason for granting or denying your consent. You can just not want to give it.

That's where the experts get antsy, because they not only don't necessarily have access to all the objective information (Does the doctor understand that your mom can't come out and help with the kid while you recover from surgery?), they certainly do not have the subjective information (Does the sawbones understand just how much you want to have a natural birth?). Here's the thing—experts can talk and talk and talk, and the decision maker might still choose "wrong."

What if the doctor said, "Well, statistically, it's clear that the best outcome will come from a caesarean. So, prep her, and gag her if she won't shut up." Based on the purely objective facts he knows and based on his priorities, he is likely correct. But he only knows some of the objective facts and not necessarily any of the subjective facts, and it is not his place to put a value on any of them.

A citizen sets his or her own priorities. A subject is subject to the priorities of others, even if those priorities are set with some level of a desire to help.

Now let's apply this same principle to society. We hear a lot about how Normals hate science because they refuse to yield to the demands of the Elite and its menagerie of pet experts, who insist that we are on the verge of dying from climate change if we don't comply right this minute. But Normals have yet to follow their advice. Carbon remains untaxed. Barbecues roast rib eyes and spare ribs across the land. Outside of blue enclaves, people don't post on Facebook how they are forgoing the bearing of children in order to rescue Gaia from doom.

This drives the Elite crazy. Its response is to claim Normals are Neanderthal half-wits.

There is no doubt that the Elite is generally on board with the climate change scam. That's one of the markers of admission. If you are Elite, you will almost certainly buy into it at some level, even if you are a putative conservative. All the smart people do, you know. And the refusal of the Normals to do what the Elite contends it will take to fight the threat of slightly warmer temperatures in a century simply reaffirms the sense that Normals are unfit to participate in their own governance.

You see, the Normals have chosen wrong.

Or have they?

The climate change controversy is a terrific example of the problem of expertise abuse. It has everything—self-interest by the Elite and self-dealing by the experts. It has objectively false conclusions and a rejection of the scientific method. And it has an underlying theme of disregard for the preferences and priorities of the very people who are supposed to be the ones whose interests are being protected.

At the outset, the whole premise of the campaign is focused on bum-rushing into effect a plan of action consisting of a bunch of Elite-favored policies *right now* with minimal input from the Normals. That's one reason we get the breathless alarmism—no time to think! We have to ban cars tomorrow or else the penguins will die, then the polar bears will die, and then the children will die!

Everyone will die, damn it, there's no time to talk! The experts know what's best and if we keep yakking, pretty soon the water will be up above our ankles in Denver.

Now, over the last two decades of nonstop red alerting the Elite has not been able to push its agenda forward, except in silly places like California, and we have had some time to evaluate the accuracy of these warnings of impending doom. If you credit the claims of not too many years ago, by now we should be pushing up the daisies into the searing oven that is Earth's atmosphere. We were told the ice caps were melting. They're still there. We were told that blizzards were a thing of the past. That would be news to most of the United States.

But this alarmism is nothing new. If you credit what the experts warned about back in the seventies, right now we should all be entombed in a mile-deep glacier. Back then, it was global cooling and another ice age was on the way, and the climate change crew is infuriated whenever someone brings this up. Of course, it did not quite work out as promised. Nor did the ozone hole fry us all. Nor did acid rain melt us all into puddles of pinkish goo.

It's hard to inspire folks to believe in the cult of expertise when the experts are so wrong so often—especially when they get angry and deny what they actually predicted. They weren't wrong—you are wrong for remembering what they said! Call it "greenhouse gaslighting."

It's not being wrong occasionally that is a problem. Normal people understand that one can be competent and get things wrong. Perhaps you're good at doing oil changes and you've done a lot of them, but one time you fail to put the new oil filter on right and the oil leaks. Annoying, sure, but not a referendum on your general ability to do an oil change. You just forgot to tighten the new oil filter. You swear a little, get the Camaro back on the lift, redo it, and then you are ready to zoom. A pain in the ass, but one incident does not call into question your competency to perform this basic task.

Everyone makes mistakes.

But here's the thing. When you make a mistake, you admit it and fix it. The problem arises when you ignore the criticism or, worse, deny you made a mistake at all.

No, damn it, that oil's supposed *to be leaking! You're an oil leak necessity denier!*

Admitting errors—that is, confessing that your hypothesis was incorrect—should not be an issue. The scientific method is all about making errors, all the way up until you get the answer that at least appears to be right in light of all of the available data. After all, even things science was nearly certain of are sometimes proven false—you have butter on that muffin? Science is all about proving theories false, falsifying them. That's why unthinking faith in science is ridiculous—if you have faith in your result, you aren't doing science.

And 'fessing up to errors is necessary to maintain people's confidence. Admitting mistakes show the Normals that an expert thinks accuracy is important. It gives the observer the impression that the expert cares about getting the answer right rather than his pride or his agenda. In other words, it makes the expert seem like what people expect an expert to be.

So when you have a nearly four-decade-long series of climate errors—not little errors or niggling technicalities, but big, honking errors—and absolutely no accountability, that's a problem. This is the same accountability problem the Elite always presents with. It screws up, does not make it right, and then tries to continue on as if it had not shattered its credibility while calling Normals idiots for pointing out the truth.

People notice when you tell them that the Arctic is going to broil and the fried polar bears we were promised never materialize. The vivid imagery of igniting ursoids is really useful in getting attention, but if you don't come up with the burning bears, people will have questions. And telling those people, "Well, you just hate science, you science denier who denies science" is not a particularly effective rejoinder.

Where's our ice age?

Where's our ozone hole o' death?

Where's our acid rain monsoon?

Where's our global convection oven?

Like the apocalypse cultists of the past, the prophets of doom can only roll back the big day so many times before the congregation stops marking its calendar for the next Armageddon and refuses to once again gather naked beneath the trees to bathe in the moonlight as they await the arrival of the four horsemen who never seem to come.

A track record of failure with no explanation other than "You're stupid!" is not going to inspire the awe and deference from the Normals the Elite was hoping for.

The ever-changing standard for evaluating the evidence is another problem. People notice glaring inconsistencies, and they do not build confidence. Every time there's a heat wave, that's global warming. Of course, sometimes it just gets hot—you can't have the temperatures setting new records if you didn't have records in the first place. But, for the weather cultists, every time it's a bit toastier than usual it is proof positive that Earth is on the way to becoming a kiln.

So, obviously if every time the mercury rises it's evidence that global warming is a thing, then every time the mercury drops it's evidence against global warming. Nah. You and your linear thinking! Cold is also proof of global warming. Only someone who hates science would apply the scientific method and allow data to falsify the preconceived conclusion!

It's also racist somehow.

But, after this charade goes on and on and on over the years, the way every single thing is always proof of global warming is a bit hard to ignore. You have a terrible fire season, and the weather cultists come out in force to announce that it's totally got to be global warming. But you have a recollection of prior bad fire years, and if there were bad fire years in the past with similar magnitudes of conflagration, then it's not really a trend, is it? And if it's not a trend, then it's not evidence things are getting worse. Nor is it easy to accept that a bad fire year confirms the theory, but a good fire year means nothing. Seems a little . . . convenient.

When Hurricane Katrina hit New Orleans in 2005, the staggering death toll and widespread destruction was pinned on global warming. But what about how we went for nearly a decade after without a major hurricane? Was that evidence that maybe the global warming trend line was headed south? Cease that crazy talk, denier!

But as soon as Houston got flooded, there was global warming in effect again. Better late than never.

The "heads we have global warming, tails we also have global warming" game is really quite remarkable for its audacity. After all, these are people who FUCKING LOVE SCIENCE and all, and suddenly the possibility of falsifying certain hypotheses is now off the table. It's almost like they aren't doing actual science but are working backward from a result they want.

That's not science. Call it "science" instead. "Science" is science's creepy adopted little brother who Mom and Dad discover trying to set the dog on fire in the basement.

Which is why they shuck and jive and try to weasel out of accountability in the rare instances when the voices of the people saying, "Er, uh, I don't think that's how science works," are heard over the chorus of outraged liberals screeching *"Denier!"* and wanting to set the heretics aflame. Apparently burning witches is worth the carbon cost.

So they try to hide how they switched out science in favor of "science" in a variety of ways. Global warming stopped being "global warming" after the conservative media gleefully ran footage of Al Gore walking into the umpteenth snowed-out global warming conference decked out like an Eskimo on a whale hunt. It became "climate change," which is an utterly brilliant formulation since any kind of change confirms the concept.

Hotter? Climate change!

Cooler? Climate change!

No change? Why don't you freaking love "science," denier!

Being the Elite, they also had to serve up a healthy dollop of condescension. "You're confusing weather with climate," they would say as soon as it snowed. But then, as soon as it got hot, it was, "See, I told you so!"

So, the weird weather cult had a track record of failure, and it treated the basic principles of science as optional, but we Normals were still supposed to capitulate. And to what? Well, that's the next issue.

We were supposed to capitulate to giving the Elite more power and money.

We are *always* supposed to capitulate to giving the Elite more power and money. That's the solution for every problem, not just ones involving weather.

I mean "climate."

Remember the "Here Comes the Ice Age!" fad of the seventies? What was the answer then? Come up with more money for the Elite, and more power for them to exercise over the Normals.

The answer for acid rain? Come up with more money for the Elite, and more power for them to exercise over the Normals.

And the ozone hole? Come up with more money for the Elite, and more power for them to exercise over the Normals.

Power comes in many forms, including regulatory power. "There's a crisis coming! No time to wait! We need to give the

Department of the Armageddon Du Jour the power to regulate us in order to head off our impending doom!"

With regard to the climate scam, look at what Obama did. He promised to, and nearly did, wipe out the coal industry. But don't worry. While tens of thousands of Normals lost their livelihoods as ritual sacrifices offered up by the smug enviro faithful of San Francisco and Manhattan, Obama's buddies got government handouts to let them get rich off cheesy "green energy" schemes. Coal never had a problem turning a profit; not so for scandal-plagued enterprises like Solyndra, which weren't really designed to solve the energy problem. They were designed to take government money from the public purse and hand it over to designated members of the Elite.

Oh, there's always a tax increase involved with every new crisis. With the climate change scam, it's a carbon tax. This is supposed to lower the demand for carbon and promote green energy, which is simply another way of saying, "Enrich the buddies of the political Elite." Have you noticed how, in all the talk about a carbon tax, no one ever mentioned what tax the carbon tax is supposed to replace? Income tax, death tax, property tax—what tax is the carbon tax going to replace?

Just kidding.

It's supposed to supplement the current taxes. Nothing gets repealed. They would just pile the carbon tax on top of all the other taxes. And it's the most regressive of taxes because Normals use more carbon fueling up their F-150s than the dork in the Prius with the "Coexist" bumper sticker.

It seems concern for the less fortunate only arises when it involves a demand for Normal people to give up more of their money to the Elite to redistribute to the less fortunate—after taking their vigorish, of course. And it's fine to take from the less fortunate, too, if it's in the name of "science."

Pop quiz, hotshot. Name one proposal for ameliorating the climate catastrophe that hits the Elite harder than the Normals.

Just one.

Tick, tock.

What about the impact on the Normals? Well, you don't need that big truck, the Elite has decided. The Elite doesn't drive trucks—a lot of them don't even have cars. Why don't you take the subway like everyone else, though there isn't a subway within five hundred miles? Or ride a bike—that should be bracing, pedaling across the Oklahoma landscape in January. You say you need your truck for your job? Why, what kind of job requires a truck? Maybe four-wheel drive is a necessity—do you go to the mountains to ski?

Autos are a big problem for the Elite and were long before the fake weather scare got ginned up. This is especially true among the urban planners—more experts—who find cars inefficient. It's so, so decentralized. Public transportation is the way the masses should move. Orderly, regularized, public transportation is the way to get Normals from Point A, which the experts designate, to Point B, which the experts also designate.

Notice what's missing in that Elite calculation?

What the Normals want.

Maybe they don't want to go from Point A to Point B. Maybe they want to go from Point C to Point D, or Point E, and maybe they want to stop on the way home and buy a gallon of milk at the supermarket located at Point F.

Maybe they want the flexibility of traveling when they want

to travel, not when some expert allows them to by creating a schedule.

Maybe they want to crank some Ted Nugent in their car and head bang all the way home, or listen to a book without sticking things in their ears. Maybe they want to talk on the phone in the peaceful confines of their ride without speaking in a low hush so as not to annoy all the other poor suckers exiled to the bus.

Maybe they just prefer to drive.

But none of that matters. Not one bit. Because the problem with the Elite and their experts is the same problem as always. The Normals ceded the Elite the authority to do certain work organizing and running society's institutions with the understanding that the Elite could collect certain benefits (money and prestige) in return for competently executing these tasks for the benefit of the Normals.

But they haven't competently executed these tasks for the benefit of the Normals. Piling self-dealing on top of incompetence and deceit is a bad, bad look.

The corruption of our Elite has spread to our society's technicians, the experts. Like the Elite, they misunderstand their role. It is to advise and enable, not to command and control. It is to help make policy, not make it themselves using their own criteria and their own priorities.

Of course, experts get mad at the Normals, and experts chafe under the Normals' bridle when the Normals pull on the reins. But that's too bad. If the Normals are not setting society's priorities then we have ceased to be a representative democracy and have become a technocracy.

The Normals did not vote for that.

In the wake of Trump's election, the Elite noticed the Normals' absolutely understandable dismay with the Elite attempting to assert expertise as a way to bar input from those they see as lesser men. There is nothing our Elite detests more than uppity Normals.

The December 27, 2016, *New Yorker* ran a cartoon that was the perfect encapsulation of the Elite's attitude and, unintentionally, its essential ineptitude. The little black-and-white drawing depicted a Normal with a moustache that no one in the Elite would ever imagine sporting turning to his fellow coach passengers and asking for a show of hands. The caption read, "These smug pilots have lost touch with regular passengers like us. Who thinks I should fly the plane?"[2]

Good one, nodded thousands of people who thought they were smarter than those upstart yahoos who did not know their place. Implicitly, they identified with the airline pilot, though none could fly a 777.

Here's the thing. The joke did not work. Its underlying premise was false. After all, what commercial airline pilot decides where he is going?

None. The Normals who buy tickets decide where they are going.

Now, the pilots are skilled technicians—let's leave aside the fact that computers largely fly commercial airliners these days and give them some credit for technical proficiency. And a guy like Chesley Sullenberger demonstrates that there still are experts who deserve respect and reverence out there. But that's what pilots are—technicians. They have a narrow, specific skill set, and based upon it Normals cede them the minimum level of authority needed to complete the task.

They fly the plane. They don't decide where it goes. That's

for the Normals to decide by buying their tickets. If the pilot were smug enough to decide he wanted to fly somewhere else, there would be consequences. And the Normals back in steerage would be absolutely justified at being pissed.

Are the *New Yorker* readers who chuckled at this masterful takedown of pretentious bumpkins who presume to dare object to the decisions of their superiors really nodding in agreement at the real premise of the cartoon?

Do they believe that the idea of governing with the consent of the governed is an outdated concept? Are they really saying that Normals should sit quietly in their seats, mere passengers in their own country, and be taken wherever the Elite feels like going?

Do they believe that the notion of Normals having a say in their country's big picture policy decisions is obsolete?

Do they believe that the Normals should sit down, shut up, and be thankful for the dictatorship of the Elite?

Of course they do.

Why do you think they got so furious at Trump, so uncontrollably angry that they let the mask slip in the form of this dumb cartoon and a thousand other digs at regular people?

It was because Donald Trump knew his proper role. But it was not the role the Elite considered proper. It was not as a fighter for the interests of the Elite.

CHAPTER SEVEN

Institutionalized

In 2017, Gallup's annual poll of Americans' faith in their institutions registered a big 35 percent of respondents answering that they have "a great deal" or "quite a lot" of confidence in fourteen different major American institutions.[1] So about 65 percent thought America's institutions generally suck.

That's a landslide. When is the last time 65 percent of Americans agreed on anything?

The people have spoken, and spoken wisely. America's institutions—the various entities comprising the government, the press, academia, Hollywood, business, and other sectors of society—are a disaster. They have stopped working for the people they were supposed to work for, but the Elite will not admit it. It can't admit it. In fact, the Elite's struggle to retain power in the wake of this rebellion by Normals consists largely of trying to use these institutions to avoid accountability, to crush the insurgents, and to get back to business as usual.

Sadly, the business of America's institutions has largely become to provide soft, comfy sinecures for members of the Elite and to be a club to use to beat upon the hated Normals.

The Elite are bound to society's institutions since their main function is to run them. No institutions, no Elite. That's why it's always amusing to watch the liberal version of the Elite rail against "the Establishment" as if they weren't themselves The Man. Or The Woman. Or The Non-Binary Metaphor For Some All–Powerful Oppressor.

Whatever.

For their part, the conservative wing of the Elite delights in institutions, too. That's the focus of what they wish to conserve—a status quo that conveniently provides them a comfortable place to nest and essentially do nothing. That's why you see the conservative members of the Elites sometimes dismiss substantial evidence of institutional corruption as mere "conspiracy theories" and oppose even the most minimal attempts to rein them in. Take the FBI. Is there an institution with a grander façade of righteousness or a more sordid track record of failure? Even the Bureau's yeoman efforts to dispute the Efrem Zimbalist Jr. image of squeaky-clean pros just doin' their job can't keep Bill Kristol and his buddies from donning their evening dress and listening to the string quartet cranking out "Nearer to God than Thee" as the iceberg-ruined ship slips under the water.

Here's the problem: Our institutions are terrible.

Actually, that statement is incorrect. It's only a problem for Normals. Failing institutions are not a problem for the Elite except to the extent the failure of those institutions riles up the rubes.

Well, the rubes are getting riled.

All across our society, in government and out, prominent and hidden, our institutions have been generally failing Normal Americans for the last half century. Sure, there have been intermittent successes, but their very rarity is what makes the few and far between successes so noticeable. If the Elite was working with the level of talent and competence that the Elite imagines it possesses, then we would be shocked by the statistically inevitable failures. Instead, we're shocked when an institution doesn't completely screw something up.

Were you to survey the major institutions of American life, what you would see is a major disconnect between the principles and values they seek to portray and the sordid reality. That gap between how the Elite wishes its institutions to be seen and how they truly are is the key to the unrest, and the gap is a result of the Elite's utter refusal to accept even the most modest imposition of accountability by those the institutions are purportedly chartered to serve.

That's because today, the major institutions of American life do not exist to serve the Normals. In fact, when they actually serve the Normals it is a pleasant surprise and often, as we have seen in the wake of Trump's regulatory rollback, the cause of much Elite wailing and gnashing of sparkly white teeth. They have grown used to serving only the Elite who man them, and the Normals have noticed. This is a big reason why we now have a president who specializes in denying the Elite members of these institutions the reverence they demand.

Let's start with the government, and why not the FBI? Because since J. Edgar Hoover slipped into his nightie and sipped the tea Clyde Tolson brought him as he rifled through the surveillance reports on his political opponents his agents gathered, the FBI's image has been about 180 degrees off from reality.

For those of us who grew up watching *The FBI* and immediately have the urge to follow those words with the stentorian phrase "A Quinn Martin Production," we default into thinking of the Bureau as the world's preeminent law enforcement agency. That image was part of Hoover's cunning game plan to protect himself and solidify his reign—to make the FBI's integrity and professionalism so beyond question that to attack its leadership is to tread on the flag and curse the very concept of motherhood. And the legacy lives on, notably in the tiresome form of the shameless James Comey, whose post-firing life has been devoted to working with his friends to avenge his humiliation and to tweeting out a nearly endless series of quotations designed to restore the "sterling reputation" he once enjoyed and subsequently defecated upon.

Professionalism. Integrity. Crime-solving savvy that leverages highly trained experts and the latest technology to nab wrongdoers and bring them to justice. That's what we are supposed to think of when we think of the FBI. And here's their professionalism and integrity, as reported by the *Washington Post* on April 18, 2015: "Nearly every examiner in an elite FBI forensic unit gave flawed testimony in almost all trials in which they offered evidence against criminal defendants over more than a two-decade period before 2000."[2]

It gets even better: Thirty-two of those cases resulted in a death sentence.

So, basically, for twenty years the FBI was sending its techs into court, having them swear to tell the truth, the whole truth, and nothing but the truth, and then they proceeded not to do so. Those jurors took notice when the district attorney announced in their openings, "And ladies and gentlemen, we will offer you testimony regarding unquestionable forensic evidence of guilt supplied by a technician from the preeminent law enforcement agency in the world, the FBI." Might as well skip the trial and get right to the conviction.

But hey—we can't dare damage the institution by pointing out that it is unable to perform its most basic task in an honest and accurate manner. Instead, let us lavish it with praise.

Maybe those thirty-two guys sweating it out on the Green Mile thanks to bad testimony ought to disregard those horrendous conspiracy theories. The same with the families of the people murdered by killers the FBI let slip through its fingers—fingers that were likely occupied sexting on the job.

Of course, it goes without saying that there is nothing wrong with a conspiracy theory if it is true.

Accidents happen. Twenty years of almost universal false testimony *could* be just an error, a simple mistake. Maybe it was just an oopsie we all just need to move past, though those thirty-two guys might not be so indulgent. We don't want to throw the baby out with the bathwater, though if it's really more like Rosemary's Baby maybe we ought to give that some thought. In any case, we still have the FBI's shining reputation for integrity. J. Edgar used to hire only lawyers and accountants as agents and held them to the highest standards—the best people, taking on the mob and commie spies and civil rights leaders with total integrity.

So, we come to the 2016 election and the revelation—partly obtained from the thousands of texts between a couple of married FBI employees who were banging each other—that the big bosses had decided early on that Hillary Clinton was never going to be held accountable for what anyone who has been in the same ZIP code as someone holding a security clearance knows were multiple criminal acts involving classified material that would have gotten a Normal clamped in irons.

Let's leave aside the texting on company time part and the cheating on their spouses' part, even though back in the day both shameless time wasting and shameless adultery would have gotten these bureaucratic bums booted. Let's get to the key part—the FBI was completely in the tank for one political party and gleefully helped cover up crimes for which it would have charged anyone not at the pinnacle of the Elite.

Hillary Clinton got off because the political party in power wanted her to, and the FBI leadership made it happen.

Think about that.

Think about what would happen if you were the one with the email shenanigans. Do you imagine you would have gotten the benefit of the doubt? Do you think the FBI leadership would have thought, "Well, for the good of our country, we should totally pass on prosecuting this person who is likely to be our boss and would be totally grateful to us for our help in her time of need?"

No.

You would be in prison, making new friends.

And the Christopher Steele dossier, packed with tales of collusion and water sports, was just another example. The FBI was absolutely delighted to take a political campaign's sketchy oppo and use it to get warrants to listen into the party-out-of-power's presidential campaign.

Think about that. If Nixon were alive, he would be kicking himself. Why send some bumbling hacks to break into the other side's offices if you can fast-talk a court into giving you a warrant to do it using the dirt your own campaign guys dug up?

But hey, the Elite has to protect the Elite. Today, that's the FBI's real mission statement.

The judiciary is another institution that has chosen to trash its reputation in order to pursue Elite goals, which means largely liberal goals. You see statues of Lady Justice holding the scales and you see the blindfold and you recall the saying, "Justice is blind," and then you watch what happens and you think, "Well, this is just more bullshit."

The FBI is merely an agency. The judiciary is a branch of government, and it exists both within each state and within the federal government. As such, its fall from respect and reverence among the Normals is even more dangerous to the long-term health of the Republic than that of the Bureau.

The failure of the judiciary is a failure of democracy. The idea underlying the United States of America is that the people of the United States of America, the Normals, should have some say in how they are governed. Our Elite, as manifested by the courts, no longer believes this. And it has not for a while.

You go back to *Roe v. Wade*, 410 U.S. 113 (1973), the decision that somehow located the right to an abortion somewhere in the Constitution, and you wonder if there is a secret footnote in that document you did not learn about in civics class. Of course there is no right to an abortion in the Constitution, not behind any penumbras, not lurking adjacent to some emanation. But the Supreme Court found one, because it wanted to find one.

And it was perfectly willing to strip away the say of Normal Americans on the issue of abortion to do it.

Now, perhaps this could be understood in the context of a consistent reading of the Constitution that broadly and liberally (in the true sense of the term) construes the protections offered by our Bill of Rights. A judicial philosophy that consistently and without favor finds that the Constitution broadly bars the government from the regulation of individuals' decision making regardless of those protections being expressly enumerated might be a coherent one, even if most people might disagree.

But that's not what is happening here. There's no philosophy; this is cafeteria jurisprudence imposed by a prix fixe judiciary. As law professor Glenn Reynolds points out in *The Judiciary's Class War* (New York: Encounter Broadsides, 2018), the judiciary is composed of people with the same background, the same degrees, and the same world view. It's a branch of government that requires you to possess an advanced degree to enter. He calls them "front-row kids," and he is talking about the Elite.

And this means the liberal wing of the Elite in particular. Through the judgeships it holds, it regularly invents rights that the liberal wing of the Elite favors, despite their absence from the text, while negating the rights that are right there on the parchment in black and tan.

Freedom of speech? It's protected if you wear a jacket in a courthouse that says, "Fuck the Draft." That's a form of self-expression, don't you know. Under *Cohen v. California*, 403 U.S. 15 (1971), this powerful intellectual statement gets First Amendment protection, and it should. But what if you want to display the American flag in a school? Nope. The notorious Ninth Circuit does not think that deserves First Amendment protection, and the Supreme Court refused to review the decision. *Dariano v. Morgan Hill Unified School District*, 767 F.3d 764 (9th Cir. 2014), *cert. denied*, 2015 WL 1400871. Well, it's a school, and schools are different. Except, no. The First Amendment does not stop at the schoolhouse doors if the expression at issue is one the liberal Elite approves of, like wearing armbands to protest the Vietnam War, per *Tinker v. Des Moines Independent Community School District*, 393 U.S. 503 (1969).

Funny how the Constitution always seems to support what the Elite prefers.

And then there is the right to keep and bear arms set out in the Second Amendment. This is the most basic of rights, as it establishes the ability of the people to maintain the means of replacing their government if and when it becomes tyrannical. After all, that's what the Founders did starting in 1775 when they got tired of the British elite governing the colonies for their own benefit and not for that of the colonists.

The Elite also hates that idea with a burning passion, of course, since they are the ones who would be overthrown if the Normals got so sick of their nonsense that they went into their gun safes and decided to enact some large-caliber hope and change.

But the Elite hates the Second Amendment for another reason—it hates it because it's so important to the Normals. The Normals see their right to keep and bear arms as central to their dignity as citizens, a physical manifestation of their ultimate right to cast a veto of the acts of those appointed to lead them, or who seize those positions of leadership without the benefit of the consent of the governed.

The Second Amendment both empowers the Normals and imbues them with dignity. Naturally, it has to go.

It has not gone quite yet, though, with a thin conservative Supreme Court majority twice speaking out in *District of Columbia v. Heller*, 554 U.S. 570 (2008), and *McDonald v. Chicago*, 561 U.S. 742 (2010), to reaffirm what is right there on the paper—that "the right of the people to keep and bear Arms, shall not be infringed." But it does not matter to the liberal Elite what is there on the paper, because when the Constitution becomes an obstacle it should be either disregarded completely or interpreted in such a way as to yield the precise opposition result intended. And that is why in the decade since *Heller*, the party of the liberal Elite, the Democrats, has engaged in a campaign of massive resistance against gun rights whose only parallel is the Democrats' campaign of massive resistance against school integration, and civil rights in general, in the wake of *Brown v. Board of Education of Topeka*, 347 U.S. 483 (1954), the decision desegregating the schools.

There are myriad other examples of this behavior from the courts, of laws that Normals enact being overturned on shaky or nonsensical grounds, of criminals being set free despite evidence of their guilt, of judges taking unto themselves the powers reserved to the people or their representatives. The courts will never be perfect—there will always be bad decisions, thanks to the cruel laws of probabilities—but this is different. This is not a few blips but a theme.

This is the Elite using an institution to usurp the right of the Normals to govern themselves. The courts are not there to do so except to the extent the Constitution authorizes them to do so. The courts are a check on the people, but checking the people when the people overstep the bounds of their Constitution is quite a different matter. Telling overwrought Normals that they cannot ban the building of any mosques in their town is a proper exercise of the judiciary's power as granted by those Normals via the Constitution's First Amendment. But telling the Normals they cannot place a menorah and a nativity scene in the park during December is overstepping the authority granted to the courts.

The decline in respect for the courts as an institution is, as with all of these institutions, a direct consequence of the Elite members in those institutions trying to use those institutions not to perform their proper task but to impose Elite (usually liberal Elite) values upon the Normals.

Normals see the courts ignoring the laws that the Normals passed and, instead, imposing what the liberal Elite considers better ones through judicial fiat. That is disenfranchisement. That is the elimination of the Normals' sovereignty, and it is no wonder that they so greatly resent it.

In the end, the courts depend on the respect the institution holds among the people. The courts have no men with guns to impose its dictates. They cannot make anyone do anything, except by the power of their own moral authority. And when the judiciary loses that, it's just a bunch of eggheads in black dresses banging little wooden hammers.

Not all institutions have yet come in for the intense contempt that others enjoy. The military remains America's most respected major institution. In 2017, 72 percent of respondents reported to Gallup that they had "a great deal" or "quite a lot" of confidence in America's armed forces. But don't worry—the Elite running the military bureaucracy can still come through and tank those numbers.

The defeat of ISIS under President Trump and Secretary of Defense James "Mad Dog" Mattis have partially reversed a disturbing trend that had not gotten a lot of attention—the inability of the United States to decisively win a ground war since Operation Desert Storm in 1991. While the Iraqi insurgency seemed to be on its back foot by the time Barack Obama decided to turn tail and run instead of finishing the job, it was far from dead. It came roaring back in the form of ISIS.

Iraq dragged on and on under Bush and Obama, and Afghanistan is still dragging on, and in Asia, China is getting feisty in the South China Sea, and North Korea is testing American resolve, as it always does. We hear lots about how a war with either one would be violent and bloody but short, and how America would eventually emerge the victor. Are we so sure?

The Air Force is running out of pilots because they can't wait to bail out and escape the soul-crushing double-whammy of too many deployments and too many chickenshit administrative tasks. The Army has been trying for years to get its troops a new rifle that will actually hit bad guys at a distance; it figures that it needs a better part of a decade to do that, though a civilian can buy a better rifle off the shelf than the aging M4, albeit without the selective fire option. But fear not—the Army is rolling along toward yet another dress uniform changeover because if you want to win a war, you need snazzy dress uniforms. By the way, the Army is down to ten active duty divisions.

Ten. It had over ninety during World War II.

But interservice rivalry being what it is, the swabbies are doing their best to compete with the ground pounders. The Navy has about two-thirds of the minimum number of ships it needs and can't train the crews for those. In a few months, it managed to lose major surface ships to collisions with civilian cargo vessels not once but twice. Its new, super-pricey Zumwalt-class guided-missile destroyers are stealthy and can sneak right up on the enemy and not shoot its gun at them; the Navy has not figured out what ammunition to buy.

So, no bang for the 4 billion bucks. Literally.

It does not take an expert to see that a ship that cannot shoot its main gun is problematic. In fact, veterans of the service have been trying to raise a ruckus about the disaster of modern American military readiness. They have a vested interest not only because of their own service, but because America's military is now a family affair, with the forces composed largely of the relatives of veterans. Their own kids and grandkids are going to be the ones sent out to fight outnumbered and outgunned. And since few of them are Elite, it will be the Normals who once again pay the price in lives and limbs for the Elite failing to prepare.

The guy from Fontana spills his blood in the sand and Kaden spills his artisanal pumpkin ale at a trendy gastropub.

Much of this has to do with funding, but it is not as if the United States Treasury cannot fund the military America needs. It's that the Elite with the checkbook won't say no to deadbeat Democrat constituents and yes to our fighting men and women. Entitlement spending is pre-rigged. It goes up up up on auto-pilot while the people actually serving the country, rather than demanding that they be served, end up last in line with empty bowls going full Oliver Twist and begging Congress, "Please, sir, I want some more."

But another deadly problem is the same one we see in other institutions—a gross lack of leadership followed by a gross lack of accountability. Let's leave aside the dozens of senior Navy officers under investigation in the "Fat Leonard" corruption probe—how many of these guys took money or gifts of hookers from this or some other contractor? Let's also leave aside the Air Force nuke general who went to Moscow—Moscow!—and got completely shit-faced and had to be relieved of command? And let's leave aside the 82nd Airborne general who used his staff as a sex harem, and let's leave David Petraeus aside, too—he pleaded guilty to a misdemeanor for classified materials antics. He walked on the adultery charge for nailing some adoring light colonel.

Let's leave all those fiascos aside and focus on the guys who couldn't win a war. Who got fired for failing to win a war? What was the name of a general who got canned for failing to defeat the enemy in Iraq or Afghanistan or anywhere since maybe Vietnam?

Not transferred. Not retired. Not rotated. Relieved. Because that's what happened in World War II. You performed or you were gone. But these days? It is like every other institution. You perform and you get promoted, or you don't perform and you get promoted anyway. Look at retired Army Lieutenant General David Sanchez. He was the commander of Coalition ground forces in Iraq from June 2003 to June 2004. That was a pretty memorable period, when the insurgency got kicked into high gear and Abu Ghraib happened. It was memorable because it was a total disaster. So did the military fire him for his terrible performance in command, or did it reward him?

It rewarded him.

Sanchez got rotated to Europe and issued a third star. After he retired, he ran for a Texas Senate seat as a Democrat. The message is clear—accountability is for the buck sergeant who misplaces his night vision goggles, not for the brass. Not for the Elite.

We all know who will pay the price if a serious, cunning enemy with top-shelf equipment decides to take on a military that spends a decade and a half stymied by a bunch of glorified bandits with old AK-47s.

Normals. And when the Elite leads them into a bloodbath, it will be everyone else's fault.

———————

If you drive through a Middle American neighborhood in the early morning, and you are of a certain age, you notice something missing from peoples' driveways and front lawns.

Where are the newspapers?

Our key institutions are not all, or even mostly, governmental. The mainstream news media is a key institution with an important role in a democratic republic. It earns respect by being an objective, neutral truth teller that courageously brings the public the facts in a fair and impartial manner so that the people can exercise their right to self-determination in a wise and informed way.

It is by those very principles of objectivity and neutrality that the news media lays claim to the respect and reverence of the people it serves. And, since the mainstream media generally practices none of those highfalutin principles, Gallup's 2017 poll had newspapers at 27 percent approval and television news at 24 percent. There are STDs that could poll higher.

It should have been an indicator that when candidate Trump mentioned the mainstream media during his rallies, it provoked boos. And it was not because Americans were outraged that reporters were being objective, neutral truth tellers who courageously bring the public the facts in a fair and impartial manner so that the people can exercise their right to self-determination in a wise and informed manner.

But the Elite did not take it as an indicator. It took it as an outrage. The very institution charged with keeping other institutions accountable was, itself, being held accountable for failing to perform its assigned task adequately, and it couldn't handle the criticism. It fell back on the oldest and lamest of canards, that a criticism of Institution X is an attack on the very concept of Institution X.

It was the same lame excuse every other institution reflexively offered whenever the press focused on them.

The problem, which the press shared with the Elite that ran every other institution, was its hatred of accountability. The media simply did not feel that it was subject to criticism, particularly not by . . . well, those people.

The Normals.

And worse, the Normals dared seek out alternative voices. This was made possible largely by the internet—one of the few transformative success stories of our institutions in recent decades, though there is a good argument that it really came into its own because of the decentralized work of millions of individuals. Sites created by Andrew Breitbart before his untimely death, Glenn Reynolds (*Instapundit.com*) and clearinghouses of conservative and/or traditionalist writers like *Townhall.com* all built a space for Normal-friendly dissent. But mostly, they built morale—Normals who looked at the mainstream media and wondered if anyone else felt like they did learned that they were not alone.

There was also the explosion of talk radio, which gave voice to Normals' interests and demands in a media space vacated by the Elite. The Elite media focused on print and television and left the door open for people like Rush Limbaugh, Hugh Hewitt, and Sean Hannity to build audiences among the underserved Normal audience. Certainly, these hosts were not all themselves Normals, but they were Normal-friendly. Hewitt, for example, had a long history in government and academia and revered the concepts of experts and institutions while criticizing their individual short-comings. Yet he remained grounded in his Normal upbringing in suburban Ohio. Mark Levin was a distinguished constitutional law litigator. Younger commentator Ben Shapiro was a Harvard-educated lawyer. Both retained a connection to the Normals and their values, Shapiro in no small part through his Orthodox Jewish religion, something the Elite could not fathom.

These alternative media outlets differed from the mainstream,

Elite-run media. They made no pretense toward objectivity. They were advocates, but they did not seek to hide it. When they took a position on an issue, they were not betraying a principle. When the "objective" mainstream media did, it was.

The media seeks all the prestige that comes with being a caste of honest brokers, but it does not want to give up the power that comes from *not* being an honest broker and putting an ink-stained thumb on the scale. Journalists wanted the respect, but they didn't want to actually earn it. And, of course, it was that residual respect—for the media had been slowly shedding the trust of the Normals over the last few decades—that gave the media the influence that might tip the scale in the first place. So, ironically, the more they tried to leverage their respect to influence events, the less respect, and therefore leverage, they had.

Pretty much every single major paper in America told its readers not to vote for Donald Trump. Pretty much every single television news outlet, cable or terrestrial, drummed his evil and unfitness into their viewers' cerebellums for nearly eighteen months.

President Donald Trump won in spite of that. Maybe because of that.

The problem is that journalists today want to be Woodward and Bernstein, though many of them probably have no idea what those old people did to get on TV all the time. They want to be liberal activists in bad suits. What they don't want to be is anonymous reporters toiling away in front of some video monitor and cold-calling sources. But that's what reporting is. And it needs to be anonymous in the sense that there are no particular brands of truth—not Maggie Haberman's, not Robert Costa's. To the extent their byline should matter at all should be the art of their writing, the depth of their knowledge, and the insight of their sources. But today's reporters don't want to be like Woodward and Bernstein because of those things. They want to be like Woodward and Bernstein because of the book deals and the celebrity ex-wives.

And the Normals see that.

They see it when every time they are involved in a story and see it reported in the media, they see it is reported incompletely at best, and most likely inaccurately.

They see it when the news reports nothing but scandals, often based on anonymous sources, which often have to be walked back or disavowed entirely.

They see it when CNN gathers a half-dozen talking heads to yak about Donald Trump and their views range from mild disgust to wanting to put his orange noggin on a stake for the treason that Robert Mueller will totally find, fingers crossed.

They see it when the stories on guns or religion or the environment or family or standing up for the National Anthem always— *always!*—end up precisely aping the Elite views on the subject.

Every. Single. Time.

If the media's target is the Elite's priorities, it should say so. If the media's goal is to guide and determine the debate, it should say so. If the media is going to be just another subset of the partisan hacks at the center of American culture and politics, it should say so.

But it won't say those things. It can't and still retain its power.

The irony is that to recover its power the media has to eschew its own power. But there's no stomach for that. The new generation of reporters, the same ones who decided that Trump was so awful that they needed to jettison all those pretty principles they learned in J-school, has no concept of fading into the background and simply grinding out the truth. This is the selfie generation—what in a young person's life experience or education has ever taught them to minimize themselves?

So, the media has a problem. It can return to its principles, or it can keep on this path and become a niche industry dedicated to its narrow readership. President Trump is wrong: The *New York Times* is not failing, sadly enough. Other papers are—the *Los Angeles Times* has shrunk down to a brochure and is likely to disappear entirely in the wake of its workforce treating its problems with the equivalent of leeching by voting to unionize. But the *NYT* is growing its readership. The problem is, its readership is tuning in for the Trump-bashing, and taking a more dispassionate, even objective tone toward the president might alienate the new subscriber base. Sure, lots of Elites read it today, and that could certainly sustain it, but no one else will.

In their pursuit of being thought leaders, the media—those that survive in the media—risk becoming mere thought reinforcers.

The Normals will never notice that the mainstream media has shrunk to a shell of its former self. And without the attention of the Normals it will fade away into a largely irrelevant circle of Elite onanism.

How apt.

The mainstream media's sister institution is Hollywood and the entertainment industry. And it's a more attractive sister—sexier, richer, and a lot more fun. In fact, a significant part of the mainstream media's current troubles can be traced back to it trying to be like Big Sis.

But where attention and self-aggrandizement are counter to the mainstream media's alleged purpose, attention and self-aggrandizement are the whole purpose behind Hollywood. News sells the news, but the entertainment industry sells the stars. You don't go to see *Action-Adventure Film*. You go to see *Die Hard* with Bruce Willis. You don't buy *Rock Album*. You buy *London Calling* by The Clash.

Hollywood offers money and prestige, and that really should be enough. It sure was in the Golden Age, when stars kept their politics (and their personal proclivities) well under wraps, while still paying at least lip service to the values of the Normals. After all, everything had to play in Peoria.

And even where they tried to slip in some leftist message, they cloaked it in Normal terms. *High Noon* (1952), the story of a sheriff forced to face a gang of outlaws alone, was an allegory of blacklisting. The film treats the cowardly Normal townspeople as aberrations and Gary Cooper's lonely sheriff as the true epitome of the individuality and courage Normals see as two of their most important characteristics. In doing so, they made a movie about standing up to the popular will into one Normals saw as validating their self-image.

Not so much anymore.

By the late sixties and seventies, the younger Elite was getting a toehold in Hollywood and aiming its hatred not just at the older Elite but at the Normals themselves. In *Easy Rider* (1969), slack-jawed yokels wax the laid-back heroes just because. In *Bonnie and Clyde* (1967), it depicted the villains as stylish, sexy folks who refused to be dragged into the hell that was normality; the cops, all Normals, were worse than the supposed criminals. Even *The Godfather* (1972) attacked what the young Elite saw as the hypocrisy of Normal values; the murderous Corleones were all about the faith and the family, and when Kay laughs off the idea that the government doesn't have people killed, Michael calls her "naïve."

And John Boorman's *Deliverance* (1972)? That Elite paranoia about Normals (or their caricature of Normals) could not have been more on the nose, or on the snout, as the case may be.

But at first, it was hard to notice that Hollywood was now biting the hand that fed it. *The Godfather* is a great film. It's easy to overlook the fact that the film is deeply cynical about Normal values. It became more and more obvious that instead of celebrating Normal values, Hollywood's edgiest players were targeting them. *All in the Family* was a frontal assault on those values, with some (very) light mockery of Meathead's new left antics tossed in. Its message was the same one the liberal Elite howls to this day: Normals are dumb and bigoted and proud of it.

Hollywood certainly got dirtier since the sixties, but this was not quite the same as Norman Lear's blistering attack on the Normals. In fact, Normals were not anti-sex—to this day, they are the ones making most of the babies. It was just that the liberal Elite enjoyed depicting them as frustrated, sexophobic prudes. That's how you got the eighties flick *Footloose* (1984), where Normals out in some generic farm town hate dancing because, well, everyone knows that everyone outside the New York metro area hates dancing because of Jesus, somehow.

Hollywood occasionally got it right. It depicted real Normal life in 1982's *Fast Times at Ridgemont High*, a crude but accurate account of the ambiguities and issues around suburban teen sex that resonated with its young audience, though Phoebe Cates's famous pool scene probably greatly assisted in said resonation.

Hollywood continued on two tracks, the projects celebrating (or at least treating with respect) Normals and their values, and the projects that attacked them. And there were some in-between. *The Simpsons* mocks Normals, and especially the value of faith (those few viewers still watching the third decade's episodes have noticed it has gotten more virulently anti-Christian). The show wears its Elitism on its sleeve (Harvard and its ilk have traditionally provided it with writers) but for an Elite show, it does pay some respect to other Normal values, like the family. It's just not as funny when it does so. Particularly in its later and weaker years, it gets somewhat maudlin with "Let's hug it out" endings that reaffirm the value of the—pardon the pun—nuclear family.

The Elite's double standard regarding those Normal values is especially obvious in Hollywood. The Elite, particularly the liberal Elite, is always willing to make excuses when some favored demographic, like the underclass Normals, indulges in actions that violate traditional Normal norms—single motherhood, petty criminality, drug addiction—the transgressive stuff that makes for Oscar-winning roles and critical hosannas. The real underclass gets a pass because they are obedient to their betters, who feed them scraps from the proverbial table in the form of welfare. Of course, the Elite would themselves rarely indulge in those kinds of self-destructive behaviors—they tend to hamper one's future success.

Having babies out of wedlock is one example. Though certainly not unknown to Normals, it is hardly a traditional American value and remains disfavored. Similarly, Hollywood Elites are rarely going to do it themselves (and the ones who do generally have the financial wherewithal to ameliorate the consequences, such as by hiring nannies). But often the shows they write and produce gloss over the reality of that situation. You get a brave and plucky heroine and she has a kid and she decides to keep it, though the script always notes that it could totally be her choice to abort it if she felt like it. What you don't see is her alone when the baby cries at two a.m. and she has to be up in three hours to go to her job.

Liberal Elites are unwilling to side with the Normals in public by including those principles in their art where they absolutely include those principles in their own lives.

Pregnant at seventeen? In the movies, the Christian father inevitably shrieks that she has ruined her life because of her sin. In real life, the Elite parents shriek that she ruined her life by jeopardizing her admission to Oberlin.

Of course, there is one noted exception—the elephant-sized creep in the room. Starting with the revelations about Harvey Weinstein, Hollywood was rocked by the fact that many of the leading lights of cinema, music, and the other arts were skeevy pervs of the most grotesque kind. But the Normal values that forbade these kinds of activities were exactly the kind of values that the modern Elite has been happy to cast off as puritan shackles on their self-expression. Values that helped them succeed in business? Embrace those, at least in private. Values that let them succeed with that busty new production assistant? Don't let the sex dungeon door Matt Lauer controlled with the red button under his desk hit you on the ass as you leave.

Sure, Normals get that the casting couch is going to be a thing. And part of the reason people want to be famous, particularly men, is the implied easy availability of high-end romantic attention. Being on camera may add ten pounds, but it also adds a bunch of points to your attractiveness. Normals get that some side action is part of the skim the Hollywood Elite gets to take for doing its job. But cornering women and forcing them to watch you punish the primate and finish on a fern—there are lines, and that behavior crosses them.

That behavior bulldozes them.

There was a reason movie stars back in the day hid their perversions—and they were perverted. But they wanted audiences to like them, and, moreover, the studios that owned them wanted audiences to like their chattels, so they kept the cauldron of fornication to a low simmer. Sometimes it boiled over—Charlie Chaplin was ruined by a public paternity suit. But by and large, old-school stars may have had reputations as rogues and men about town and temptresses, but allegedly drugging dozens of women between Jell-O pudding pop commercials like Bill Cosby? Nope.

Not coincidentally, there are few real movie stars left today, people who can not only open a film to gangbuster box office on the power of their names but who walk on the screen and you know you are in the presence of a star. Denzel Washington probably; Tom Cruise maybe, despite his bad press. Perhaps not coincidentally, neither tweets.

But who else? Can you tell Brie Larson from Jennifer Lawrence? They both won Academy Awards for movies probably 98 percent of America has not seen. They also both tweet. They both feel they have much to say of importance regarding today's political and cultural scene, like many of today's Hollywood crowd, and they are wrong.

Moreover, they are dumb. Injecting themselves into polarized debates necessarily alienates the people who disagree. Lawrence, who grew up in Kentucky but has bought into the Elite completely, decided the smart career move for her was to make an anti-Christian allegory called *Mother!* (2017), with the emphasis on *gory*. Among other things, a baby gets eaten, which would seem more apt for a Planned Parenthood allegory. Lawrence plays a sort of Mother Earth (someone else is Eve) who gets set on fire and has her beating heart ripped out, just like in the New Testament, except totally not. She got lots of Elite praise for her courage in taking it to those backwoods Bible thumpers onscreen, and in case anyone missed the point she emphasized it in interviews. And she can't open a movie.

She followed it up with a spy melodrama called *Red Sparrow* (2018), which she promoted by doing lots of press talking about the courage she displayed to do a bunch of nude scenes, subtly emphasizing that she did a bunch of nude scenes. But it tanked, too. When Hollywood can't sell a naked Jennifer Lawrence, then they can't sell any Jennifer Lawrence.

What's the name of a Normal who says, "Jennifer Lawrence? I don't care what the movie is about—let's go spend fifteen dollars for a ticket"?

Well, she and the other outspoken liberals who can't seem to come up with a hit lately—like Tom Hanks, George Clooney, Jessica Chastain, and Matt Damon—can still count on the support of their Elite pals. At least until their pals realize that these folks aren't putting butts in seats. And that's when it will get real.

Look at Dwayne "The Rock" Johnson and Chris Pratt. When you hear from them outside of the theater, they are visiting some sick kid in their superhero getup or tweeting about how much they appreciate veterans. They embrace the values of Normality and celebrate them. And people usually flock to their movies.

The guy from Fontana took his kids to see The Rock in

Jumanji: Welcome to the Jungle. Kaden, who won't consider having a family until his late thirties, would sooner be caught at an anti-Trump protest without his gyno-beanie than see a Dwayne Johnson movie.

It is not all the slow accumulation of programs that mocks Normals' values and the essential scumminess of so many in Hollywood that has hurt the box office. Technology is also an important reason for the change in viewing habits by Normal audiences over the last decades. The fact is that audiences are no longer at the mercy of what's in *TV Guide*, if that still exists, or what's playing down at the Bijou 26. Technology makes the viewers able to demonstrate their frustration more readily since there is always something else to watch besides the latest Normals-trashing garbage.

Not up for the latest interchangeable film about our troops coming home from Iraq as emotional basket cases in need of— wait for it—Elite expert help to regain their sanity? Noting the irony of how it was Elite experts who thought it was a great idea to send them there in the first place? There's a good chance you'll find *Where Eagles Dare* (1968) playing on Amazon or Netflix.

Hard pass on the latest independent flick about the Christian teen girl who frees herself from the tyranny of Jesus and learns to be a free spirit by embracing Elite attitudes? She's going to be a poet, damn it, even if the preacher says the Bible tells us girls can't be poets! Maybe watch a Tyler Perry film—these Christian-infused films make a boatload of money precisely because they refuse to insult their viewers' beliefs.

Tired of all the crap that tells you you're dumb and racist and that you should sit down and shut up and let the Elite make the decisions? Especially nonsense like *The X-Files*, which flatters its Elite nerd viewers by masquerading as antiestablishment while simply advocating a different faction of the Elite be in charge? Maybe shut off the television and walk your corgi. Or go get a girlfriend.

The Hollywood Elite was always among the most cunning of the Elite, and it requires massive infusions of money to maintain Hollywood Elite status in the way it is not required for Little Sis mainstream media. Unencumbered by a need to be respected, Hollywood's Elite merely needs to be loved, and we may well see a return to the old days where stars were elusive about their lives and their politics. What we have today won't work for much longer, and at its core, Hollywood is still a business.

Big Business is another institution that Normals distrust, and it's not hard to see why Gallup's respondents gave it a whopping 21 percent approval rating in 2017. Big Business, with all its yakking and posturing about social responsibility and greenness, has shafted the Normals for decades. It has also insulted them. During the 2018 Super Bowl, T-Mobile ran a spot that showed a United Nations of multiethnic infants to the strains of Nirvana's "All Apologies," as the narrator explained that T-Mobile was against discrimination. Apparently, Normals who use cell phones need big corporations to help them get woke.

Normals never expected "social responsibility" from the corporations—that was gobbledygook for the benefit of liberal Elitists, just like all the green nonsense. Normals expected jobs, the chance to work hard for fair wages and fair treatment. But the corporations did what corporations will do, especially when backed up by cynical liberal Elitists in government they could buy off and gullible conservative Elitists they could count on ideologically. Under that Elite consensus, "free trade" became unfair trade, trade where Normal American workers' interests were never, ever a priority.

The basic fact is that corporations found American workers too expensive—they simply could not be exploited like foreigners could be. Hence the push overseas, moves enabled by favorable tax treatment and laws that allowed the reimportation of often subsidized goods back into the United States so they could be sold to these same workers under cost. Manufacturing jobs plummeted. Normals watched the jobs they thought they would be able to support their families with until retirement suddenly vanish.

And the Elite did not care.

It occurred to many union workers that the unions' bosses were more interested in the bizarre social priorities of their Elite pals than with making sure the workers were squared away. In fact, a number of unions donated substantial sums to Planned Parenthood and other leftist organizations that have nothing to do with protecting worker interests. Hey, the unions may be failing their members, but at least the workers can rest assured that their dues are being spent wokely.

The Normals cried out about their economic troubles, but the Elite could not hear them over the clinking of their Champagne glasses. The good times rolled for the ruling class. The good times always rolled. They rolled right up until 2008, when Wall Street's incompetence put the whole economy on the precipice. And then, after the Normals bailed them out with their tax money, the good times resumed rolling.

It was different in the heartland. Mom-and-pop shops on Main Street, the kind of place Normal entrepreneurs owned and operated and supported their families with, suddenly found themselves under assault by big box stores selling imported goods their huge buying power could acquire at a substantial discount. Boarded-up windows across America testify to that. Hillary Clinton would take a call from Walmart; she had served on its board at one point. Fred from Fred's Fashions in Tulsa, not so much.

In fact, who would take their call? The Chamber of Commerce? It was too busy agitating for illegal alien amnesty and more "free trade."

Big Business was part of the problem. But small business? That was part of the solution, a traditional way for Normals to succeed. And the people agreed. Gallup reported that 70 percent of Americans looked favorably upon small business, second only to the military.

Let's review where Donald Trump stood while running for election in 2016 and after being elected:

- Trump thought the FBI had covered up for Hillary, which it had.
- Trump accused the judiciary of being out of control, which it was.
- Trump supported the military, but promised to help it rebuild and win again.
- Trump labeled the mainstream news media "fake news," which was undeniable.
- Trump attacked loudmouthed celebrities, who deserved it.
- Trump called out Big Business for putting Normals' concerns at the back of the line, and the CEOs acknowledged it and started changing.
- Trump praised small business, which has since blossomed.

With regard to every one of these Elite-run institutions, Trump was on the side of the Normals.

With regard to every one of these Elite-run institutions, Hillary Clinton was on the side of the Elites.

And most of the Elite is still stunned that Trump is in the White House, and that Hillary is reduced to tweeting embarrassing shout-outs to her fans in the "activist bitches" community.

CHAPTER EIGHT

Looking Down Their Noses

Is it too much to say that the Elite wants Normals dead or enslaved?

It sure seems a bit extreme.

Dead or enslaved?

Wow.

That's pretty harsh.

It is harsh, and also accurate. Some of the Elite want the Normals gone, and the rest merely want them obedient.

The dead part is the trickier one. Some of the Elite definitely want the Normals dead. How they differ tends to be based on the means and the timetable. There seems to be a disagreement among the pro-dead faction as to whether the process should be facilitated, or whether the Normals should die off over time. But the rationale is the same for wanting Normals gone. No uppity opponents, no problem. Seems straightforward. Many of the Elite fantasize of a world free of icky Normals; just how the world becomes free of them varies.

Some are hoping for fate to intervene—they are the passive hell-wishers. Get on Twitter for long enough and offer Normal-like views such as "I approve of God and America and the Constitution," and pretty soon someone with a handle like @OpenMindedBookLvr and a bio that quotes Gandhi is going to respond with a tweet along the lines of, "I hope you die from your Jesus-guns, Flag Bitch!"

Someone like that is Elite, to be sure, but affiliation Elite. Most of them have never achieved anything, like a decent relationship with their parents or a job.

The tough-to-swallow fact is that some of them would like to literally see Normals dragged from their homes, put on trains, and shipped someplace far away to be disposed of. Rounding up the kulaks and shipping them away for disposal is a classic collectivist go-to move. And thanks to the power of social media to compel sociopaths to reveal themselves, these active measures advocates are happy to tell you they hope you die.

They will inform you that your time is running out and that the Normals—usually referred to as "racists" or "Xtians" or "gun lovers" or the whatever unpersons they are screaming about at the moment—will pay.

Oh yes, how they will pay...

Presumably, the ones threatening these horrors will be the ones doing the eliminating of the undesirables, though logistically this seems unsound. The concave-chest crew of pasty couch dwellers who usually traffic in this low-grade trolling are unlikely to muster the combat capacity required to scrub the continent of the Normals. The average Normal's gun safe likely houses exponentially more firepower than the whole of Final Solution Boy's entire Marxist-theme dorm could ever muster.

When the revolution comes, its vanguard will be disturbed to discover that its intended victims are significantly feistier—and shootier—than the spineless administrators and complicit academics they are used to pushing around. The Normals are heavily armed, many of them are military trained, and after seeing the Antifa posers doing their thing while the cops were restrained by the radicals' fellow travelers in government, Normals are not in a playful mood.

Others do want Normals dead but aren't fronting about going out and making that happen. They are talking about how the Normals are going to die off on their own. This is where a shocking number of the Elite—not all, by any means, but a surprising number—will jump in and own up to their preferences. But the fact remains that every time some frustrated Bernie supporter, Black Lives Matter nut, or immigrant member of the Religion of Peace decides to open fire in a gun-free zone, there's always some scribbler for a mainstreamish liberal website or an assistant adjunct sociology professor at a second-tier college who makes him/her/xirself notorious for tweeting "NEXT TIME I HOPE THEY GO TO A CHURCH AND SHOOT ALL YOU MICRO PENIS JESUS GUN FREAKS' KIDS."

With this bunch, it's always about the Jesus and the guns and the penises.

But generally, they are happy to run out the clock on the Normals, sure that time will grind finely and that the Normals of today will eventually meet their Savior. In this they are correct, but at the same time they make the unsupported assumption that the follow-on generations are going to be so thoroughly infused with the same weird psychoses that spawned the current crop of young leftist Elitists that in the future there will be no Normals.

Of course, most people are Normals. In any group, people will eventually divide into the ones who run things and the ones who just want to get on with their lives. That's simply human nature, but leftists probably are not the right people to talk to about human nature. Their entire ideology is dedicated to defeating it.

In any case, the long-run death wish for the Normals would be doomed to failure even if it worked at first. If there were no Normals, there would be no Elite, since as we have seen, the Elite in America exists purely in opposition to the Normals. Everyone will identify as Elite, and therefore the Elite itself will have to itself be broken apart into the equivalent of Formerly Elite Normals and a New Elite that can differentiate itself in its opposition to the Formerly Elite Normals. Whether there are material benefits and the power and prestige available to the top ranks of the Elite, or just the smugness the affiliated Elite gets from feeling better than the Normals, you cannot have the perks of being Elite if everyone else is Elite, too.

It all sounds very confusing and tiresome, but on the bright side, if it were to happen, today's Normals would by definition all be dead and would not be around to be bored by the post-victory Elites' tiresome antics.

The fact remains, however, the Elite's desired end state for the Normals is that they go away. No, they have not thought that through, and no, that can never actually happen, but that's what they *think* they want. Whether it is today or tomorrow or in a few decades, they wish for the Normals to be gone so that they can be free of the last vestiges of restraint, of fealty to the traditional mores of the bourgeois, and create the Elite utopia.

But what the Elite really wants is for the Normals to be enslaved.

Not in literal chains, though that's certainly an option for the most uppity of the Normals who insist on flouting the New Rules. The enslavement they would impose is not something out of *Roots*, but one where the Normals continue to work to create the wealth and perform the basic functions within society that allow the Elite to enjoy the perks of their position in comfort and safety, while depriving the Normals of any meaningful ability to govern themselves.

Kaden is horrified that the guy from Fontana has the same say, the same vote, as he does. After all, the guy from Fontana is not even remotely woke and is certain to vote wrong. Democracy is far too important for the people to be any part of it.

Until the administration of Donald Trump, with its assault on political correctness and regulatory rollbacks, everything we have seen in recent decades has been consistent with that one goal—to slowly whittle away the power of Normals, collectively and individually.

Then the Elite can rule without accountability, without limits. It can do as it pleases.

And the Elites move toward this goal by exercising government power and cultural power to limit the ability of Normals to live as they see fit.

The First Amendment protects freedom of speech, of assembly, to petition, and of the press, a placement that is a recognition of the centrality of these rights to a free people. And those rights are under assault.

Those rights are under assault because Normals are daring to exercise them and it's getting in the way. The danger to the Elite from unfettered Normal expression has grown exponentially because technology (particularly the internet) has enabled Normals to express their ideas to a wide audience by bypassing the Elite gatekeepers who controlled discourse in the past.

Free speech for...those people...was fine when it was purely theoretical. But now every housewife, insurance agent, and beat cop can jump online, sometimes anonymously, and say whatever they want.

Which is often what the Elite do not want said. So they try to stop it.

Sometimes they do it with the blunt instrument of state power, though all that talk about free expression has—until now—made outright punishing speech kind of awkward in America. But in Europe, which our Elite feels has so much to teach us, the Elite has already seen fit to dispense with those obsolete Enlightenment ideas like free speech since their own Normals started to use those rights and used them wrongly. In Britain today, you can be arrested for offending someone. You can go to one of the local squares, express some doubt that the green and pleasant land ought to be importing a whole new electorate for the benefit of the Labour Party, and some bobby will haul you off. The police regularly use social media to inform the electorate of their new legal obligation not to make statements in public or online that their betters find unacceptable. Britain and the rest of Western Europe was freed or kept free at the cost of considerable blood, including American blood, and today its Elite has chosen to squander that gift.

America's Elite turns its collective eyes to the Old World and nods in appreciation at their overseas siblings' achievement in casting of the shackles of civil rights for the Normals. For civil rights are a fetter that binds and limits the power of the Elite, and therefore civil rights are hateful. Had Hillary Clinton managed not to be crushed by Donald Trump, is it too much to imagine that she and her ilk would have pressed for similar laws?

The Elite already used the Internal Revenue Service to stop political activism by Normals. It used the Department of Justice and the FBI to spy on the Normals' candidate in 2016—and to try to frame him for the kind of "Russian collusion" Hillary and her seedy coterie of grifters manifestly engaged in. How far a leap would it be for an Elite with Hillary at the helm and willing Congress (or merely a willing bureaucracy) to impose the kind of speech rules the European Elite has been able to use to silence its own Normals?

Spoiler: It's not much of a leap at all.

After all, the Elite has managed to impose restrictions on expression where their power is already unlimited. Free speech does not exist on college campuses, except in the insincere recitals of clichés about free expression by administrators who ruthlessly suppress any expression of any idea that does not come with the stamp of approval of the faculty senate and the pierced, freak show radical contingents that are always milling about our universities. If you want to see the America the Elite dreams of, stroll across a campus. Maybe you will find some poor schmuck offering non-Elite-approved ideas off in the ten-by-ten-foot "free expression space" out behind the shed where they store the broken riding mowers.

Those who dare express wrongthink are hassled and persecuted by fussy bureaucrats investigating "hate crimes" and "hate speech" and who can always detect wrong thoughts among the dissidents but never manage to detect the hate being spewed by the good little boys and girls and others who toe the Elite line.

Try to run a conservative student publication on a college campus. It will be nonstop war, on the off chance the student council manages to find a few bucks in the alternative media

budget after funding publications for nineteen categories of radi-
calized ethnic agitators, twelve brands of socialists, and forty-
seven flavors of LGBTQ&D!H&$.

The Elite unleashes the power of hassle. What they can't ban
outright they make such a pain in the ass that Normals censor
themselves. And if you can't say what you think, are you really a
citizen, or are you merely a subject?

And that is what they wish to bring to society at large. If they
can't pass a law that you may not say "Z" or "Y," they will seek
to make it so miserable informally that you will not even dare
try to say it. You cannot call illegal aliens what they are—"illegal
aliens"—without some huffy Elitist screaming that you are "racist." No, they must be called "undocumented immigrants" or,
better yet, "undocumented workers." Always watch for language
that obscures reasonability by portraying the actors as passive
spectators—"undocumented," as if being without the documents
allowing them to be in our country was some mysterious act of
Gaia, mere happenstance that the alien had no control over.
"Alien?" Oh, I mean "worker," because everyone who comes here
illegally—oops, I mean "suffered undocumentation somehow"—
is a worker. But workers typically work, and many illegals—darn
it, I mean "document-challenged persons"—do not actually work.

What about the Dreamers, brought here as kids? Were they
workers? Isn't the whole point of them that they were just kids?
Were they doing child labor here in America? Damn, then their
homelands must really suck. So really, the word *workers* is inac-
curate factually, but it is accurate in the meta sense that it supports the narrative. That means it is therefore somehow truer
than something that is merely literally true, or what we used to
call "true."

One could get really confused. Which is almost certainly the idea.

George Orwell, whose books were never intended to be how-to manuals yet here we are, would appreciate the Elite's use of language to constrict the possible range of ideas. But in this case it is not some mentally superior class of supervillains trying to starve the Normals of their sovereignty by compressing down the Normals' access to the vast landscape of knowledge the Elite enjoys. The Elite willingly constricts its own thoughts.

This is the core irony of an Elite that is often in no way elite. They are not trying to make the Normals as open-minded as the Elite. They are trying to make the Normals as narrow-minded as the Elite.

If this was a carefully conceived and laid-out plan, it could hardly be more dangerous. But instead of being a conscious effort, it is the natural result of having a meritocracy that does not require its members to demonstrate merit. The Elite simply seeks obedience and control, and it tries to strangle any new birth of freedom in its crib. In every instance, the Elite seeks to maximize its own authority at the expense of the Normals.

It attacks the basic concept that Americans are suited to govern themselves, and substitutes the reign of experts.

It prioritizes the institutions of society over the purpose for which those institutions allegedly exist and over the interests of Normal citizens.

It resents and rejects accountability, because those concepts assume that the Normals have the moral standing to hold the experts and the institutions to account, to weigh their successes against their failures, as if Normals were created equal and endowed by their Creator with certain unalienable rights.

Nonsense! A master is not accountable to his slaves, and that is why the Elite refuses to be accountable to the Normals.

Enter the Trump administration and the so-called #Resistance. Leave aside the breathtaking chutzpah, of nearly stolen valor proportions, of adopting a moniker made glorious by the sacrifice of those who risked torture and death to fight actual Nazis behind the lines in Europe. Instead this pampered Elite, safe behind the civil rights and liberties it holds in contempt and seeks to undermine for others, acts not merely to reject the authority of President Donald J. Trump. The Elite acts to reject the authority of those who elected him.

How dare that guy from Fontana presume to have a say. Says are for people like Kaden.

Remember the heady days of October 2016, when Hillary Clinton was turning in some of her most lifelike performances as she pretended to be outraged that Trump would not commit in advance to overlook her attempts to rig the election? Considering that her minions were in the process of rigging the election and her taste for booze, she kept a remarkably straight face. One might almost have believed that she was committed to the principle that the results of fair elections must be respected if our society is to function as a Republic.

And then she lost Wisconsin and all those cheeseheads suddenly became pawns of the Kremlin. Hillary lost her taste for recognizing the legitimacy of the election faster than she lost her shoe passing out on the sidewalk that previous September.

Do not be fooled by the gyno-hat-clad hags and militant visual arts majors marching in the streets, pausing only to listen as Ashley Judd shares slam poems about her oppression as a woman of womynhood. This is not about Trump, though they do hate him and how he holds the Elite in utter contempt. Donald Trump is merely the avatar of a greater movement, of the Normals themselves. The Elite pivots to attacking him because that is its go-to move; Alinsky Rule No. 13 demands they personalize a target in every battle.

But make no mistake; they are protesting the Normals for daring to assert their authority to enact a macro change in the direction of society. Of course, enacting these macro changes is precisely what the Normals are supposed to do. The Normals cede control of day-to-day operations to the Elite-dominated experts and institutions and reserve the right to reassert control if the Elite fails to perform. Look at the Elite's track record—failed wars, economic stagnation, rampant self-dealing among those entrusted with the keys to the culture. The Elite should not have been surprised that the Normals got tired of their crap and kicked them in the ass.

Except the Elite had changed over time. It got high on its own supply, so to speak, that supply being the Frankfurt School bullshit pushed by the dealers in academia harping on the total moral bankruptcy of Normal American society.

As the Elite grew to hate the Normals and their values, and to oppose those values rather than at least pretend to honor them even if they did not do so in private, the calculus changed. In prior generations, the Elite understood that the Normals had a reasonable expectation of a competently run society, and the Elite more or less accepted that notion. After all, the Elite and the Normals shared basic beliefs about family and faith and patriotism. The Normals were dumb and boring and really, really square and when you were a young Elite it was fun to scandalize them with the occasional dirty book by Henry Miller—but they were harmless. And they were necessary.

But then the Elite began to teach itself that the Normals were not harmless, that the Normals were not merely dumb and boring and really, really square, but evil, sexist, racist, imperialist war-mongering monsters. And now the Elite were not only smarter and more sophisticated but also morally superior for having adopted the moral framework of the predominantly liberal Elite.

Hence the hatred that results in the Elite wanting those it is supposed to be serving dead or enslaved.

The Elite went from tolerating the Normals to hating the Normals over the several decades since the sixties, when the young Elites rebelled and were beaten back by the older Elite and the Silent Majority of Normals. But now yesterday's young Elite is today's old Elite. They were now the experts. They were now in the driver's seats not of a fleet of chartreuse 1966 VW vans but of the Elite institutions that ran the country.

And they hated the people they were supposed to answer to, so they stopped answering to them. They ignored the Normals and ran the operations of the institutions not for the benefit of the masses but for themselves, for their own material and ideological interests.

And the rift between the Elite and the Normals grew. And grew. And grew.

And when the Normals rose up in 2009 as the Tea Party and were suppressed temporarily, the frustration built up instead of dissipated as it had after Howard Jarvis's tax revolt and the election of Reagan in the seventies and after Bill Clinton good-ole-boyed his way through two terms after besting Ross Perot in the nineties.

Trump was the explosion, the Mount St. Helens of American politics.

It stunned the Elite, which immediately decided this rebellion was an outrage. The #Resistance saw Trump as individually illegitimate, but more important, it saw the people who elected him as illegitimate. They were bad people—haters and gun nuts, Jesus freaks and canoeist-raping perverts. And they had no moral right to power.

That is the rub. The Elite no longer recognizes that the Normals have any moral right to participate in their own governance.

Everything that has happened since the president was inaugurated reinforces this undeniable truth. The phrase they use is "normalize"—"Don't normalize Trump." Don't treat Trump like he has a right to be where he is, to exercise the powers the Constitution invests in him, to the respect or reverence that they had demanded for Barack Obama.

What they really mean is that they refuse to normalize the exercise of power by those not approved by the Elite. And they consider this a moral duty, since in their shriveled conception of morality—one divorced from the Judeo-Christian tradition and largely manufactured from whole cloth by leftists like the Kwanzaa holiday—the Normals are fatally tainted by their original sin.

They are not Elite, and they cannot be allowed a voice in how they live their own lives.

Look at the way the bureaucrats closed ranks in what they considered "their" agencies to fight against Trump keeping the promises he made to the American people before they voted. Heartbroken Deputy Assistant Underdeputies for Twigs and Toads from the Environmental Protection Agency would seek out receptive journalists, who would offer them the professional Elite courtesy of a sympathetic hearing when the poor bureaucrat whimpered about how Scott Pruitt was daring to undermine all the wonderful work Obama had done in addressing the growing twigs and toads crisis.

The mask came off completely during the Trump/Russia grift, where the Deep State did not even pretend there was no Deep State. Beyond the self-dealing and self-service of the allegedly self-sacrificing Elitists at the top of federal law enforcement's food chain, and past the media's slobbering obedience to the narrative the Elite generated to cover up its malfeasance, what started as a scam veered into extortion and threats against those the people had chosen to lead.

On February 2, 2018, just after the Devin Nunes memo dropped, CNN—what else—issued a tweet that read, "Former CIA counterterrorism official Phil Mudd: The FBI people 'are ticked' and they'll be saying of Trump, 'You've been around for 13 months. We've been around since 1908. I know how this game is going to be played. We're going to win.'"[1] So, basically, the unelected bureaucrats in the executive branch were going to somehow defeat the elected president of the United States because he dared defy them?

Way to completely substantiate the critique of the Deep State.

Remember, when people like this hack talk about "Trump," they are talking about Normal Americans. Trump is just one person, a symbol, and a not untalented politician, but he is not the threat to them.

Normals, particularly the Militant Normals, are the threat. If that beast gets loose, they are done.

The campaign against "normalizing" what should have been a routine transfer of power is simply a desperate rearguard action by an Elite that feels its power being challenged. The Elite lived with past uprisings and adapted to them. But back then, the Elite did not have the visceral hatred and contempt for the Normals that is at the core of its class ideology today.

They *can't* let the Normals exercise power. The Normals are evil.

The guy from Fontana is evil, not because of anything he has done, but because of who he is. And, conversely, Kaden is good, not because of anything he has done, but because of who he is.

For the first time, we have an Elite that actively hates the people of the nation it purports to run.

Not merely looks down upon them as dull and ignorant, though it does.

Not merely holds them in contempt for their parochial habits and bad taste, though it does.

It hates them for who they are and for the values they hold.

The Elite considers the people over whom it places itself not merely moral inferiors but morally bankrupt, possessors of parochial and provincial beliefs that are contrary to the most deeply held modern Elite values.

Morality? Hollywood's tropes best describe the Elite's view of the traditional morality of the heartland. Behind those picket fences and waving flags lurk hate and violence and bigotry and, worst of all, real Christianity. In Hollywood's product, almost every small town is a seething cauldron of racial menace, every suburb an intellectual wasteland steeped in hypocrisy, every small businessman corrupt, and every minister a drooling Bible nut or closet pervert on a quest to stop those sinful kids from shimmying.

That's not just the movies and television, and practically every Netflix series ever. That's what the Elite really thinks. Hollywood is not a thought leader; it is an Elite mirror. It reflects back the values of its Elite audience to flatter it by reaffirming how so very right and moral it is.

The Elite moralism angle is key. It's the part of the puzzle that is new and changes the prior dynamic. But the old conflict of interest is still there, the temptation toward self-dealing. Normals never expected the Elite not to skim a bit of the take for itself. A reasonable bit. That they would enrich themselves was part of the cost of having an Elite. Not that the Elite would admit it.

But now you have an Elite that actively despises and seeks to punish those it looks down upon. Plus, the spoils are nice, too. If the Normals step in to exercise power then their own power necessarily declines. So does their take. But they won't acknowledge that.

Instead the Elite denies the obvious. Why, this is about protecting the morality! No, none of this is about maintaining their positions and prestige! No, none of this is about securing their own rice bowls! Ignore that fact that several of America's richest counties now surround Washington, DC.

They are not venal and self-serving. No, they are the selfless resistance to the tyrant in the White House and those deplorable people who support him.

You know, the Normals.

CHAPTER NINE

Pitchforks, Torches, and Conservative, Inc.

The Elite is largely out and proud liberal—typically, they make no excuses and rarely deny it—except when trying to seize the moral high ground that comes with being disinterested and neutral. When they are posing as disinterested and neutral, they deny being liberal. Why, they are merely using "common sense" in a "pragmatic search for solutions."

What they call "common sense" and "pragmatism," of course, always lead to liberal solutions. Amazing how that works out so well for them.

But there is another branch of the Elite, a portion of the establishment that is arguably much, much more annoying to the Normals. Those are the conservatives—often alleged conservatives—who look on the people who they are supposed to defend and represent with horror and contempt.

They are the members of Conservative, Inc. And they are terrible.

Conservative, Inc., is the intertwined web of donors, intellectuals, media personalities, activists, and politicians who used to be the face of conservatism in opposition before Trump came along and derailed their gravy train. They are also members of the Elite, and many are quite proud of that. They deny that their Elite status turns them toward liberalism—instead, they see themselves as the torch-bearers of True Conservativism™ and the Keepers of the Sacred Principles.

But they have a big problem, the same problem that caused the Normals to revolt against the Elite in general. They did a terrible job. They are now marginalized by the people who used to care what they had to say because they never managed to actually conserve anything, and because their vaunted principles never seemed to include actually winning.

The loudest and whiniest voices of Never Trump come from inside Conservative, Inc. And that should be no surprise. By choosing Trump, the Normals expressly rejected the conservative Elite. Worse, they *disrespected* the conservative Elite. And still worse, they exposed the scam that is Conservative, Inc.

With Trump in the Oval Office, who's going to sign up for one of Bill Kristol's *Weekly Standard* voyages? Bill's not a player anymore. He's a drunk in the stands hooting at the guys actually out on the field. But instead of Budweiser, he's buzzed on white wine spritzers and his own former middling glory.

After all, there's not a lot of alpha male action in Conservative, Inc., which is one of its many flaws.

Conservative, Inc., was not always useless. Actually, that's not quite fair, because it's not entirely useless today, either. It's just largely useless, because it's less concerned with conservatism than with filling the troughs of professional conservatives. Its limited usefulness is merely a side effect. Conservative, Inc., you must understand, is about maintaining sinecures for professional conservatives who identify with the Elite over the Normals.

Go back in time to the fifties, when conservatism as an ideology was at its nadir. The communists looked ascendant around the world, and here at home everyone who was anyone—that is, everyone in the Elite—was embracing the kind of can-do liberalism that hung in the air after the New Deal. Even the Republican president, Dwight D. Eisenhower, was a career government employee. While he certainly respected the kind of yeoman farmers and small businesspeople he had grown up around, he was also a believer in top-down solutions, of planning and central organizing. After all, he had been a general, and planning and central organizing is what generals do. No wonder big corporations found a friend in the White House.

What was good for General Motors was good for America.

But then William F. Buckley showed up and gathered the scattered remnants of conservatism together by founding *National Review* in 1955 with a promise that the publication "stands athwart history, yelling Stop, at a time when no one is inclined to do so, or to have much patience with those who so urge it."[1]

William F. Buckley was not a Normal. Not even close, nor would he ever pretend to be. Instead, he wore his Elitism on his chest like a medal, both in his attitude and in his boundless vocabulary—you didn't read a Buckley column without a dictionary handy. And the *National Review* itself was openly Elitist—that was part of its charm, part of why it was so dangerous. It was of the Elite and inside the Elite, and the Elite could not ignore it. Buckley came from Yale— one of their Ivy League meccas—and if you were Elite, you might well hate and despise what he had to say, but you had to take him seriously. After all, he had your credentials.

But Buckley was also "obliged to confess I should sooner live in a society governed by the first two thousand names in the Boston telephone directory than in a society governed by the two thousand faculty members of Harvard University."[2]

He also wrote, in *Up from Liberalism* (New York: McDowell, Obolensky, 1959), "I will not cede more power to the state. I will not willingly cede more power to anyone, not to the state, not to General Motors, not to the CIO. I will hoard my power like a miser, resisting every effort to drain it away from me. I will then use my power, as I see fit."

Buckley, a man no one could deny was actually elite as well as a member of the Elite, probably summed up the Normal mindset more than anyone before or since. He had boundless faith in Normal Americans to capably exercise the rights God endowed them with.

And Conservative, Inc., today? Not so much.

In 1964, Barry Goldwater tried to put those ideas into effect and got trounced by Lyndon B. Johnson. There were many reasons for Normals not rallying around him, most of them not in play today. The assassination of John F. Kennedy was a unique factor. Some of it was sympathy. Some of it was Goldwater's personality. Conservatives adored his stridency ("But he fights!" is a recurring theme among successful conservatives), yet that also turned off many Normals. A lot of them had served in the Big One, and when Goldwater talked about war, they saw he meant a war their kids would have to fight. Of course, their kids *did* end up having to fight one—it just wasn't Barry's war.

Yet those were not the most important factors.

At that point, liberalism had not utterly failed. We had just won the greatest war in the history of mankind, and the United

States was the unchallenged economic superpower. The depression of a quarter century before was not a history lesson or a tale told by elderly grandparents but still a fresh memory for millions of Americans who understood deprivation—and credited Franklin D. Roosevelt and the Democrat Party with pulling them out of it. In 1964, you looked around your neighborhood and people had cars, refrigerators, television sets, and hope for the future. Sure, there were warnings that liberalism was a house of cards that would have to collapse eventually, but that had not happened yet. Liberalism was riding high, though not for long.

We had not yet seen the growth of the welfare state, the destruction of the cities under the blue state model, and the explosion of crime that was coming. It was still a time when liberals would still call themselves "liberals" instead of trying to find some euphemism to cover up who they really were.

You also had a media united behind LBJ, with just as much lock-step unity as it had in 2016 behind Hillary. Except back then there were no alternative outlets—except a few fringe magazines like *National Review*—and there was certainly no internet or social media where non-Elite voices could articulate and promulgate a conservative counternarrative. Moreover, the media had something then it does not have now—trust. People generally trusted the media, just as the people generally trusted all of America's institutions. The turmoil of the late 1960s and the 1970s were off in the future, and the media had not yet completely disgraced itself by casting off its pose of objectivity. When the evening news hinted darkly that Barry Goldwater was nuts—that was the beginning of the hoary tradition of liberal shrinks offering long-distance diagnoses of Republican figures as mentally ill—people took notice. Heck, if Cronkite said it, it had to be true. Right?

But the biggest reason Lyndon Johnson won is that he did not alienate the Normals. In fact, he cultivated them. In 1964, unlike 2016, the Democrats did not come across as despising Normal people. Quite the opposite—the Democrat Party aimed most of its efforts directly at the working man. Private-sector unions were much bigger and more powerful, and the Democrats partnered with them. Those guys in Wisconsin who handed the election to Trump in 2016 would have all lined up behind LBJ in 1964. In 2016, they went for Trump in no small part because they saw clearly that Hillary hated their guts.

The voters gave the White House to LBJ in 1964, but the conservative movement got a not inconsiderable consolation prize in the form of Ronald Reagan.

Reagan was the ultimate Normal, and the Normals justly revere him even if today they would strongly reject some of his specific policy positions—amnesty and, later, guns, though that may have been under the heavy-handed guidance of Nancy while he was in decline. He was never destined for the Elite, and no matter how high his talents took him, he never made the decision to become a member.

He was born in a small town in Illinois in a second-floor apartment over a tavern—hardly auspicious. He grew up in a variety of small Midwestern towns and eventually went to Eureka College—again, hardly an invitation to join the Elite. During the War, he served stateside due to bad eyesight and hearing. Afterward, he went back to Hollywood and fought against communist infiltration of the industry—that taught him all he needed to know about the commies. But it was self-study, combined with an instinctive love of country and its Constitution, that developed him into what he became—perhaps the greatest advocate for Normal Americans in history.

The Elite, for its part, hated him. And so did many in Conservative, Inc.

Much of the Republican establishment hated Reagan from early on. His anti-Elitism gnawed at them, and the fact that he was (by then) from California further demonstrated that he just was not fit to have a leadership position in the Republican Party. Of course, many of them also detested Richard Nixon, but in his case it was because Nixon so obviously wished to be accepted as one of the Elite. They put up with Nixon because Nixon won (until he stopped winning, and then they deserted him). And they put up with Reagan because he won, then claimed his mantle as their own even as they ignored everything he did.

Remember that it was the Republican Elite, the best and brightest minds of the Grand Old Party, who thought the guy to beat Jimmy Carter in 1976 was Gerald Ford. Ford was already walking wounded after pardoning Nixon. The loudly and tiresomely born-again Christian Carter was still benefitting from the Democrat Party's temporary refocusing on the working man after the disaster in 1972, where a new generation of Democrats followed their tiny, shriveled hearts and nominated George McGovern on a platform of acid, amnesty (for draft dodgers), and abortion. In their wisdom, the GOP geniuses chose the quintessential insider after a shocking scandal had rocked Washington. It was the culmination of a seemingly endless series of earthquakes that had shaken the citizenry's faith in America's institutions, and the last thing the GOP needed was to nominate Mr. Institutions.

Of course, today a president pulling on the levers of executive power to spy on political opponents is the height of patriotism—assuming it's a Democrat doing it to a Republican.

Not for the last time had the Republican Elite utterly misread the very people it was expecting to vote them back into office. When Reagan finally got a crack at Carter four years later—no thanks to the GOP Elite—he kicked that sanctimonious incompetent's peanut-farming ass.

But it was under Reagan that Conservative, Inc., truly began to flourish. In the twelve years of Republican rule that followed, donors began to take notice, and conservative entrepreneurs began to build a right-wing extragovernmental infrastructure of think tanks and activist organizations. Back in the day, for most conservatism was just a hobby (even Buckley wrote a series of best-selling, largely apolitical spy novels). Now, it was a living, and for many, a lifestyle.

We began to see the rise of the professional conservatives. These were the pundits, the thinkers, and the talkers, and they were determined to continue the *National Review*'s work of building an intellectual framework for conservatism. But it was only a nascent campaign in the 1980s. For those conservatives outside the Beltway, their conservative fix only came every couple weeks when the postman delivered a copy of *National Review*, or maybe the more feisty and irreverent *American Spectator*.

However, the movement had learned from the left that you gotta get 'em young, and money and support began to pour into college campuses to fund conservative papers like the *Dartmouth Review* and the University of California, San Diego's *California Review*. These papers had the advantage of creating a farm team for talent; both Dinesh D'Souza and Laura Ingraham started their activism at the Dartmouth paper.

Then Reagan left office and George H. W. Bush took office and everything started turning to shit.

The Bush family was the definition of elite, even if George W. Bush would later cultivate a connection with the Normals that was big on talk and short on actual connection. Bush 41 had run against Reagan in 1980, and you always got the idea that he was gritting his teeth waiting for Reagan to clear out of the Oval Office that was his by right. Bush 41 was a patriot and a legitimate war hero, but he was no Normal and he had no desire to cater to them. A lifelong "public servant," Bush 41 was most comfortable with those who shared his moderate, sensible conservatism—which translated to "liberal conservatism," which of course made absolutely no sense.

He came into office promising a "kinder, gentler nation." Of course, that meant that the Normal agenda that Ronald Reagan had been carrying out was anything but "kind" and "gentle." Bush 41 was determined to steer the ship of state back in the kind of sensible direction that the sensible people that he met at his sensible functions felt comfortable with.

He just didn't get it. In fact, it appeared that he was a bit ashamed of the kind of demands the Normals pressed on him. But then, he had absolutely zero idea, having been at or near the pinnacle of society all his life except when he was flying dive bombers in the Pacific, what a Normal life entailed. Nor did the majority of the people he was listening to.

He got America into Operation Desert Storm, which was not a bad thing in and of itself. Normals are not antiwar in any meaningful sense. What they are is anti–their sons and daughters dying in indecisive battles where America seems to have no real interest at stake and the people in charge don't have the guts to

win. That was the problem in Vietnam—Normals had no problem killing commies. They *liked* the idea of killing commies, and
most were perfectly happy to join in that laudable effort. But they
didn't understand why they could smoke Charlie on one side of
a line on the map of Southwest Asia, but when he crossed it,
Charlie could sit there on the other side and make faces at the
Americans and not get smoked. And then there was Hanoi and
the ships in Haiphong harbor, just sitting there, unloading the
bullets killing American boys down south. In World War II, they
knew what to do with enemy cities—you leveled them, and the
Japanese and the Nazis surrendered. But in North Vietnam, they
were off-limits—why?

Why did our Elite betters—the "Best and the Brightest" and
Robert McNamara's "Whiz Kids"—get us into a war they didn't
feel was worth doing what was necessary to win? Of course, when
Richard Nixon finally unleashed the B-52s over Christmas 1972,
the North Vietnamese couldn't scramble back to the table at the
Paris peace talks fast enough to make the pounding stop.

So, Americans were okay with going in and kicking Saddam's sorry ass out of Kuwait and leaving his formerly feared
army in smoking heaps across the southern Iraqi desert. And they
rewarded Bush 41 with Gallup approval ratings of 89 percent (the
record) after the war ended.[3] But there was the nagging thought
that this wasn't over, that it wasn't a final victory because the dictator was still feeding opponents into industrial shredders instead
of swinging from a lamppost.

We all know how that worked out. And we all know who
supplied the blood and sweat to finish what Bush 41 left undone.

Leave it to a member of the conservative Elite to take an 89 percent approval rating and lose, less than two years later, to a skeevy serial adulterer who had weaseled out of the draft.

Normals understood both that they were already taxed too much, and that Washington's money problems were not the result of hardworking Americans keeping too much of their own money but a consequence of an out-of-touch ruling class back in the capital spending too much damn money. And making it worse, the money was too often going to people who didn't work. Entitlements—even the name is obnoxious, since it presupposes that someone has a right to the fruits of another's labor—were the problem. Not a lack of kindness or gentleness. Not greed by Normal Americans.

George H. W. Bush decided to lie, right to the Normals' collective face. He had promised "No new taxes." And when he said it, he had even invited Americans to "Read my lips." But the Washington consensus was that the people were keeping too much of their own money, so the heck with that. The Normals surely wouldn't remember some throwaway line from a speech, would they?

Oh, they remembered.

And they remembered hard. The GOP wing of the Elite had decided to try to shaft the people who sent them to Washington, and George H. W. Bush paid the price.

But gosh, all the smart people said it was a good idea to raise taxes.

Conservative, Inc., entered the Clinton years and found out something that would inform its behavior in the decades that followed. It was a lot easier—and profitable—to be in opposition.

The thing about being in opposition—about working against

the Democrats holding power—is that you don't even have to fake accountability. Under Reagan and Bush, the Senate had been on and off Republican, but the House had been a Democrat lock for decades. Conservative, Inc., could generate all sorts of swell ideas, but as long as Tip O'Neill and his successors were opposed, nothing was happening on the legislative side. With Bill and Hillary, his scheming, striver wife, holding down the executive branch, America would not change course.

Not only was there no accountability, but there was a really good excuse for no accountability. Conservative, Inc., could fulminate and screech and rake in donations all day long and shrug when asked what it was accomplishing.

The Democrats made us not do it!

What changed when Newt Gingrich and his rebels took the House in 1994 was that at least there was a political pulpit for their views, and there were some victories. Bill Clinton was forced into accepting welfare reform. That was something. Yet between the Clinton permanent campaign model and the rise of conservative media, like Rush Limbaugh's show and the new Fox News cable network, the political struggle began taking on a new urgency. Eventually, once social media came online, politics would embrace the modern 24/7 news cycle model.

The razor-thin victory of George W. Bush over global warming huckster Al Gore revealed a problem for Conservative, Inc. The think tanks and the media outlets that had prospered during the pitched battles with the Clinton cabal provided a wealth of recruits for the thousands of newly opened posts in the federal government. And the conservative pundit community now included Bill Kristol's *Weekly Standard*, which prided itself as an idea incubator for some amorphous new kind of conservatism for the modern age. But the problem was that the conservatism of Conservative, Inc., was still at odds with the conservatism of Normal Americans.

Obviously, Bush 43 had 9/11 thrust upon him, and the Normal consensus was to hunt down and kill everyone who had anything to do with it, as well as all their pals and their goats. But Iraq was a war of choice, and it turned out to be a bad choice since all those chemical weapons we were promised were never found. Still, Americans were none too broken up about marching on Baghdad and booting that dirtbag out of power. It's just that when the insurgency started, there seemed to be no sense of urgency about ending it. Veterans began trickling home—those not on stretchers or in body bags—with dire reports of rules of engagement that tied our troops' hands. And on television, there was an endless series of commentators explaining "counterinsurgency strategy" and how it would take time to win over the Iraqi people's hearts and minds.

To which sensible Normals like the guy from Fontana wondered, why, instead of winning these *jihadi* freaks' hearts and minds, we don't just put bullets in them? Kaden would have been horrified by the thought, but then Kaden never saw the *jihadis* up close like the guy from Fontana and his brothers-in-arms.

Normals will tolerate a war. They will tolerate their sons and daughters—and it was the Normals' sons and daughters—coming home in boxes. What they refuse to tolerate is those lives being squandered on poorly thought through wars fought for no discernable purpose and that the genius architects refused to win.

But that is how the Elite rolls, even the Republican wing of the Elite.

Actually, their roll is much worse than that.

Bush 43's thing was "compassionate conservatism," a conservatism that flatters the advocate by allowing him to adopt the mantle of caring. This is in opposition, of course, to those conservatives who aren't compassionate—you know, the ones who are actually conservative.

Guess who foots the bill for all that compassion?

Compassionate conservatism is the perfect vehicle for Elite Republicans because, like everything else the Elite does, there is no cost or accountability. You adopt the mantle and you get the credit. Who picks up the tab for this compassion? The Elite? Of course not. They have already done their bit. They are compassionate because they call themselves compassionate.

It's the Normals who pick up the tab, the Normals who have to work that much harder to pay that much more, either now or down the road when the tab for all this compassionate deficit spending comes due. When Warren Buffett complains that his secretary gets taxed at a higher rate than him and therefore people should be taxed more,[4] remember that if he's taxed another $10 million that means he's still got the other $90 million he made. The guy making $50,000 now has $45,000. The $10 million to Warren is nothing, but that $5,000 is everything to the guy from Fontana.

And when Kaden offsets his 787 flight to his vacation in Tuscany using carbon credits he got on a website by paying twenty dollars for someone to plant a banana tree in Ghana, that's not sacrifice. It's posing. The Elite has mastered the art of signaling their noblesse oblige without actually being obligated to do anything noble themselves.

And the GOP establishment did it hand in hand with the Democrats, who had to be pinching themselves at their good fortune to have such an eager sucker at 1600 Pennsylvania Avenue. No Child Left Behind? Didn't that just give even more power to the education Elite that had already screwed up the schools so badly in the first place? Normals wanted more control over their kids' education, and compassionate conservatism—with significant support from the Conservative, Inc., intellectual wing—handed even more over to the bureaucrats. After all, it was an institution, and everyone in it was by definition an expert—no matter how remarkably unbroken a track record of failure they had managed to assemble over the years.

But gosh, we're helping the children! And it's bipartisan! Look, Ted Kennedy is positively beaming!

This was about the time that Governor Mitt Romney was passing Obamacare in Massachusetts using ideas generated by the Elite conservative brain trust.

But nothing showed the stubborn tone deafness of the Elite better than their inexplicable fetish for giving amnesty to law-breaking illegal aliens. And Conservative, Inc., largely cheered it.

Imagine yourself a Normal, if you are not one. Imagine yourself breaking the law. You go out, and you commit a crime. What happens? You get arrested. You get put in a cell, at least until you bail out. You have to spend money on a lawyer. Maybe you lose your job. You certainly lose face in the sight of your community. You might have to pay a fine or even go to jail for a while. Say it's a DUI. You'll lose your license. You'll be out ten grand minimum.

Now imagine you are an illegal alien. You're not even an invited guest, much less an actual citizen. You shouldn't be here—you should be back in what Donald Trump memorably—because it was true—referred to as some "shithole" country. You've violated the law—*our* law. The one that our elected representatives went to Washington and voted on, and the president signed, just like you learned in civics class or from that "I'm Just a Bill" cartoon on *Schoolhouse Rock* back in the 1970s.

Our democratically passed law says that you can't be here.

A law.

Passed by our representatives.

To ignore it is to ignore...us. The Normals. The very people who ceded the Elite their managerial authority in the first place.

And it's not as if our immigration laws are arbitrary or irrational either. This is not one of those obsolete regulations you see gathered into an article on wacky statutes that remain forgotten on the books, like some 1906 provision of the Muncie Municipal Code prohibiting walnut gathering on St. Swithin's Day.

These are real laws with real effects. Immigration changes the culture, *our* culture. Remember the now-disfavored melting pot metaphor? It may be unfashionable, but it's true. Don't Normals have a right to control how that cultural change happens? Didn't they already exercise that right through their representatives?

What other laws will the Elite effectively repeal by choosing not to enforce them?

Isn't it called "tyranny" when the people have no say in their own governance?

Compounding the injustice is the fact that it is a gut punch to Normals, not the Elites. The Third World is not shipping over movie producers, college presidents, and CEOs. Illegal immigrants—oh right, *undocumented workers*—affect the job market for the less glamorous gigs Normals generally take. Since these "undocumented workers" are workers and all, a worker by definition takes up a job that could have gone to—wait for it—an American citizen.

"But but but," objects the *Wall Street Journal* editorial page. "These wonderful people do the jobs Americans don't want to do!"

Well, that's sort of true, because the companies whose water the *WSJ* carries can get away with paying illegals a fraction of what an American would demand, depressing the wages in those industries. Apparently, the law of supply and demand no longer applies when it comes to importing a workforce of eager serfs.

So what happens to you, an illegal alien, for breaking this law? What are the consequences for committing this crime?

The Elite wants the consequence to be nothing. Oh wait, maybe you pay a fine. And maybe you wait a couple years before you can become a citizen and start electing Democrats. But you get to break the law and get the greatest award imaginable—American citizenship.

All because the Elite likes you, because it needs you, you get a special pass. Normal Americans, not so much.

And they wonder why the Normals got militant.

Was Conservative, Inc., making this case for Normal Americans? Nah. But it was sure pretending to have Normals' backs, especially around election time. Every election year, the politicians of Conservative, Inc., are out there conservativing it up for the Normals, and every off year they go back to Washington and do just the opposite.

The *Weekly Standard* was a particularly interesting example of the Conservative, Inc., syndrome. Bill Kristol founded it. His father was a well-known conservative intellectual. Bill got a gig as chief of staff to Dan Quayle, so winning is in his blood, and then bopped around riding the conserva-cash wave until he started the magazine as a sort of hipper, more practical *National Review*. He

ran it largely on donations and subscriptions from eager suckers
hoping for a glimpse of the inside. And, of course, there were
cruises—the *Weekly Standard* cruises are absolutely legendary. Kristol live and in concert? You can't pass that up!

It used to brag about being the idea factory for the conservative
movement. It was, but many of them were terrible, terrible ideas. Bill
is famous for his dedication to going to war again with Iraq. He has
yet to apologize. The *Standard* also pushed other ambitious domestic
programs that always, always seemed to involve the government
doing more and more in the name of empowering the people.

Message: We in the conservative Elite got this.

Truth: Those guys in the conservative Elite totally did not
have this.

Bush left office with Conservative, Inc., wiping its collective brow, relieved that the Normals would be asked to fund a
giant bailout for the very same Wall Street jokers who had risked
sending everything down the tubes with their antics. Everyone in
Washington, New York, and the other important places had gotten together and decided that it only made sense to make other
people pay for the mistakes of fellow members of the Elite.

Remember, class always trumps ideology. And since the domi-
nant ideology of the Elite class is liberalism, guess what we always
move toward?

Go ahead. Guess.

Conservative, Inc., as always, sought to surf the zeitgeist when
the Tea Party movement arose. The conservative Elite liked its
energy, meaning they liked its ability to drum up voters and
donors. But the Tea Party's insistence on specific prescriptions that
moved power out of the Elite's hands—now, that was a problem.
And the problem threatened to grow out of control.

The Tea Party was the first whiff of danger for Conservative, Inc. For almost twenty years before that, it had not really been a target of the Normals' ire, not since a bunch of Normals had gone over and supported that screechy Keebler elf, billionaire Ross Perot. Perot had many faults, including being a nut, but his greatest sin was subjecting Vice Admiral James Stockdale to ridicule as a result of the 1992 vice presidential debate. Admiral Stockdale was a true American hero of unwavering courage and integrity, and he deserved far better than to be a punchline served up by lesser men. But the Perot insurrection passed, and Conservative, Inc., got back to the business of conservativing.

That is, until about the moment Rick Santelli launched his famous rant in the midst of the bailouts on February 19, 2009. All of a sudden, rallies started happening—spontaneous ones, all over the country. And the target of the protests was the Elite.

Pretty quickly, the members of Conservative, Inc., figured out that the Normals of that most Normal of movements, the Tea Party, despised them as much as they did the Democrats.

Maybe more.

After all, many people asked of the professional conservatives exactly what they had conserved. But the pros had no good answer.

The Tea Party became utterly intolerable when it began doing the unthinkable—demanding that candidates actually support the same policies in Washington, DC, as they did back home on the stump every election year.

You mean these yahoos out in Hooterville actually want us to do the stuff we say we're going to do? Yikes!

Worse, these people were actually reading the Constitution and talking about governing in terms of the Constitution. They fetishized the Constitution, while the establishment fetishized pragmatism. Wait, Obamacare is bad because the Constitution doesn't provide for the government paying for your doctor? Huh? Sure, the Constitution is something you talk about when complaining about liberal activist judges, but using it as a guide to delineate the proper role of government?

Wait, what?

That's crazy talk.

There was a lot of crazy talk with the Tea Party, including some legitimately crazy talk. It was a reaction to a status quo that had to change, and sometimes the partygoers made tactical errors. Mike Castle, a timeserving Republican squish in Congress, would have made a perfectly adequate senator for Delaware. He would have won. He was a moderate, but then again it was Delaware, and a moderate was about the best one could ever expect from a state that kept sending Touchy Joe Biden back to Capitol Hill. Instead, the Republicans nominated Christine McDonnell, who ended up having to go on television to dispute the notion that she was a witch.

Clearly a problematic candidate, despite her cross-over appeal to the growing Wiccan community.

But while the Tea Party movement picked some losers, it also got Ted Cruz and Mike Lee into office, both of whom beat gooey moderates. They both proceeded to raise hell, making Conservative, Inc., even more unhappy about the campaigns the Tea Party won than the campaigns it lost.

Conservative, Inc.'s media and its political wings moved to distance themselves from the Tea Party, allowing the media and the Democrats to attempt to bomb it into submission. The Elite—conservative and otherwise—hoped that this would end the insanity and that the Normals would return to their slumber and allow the Elite to get on with business as usual. Except, they fundamentally misunderstood the nature of the phenomenon they called the Tea Party.

There was no Tea Party.

Sure, there were rallies with the words *Tea Party* on their banners, and certainly when grifters moved in—as they inevitably do in any movement—the words *Tea Party* got stamped on innumerable mailings targeted at conservative-leaning shut-ins. But "Tea Party" was merely a convenient label to paste on the public manifestations of a deeper dissatisfaction among America's Normals.

The Elite did not see it, because the Elite did not want to see it. That is true for both the right and the left. They still can't, or won't, though it has manifestly bit them on their collective ass.

The attack on the "Tea Party" was an attack on a conservative insurgency, but it was a rebellion that was totally decentralized. Where was the Tea Party? What building did it reside in, so that if you wished to drop the Mother of All Bombs upon it you would take out the Tea Party leadership?

There was not one.

They wanted to cut the heads off the hydra, and whenever they chopped one a couple more noggins popped out in its place. The fundamental misunderstanding by the Elite was that the Tea Party did not need (and did not want) its own Elite guiding and controlling it. The Elite could not fathom that notion.

The underlying movement was, and remains, an un-Elite movement. Sure, there were big names who grew associated with it. Take Andrew Breitbart. He was held up as a leader, even an instigator of the movement, but that's a flawed understanding of his role. Sure, through his pre–Steve Bannon *Breitbart.com* websites and his media appearances, Breitbart publicized the movement, but he didn't organize it. When he spoke at a Tea Party rally, it was because he was asked to be there. He didn't organize it. He didn't create it. The local people thought it up, set it up, and got it up and running. Andrew just showed up to get the crowd on its feet.

The Tea Party movement was the kind of movement people like the Normals would inevitably create—a bottom-up movement with little in the way of hierarchy. The Elite, both conservative and liberal, misunderstood the Tea Party because it could not imagine a great movement developing and actually influencing the course of events without the Elite pulling the strings.

The Normals created the manifestations of the Tea Party— the rallies and such—all by themselves. They were used to doing that sort of organizing. They had founded and operated their own small businesses. They had run their own sports leagues in their communities. They were often managers or military vets who knew how to make things happen. Putting together a rally? No big deal. With social media to help them—Twitter and Facebook became ways to communicate and spread the word—they did not need any help from their alleged betters.

That was the scariest part. The liberal Elite could not conceive of a real grassroots movement. They were so used to astroturfing— trying to make centrally organized demonstrations and protests seem spontaneous—that they could not recognize an authentic popular movement if it bit them on the ass, which it did.

They wanted, desperately, to believe that some mysterious, sketchy force was behind the Tea Party. Maybe it was the Koch brothers! But while some money did flow in for activist training later—it has since dried up almost completely—that was well after the main event.

But here was the thing—the rallies and so forth were only what was seen above the surface. Like the iceberg that took out that monument to expertise, the RMS *Titanic*, what lurked below was much bigger and more dangerous to the Elite. Attending a rally was a public declaration, and only a small percentage of Normals ever made it. The rest of the activated masses—some of whom would tell you then and still today that they opposed the Tea Party—made their dissatisfaction known only in the voting booth.

When the Tea Party faded away, Conservative, Inc., expected to resume its rightful place as the shepherds of their center-right flock. Yet, troubling signs remained. Speaker of the House John Boehner seemed to be drawing an awful lot of flak from the GOP base. With his clinky bourbon tumbler vibe and notorious affection for the K Street Crew, the Speaker seemed to embody the worst stereotypes of the kind of conservative of convenience Normals had grown weary of. And he just gave off the vibe that he thought you and your petty personal concerns were a giant pain in the ass interfering with his truly important work, securing the sinecures of his pals.

But Conservative, Inc., loved Boehner. He was the adult in the room—though usually it was a barroom—and he knew how the game was played. You see, out there in the hinterlands they don't know how the sausage gets made, how you have to compromise, how you can't let yourself be constrained by ideology. All these radicals the voters keep sending to Congress—they are just getting in the way of the kind of compromise we need to make real progress!

Maybe.

But maybe keeping John Boehner and his henchmen in wine,

women, and song wasn't the Normals' priority. Maybe Normals wanted some relief. After all, real wages for Normal Americans had been stagnant for years. Companies—including the big companies the Republican Elite seemed so concerned with—were shipping good jobs overseas. Illegal aliens were a problem. Welfare rolls were growing. The system seemed rigged against the very people who built the country, fed it, and defended it.

And all the John Boehners seemed interested in was partying with their Elite pals on the other side of the velvet rope that no Normal could cross.

"Do you hear us now?" the Normals asked when they sent Eric Cantor packing.

Conservative, Inc., did not. Instead, it had its own answer to a question the base was not asking: Jeb Bush—wait, Jeb! Bush, with the exclamation point that symbolized the excitement he generated.

What freaking question did they think they were being asked?

In 2012, Conservative, Inc., managed to nominate Mitt Romney, a guy who was, by all accounts, honest and decent and completely out of touch. The conservative wing of the Elite imagined that the best guy to embody the spirit of the age was a dude who seemed more like a mousier version of Judge Smails in *Caddyshack* (1980), without the laughs or the human touch.

You just knew that Mitt had never, ever seen *Caddyshack*. And if he had, he would think Rodney Dangerfield was the bad guy.

Mitt had another problem, besides being the guy who looks like the guy who tells the guy who tells the guy who tells the guy who tells your direct supervisor to eliminate your job in the interests of "efficiency." And also besides being for Obamacare before he was against it. Mitt Romney was a gentleman.

In the sense that *gentleman* is synonymous with *wuss.*

This was a theme with Elite conservatives. George W. Bush had taken a hurricane of unmitigated shit from the left during his eight years in office. Not just run-of-the-mill shit either—ultra, mega shit, right up to and including calls for his assassination. They had called him "Hitler," said he was "racist," accused him of getting thousands of Americans killed over "lies," and worse. Throughout it all, he was a gentleman. He maintained the quiet, solemn dignity of the office by refusing to lower himself to respond.

That was stupid.

His decorum was taken as weakness by his enemies. And not just his enemies. Among those not truly involved in politics, these unanswered claims do what unanswered claims do. They make an impact, fair or not, right or wrong. If you have a chorus screaming at you 24/7 that you are worse than herpes, and you don't respond, at *best* you're going to eventually be associated with herpes.

It's bad to be associated with herpes. And also with Hitler, racism, 9/11 conspiracies, and committing mass murder to enrich your Halliburton buddies.

Bush 43 never fought back while in office, or when Obama was sliming him afterward, though he finally found his voice again when the guy who crushed his brother was inaugurated. It is hard to overestimate the damage his choice to sit there and be pummeled did to the morale of the GOP base. He left it to his supporters to try to do the heavy lifting, negating the power of the bully pulpit they had handed him. There is a huge, natural inclination for human beings to hit back, and by allowing himself to be a punching bag, Bush 43 left the lasting impression that establishment Republicans not only would not fight, but could not.

If you won't fight for yourself, they reasonably concluded, you sure as hell won't fight for us.

Enter Mitt Romney, who like John McCain four years earlier, seemed to be convinced that conservatives had a moral obligation to lose. McCain was pro-amnesty through and through, so his nomination was an insult to the base. Mitt? He went hard the other way, caught heat from the media and...treaded water. He just could not deal with the disapproval of his fellow members of the Elite. And while he was a conservative within the Elite, in the end Elite opinion mattered more than sticking up for the Normals. He went wobbly, and Barack Obama beat him to a pulp.

When Candy Crowley corrected Mitt with false information at one of the debates with Obama, he did the deer/headlights thing and froze up. He could have gone for her jugular and left her a tubby, quivering heap on the stage—and maybe won the election. But he was a nice guy. A gentleman. And gosh—she was a serious reporter, the elite of the Elite—so *maybe* she was right.

She was not right. She was shilling for Obama, and he let her get away with it. And he lost.

It was this mindset that decreed that, naturally, the answer to the GOP's troubles as it faced 2016 and Hillary Clinton was Jeb! Bush.

Another Bush—exactly what American Normals yearned for. The first one had been booted out of office after lying to the people, and the last one had left office with the economy about to go into a tailspin, but this Bush—well, this Bush was going to get it right. Hey, the Bushes were due.

You look at Jeb!mania and you wonder, "What the hell were these people thinking?" What was the thought process that led the conservative Elite to think this chunky, condescending doofus was the right man for the job?

He was the scion of an American dynasty, and that was bad. America, the Roosevelts aside, has a lousy history with dynasties. Look at the Kennedys—Jack was a tramp who got us into Vietnam and almost into a nuclear war, Robert was a tramp who turned hard left, and Teddy was a tramp with a confirmed kill with his Oldsmobile.

And the Clintons? Hillary's primary qualification for getting the senate seat in New York, where she had never lived, was sleeping with Bill at least once. She got the secretary of state job as a consolation prize for losing to unaccomplished uber-Elite candidate Barack Obama in 2008. Yet Jeb! was the one guy in the entire world the GOP could nominate who would immunize her from those weaknesses.

Jeb! was the conservative liberals loved—a clueless one with a unique ability to infuriate the very people he imagined would vote for him. As the chairman of some donor-fueled boondoggle called the National Constitution Center, he presented Clinton with its 2013 Liberty Medal. *He gave his ultraliberal opponent Hillary Clinton a freaking medal for her dedication to the Constitution.* And he did it on purpose!

Oddly, it apparently never occurred to anyone within the conservative Elite that this might make it a little awkward for Jeb! when attacking her for the Constitution-defiling pinkos she was dying to put on the Supreme Court.

Nice of Jeb! to provide his opponent with ready-made campaign ads. Please clap, indeed.

Oh, and amnesty reared its ugly head again. Of course Jeb! was for it. And he was not only for it, despite the clear and unequivocal position of the very people he thought were stupid enough to vote for him. He had called violating American law "an act of love."

No. The "act of love" was when Jamiel Shaw's heartbroken family said good-bye to the son murdered by some illegal immigrant scumbag.[5]

If you want to know the Elite consensus at any given time, you can consult Jeb! Conversely, the opposite of whatever he says—he keeps talking because, for some reason, he thinks people care what he has to say—is a pretty good indicator of what Normal people think.

The priorities of Jeb! and his ilk were absolutely clear—which is why he was so decisively defeated in the primary despite spending the combined GDP of several "shithole" nations on his windmill jousting campaign. Unsurprisingly, Jeb! later chose to weigh in with some sanctimonious nonsense during the faux outrage over Trump's accurate remarks regarding certain shitty countries.

In the end, the Normals put Jeb! out of their misery. But more than that, they knocked much of the conservative Elite on its collective heels. Yet the Elite, of both ideologies, was not done. It was not going to go that easily. It resolved to resist the Normals, though it did not put it quite that way. Instead, the Elite decided to resist Donald Trump.

CHAPTER TEN

"But He Fights!"

Toward the fall of 2016, Trump was pounding on Hillary with as much gusto as she was pounding on him. But the Elite did not recognize the critical significance of a Republican who fought back. To the Elite, the election superficially looked like 1964 all over again—a looming rout. Their eyes were fixed on the future. They were With Her.

Far be it for the Elite to look back five decades and learn something from history—even something useful. The modern Elite, marinated in Frankfurt School nonsense, considers history racist and besides, past people—especially past people of pallor—have nothing to teach the Elite. The Elite knows all.

The past was at best irrelevant, if not actively evil. Back then, they thought there were only two genders—can you believe it?

There were some similarities between the elections on the surface. In 1964, the liberal Elite and their Republican fellow travelers like Nelson Rockefeller had worked together to marginalize the straight-arrow, committed conservative war hero from Arizona, as well as his followers, who were the real target, as they always are. In 2016 the Elite was making the same play with a guy who was as different from Barry Goldwater as any biped could be. The two men did share one key attribute in common—the Elite hated them both. The candidates were different, but the strategy was the same.

Destroy them, and thereby suppress those horrible people who supported them.

But there was something to learn from what went on in that election a half-century before, if you looked. The candidates were different in 2016, but so were the people the Elite were determined to disenfranchise.

Once again, the liberal Elite and their Republican fellow travelers would simultaneously work together to marginalize the candidate who captured the base's imagination. Except the new guy was Donald Trump, and the Normals had gotten woke to the fact that they were in a real fight. They had selected a candidate who understood the situation, who saw it as it was and not as he wanted it to be.

Which is why the Elite's playbook did not work.

Trump fought.

Goldwater was a fighter in war, but he was unprepared for the kind of combat taking on LBJ and the entire Elite would require. At some level, Barry Goldwater had a level of respect for his opponents and considered the system essentially fair. Oh, the good old days of such naïveté. Think of how Trump would have blown the minds of the squares.

Trump was what he was, but he was certainly the right man for the present era.

Hate the era, not the player.

Trump was no button-down Arizonan whose hobbies included

operating his ham radio and collecting Indian art. He was a play-boy who spent decades in the limelight, mingling with the Elite, and learning to have nothing but contempt for them and their minions in the press. He operated a huge company, he hosted a reality television show, and he collected beautiful women.

Trump was vulgar and prickly, and his habits—like a love of Big Macs—scandalized the smart set. But unlike Goldwater, Donald Trump did not have any residual awe for those who presumed themselves to be his betters.

Instead, he had active contempt for them.

After all, weasels like Hillary Clinton, Kirsten Gillibrand, Chuck Schumer, and hundreds of others had crawled on their bellies to him as he sat in his Trump Tower throne room, begging for his money.

They weren't his superiors.

They were his supplicants.

And he laughed at them. He was delighted to rub the fact that they had abased themselves before him in their smug faces.

To the Elite, Trump was a million times worse than Goldwater because he laughed at them.

Because the Elite didn't impress him.

Because he took the garbage they had been serving up everyone outside of their caste and shoved it back in their smug faces.

He fought.

And the Normals of 2016 loved it.

Back in 1964, the Normals had respect. They revered the institutions. They played by the rules and the Elite was wise enough to hide the fact that they were creating their own special rules from the people out there on the other side of the television screen. Think of the scandal if more than a whiff of John

F. Kennedy's reckless bimbomania escaped into the culture past the phalanx of his media praetorian guard. This guy was passing around secretaries to service his cronies in the White House pool. Middle America would have been more than shocked; they would have demanded retribution.

Back then, you could not have everyone knowing that King Arthur was grabbing a quickie with Guinevere's lady-in-waiting out by the drawbridge. It was supposed to be Camelot, and that was true to the extent that the satyr-in-chief sure came a lot.

But the truth about his needy pursuit of side action—which was so unfathomably and arrogantly reckless that it included banging mobsters' molls—did not escape into the culture while he lived. His buddies hid it for him. His Elite buddies, including his buddies in the press. Buddies like Ben Bradlee, the *Washington Post* editor lauded for his bravery and courage and dedication and stuff in movies like *All the President's Men* (1976) and *The Post* (2017)—you know, movies that made this enabler a hero for his undying dedication to exposing the truth about anybody who didn't rate Elite professional courtesy.

People like Richard Nixon.

When the truth about Cover-Up-a-Lot finally came out decades later, and the Elite snickered and shrugged, it was just one more chip in the Elite's façade. There were plenty of chips by then. The Elite had gotten comfy and had forgotten that to get the rabble to keep granting you all of the perks of being Elite—like respect and trust—you had to eventually earn them.

So by 2016, the Normals had spent decades being commanded to submit to disrespect and neglect without complaint by people who did nothing but complain about Normals. But Trump had turned the tables. Now *he* was complaining, loudly and crudely, and therefore prominently and clearly. The media suddenly could not ignore the issues that the Elite had declared off limits. How can you crucify the Orange Monster from Queens for being racist against illegal aliens without mentioning what he said? You could try, but when Trump talked about illegal aliens killing Americans and mentioned Kate Steinle, a lot of people thought, "Yeah, keeping people here who shoot young women out for walks is a bad thing."

If anything exposed the priorities of the Elite and how the interests of the Normals were an afterthought, it was illegal immigration. The Elite got cheaper nannies and gardeners and that sweet rush that comes with cost-free munificence. The Normals got the consequences. No, not every illegal was a murderer or even a major criminal, but they were all breaking the law—the law the Normals had been taught came about because their representatives had voted for it. But now it was being effectively repealed. How did that happen? No one had asked them. They never got to vote on that change. The Elite just…did it.

The Elite chose not to defend the border and chose not to deport the illegals. The Elite was delighted to let Uncle Sucker grant them handouts. Based on 2012 data, 61.9 percent of illegal alien families received some form of welfare; for actual Americans, the number was 28.1 percent.[1]

Sure, you had to have some grudging respect for a guy who would swim a river and hike through a desert to take a subminimum-wage job. But then, would not this hardworking exemplar of industriousness be more useful back home turning his homeland into the kind of place that does not inspire you to swim a river and hike a desert to take a subminimum-wage job somewhere else?

Oh, the Elite had a name for people who complained about illegal aliens, too: "racists." But, of course, when everything is racist, nothing is. What was once a verbal Mother of All Bombs was now a piddly firecracker. Normals were tired of the constant race hustling that had become the go-to move of the Elites and their media flunkies. Now, "You're racist!" was less a cutting charge that demanded a personal inventory than a punchline in a semi-funny joke.

"Dude, pour me a beer."

"Keg's empty!"

"That's so racist, dude."

Trump didn't care if he was called a "racist," which was what his more kindly inclined ones went with. The rest of his enemies went Full Hitler. Never go Full Hitler. Trump had the advantage going into the arena of having been called much, much worse, well before even the late eighties when *Spy* magazine first made Trump's allegedly tiny paws a running gag.

Today, Trump is the president and *Spy* is a vague memory from long ago.

So Trump, unlike Goldwater, was not only uniquely suited to surviving these Elite attacks, but he came into the fight skilled at converting the slings and arrows into ribbons that he could wear proudly on his chest to attest to his having exactly the right people as enemies.

That which did not kill him made the Normals like him more and more. Where the hate froze Barry Goldwater, because Barry Goldwater was a gentleman and gentlemen expect gentlemanly behavior from opponents, Trump didn't give a shit.

He fought.

He fought.

The Never Trump crew would eventually sneer, "But he

fights!" to dismiss the popularity of the guy who displaced them at the vanguard of conservatism. That would morph into "But Gorsuch," and then "But the repeal of economy-killing EPA regulations," and after that—after his string of conservative victories the Vichy Republicans had been promising but never delivering for decades grew longer and longer—they just went with their empty sigh of "We're better than that."

The Normals were sick of being better than that. They were sick of having their morals and values rejected, spit upon, rolled up tight, lit on fire, and shoved up their asses by an Elite that thought morality was a joke and decency a weakness.

See, the problem with creating new rules is that the other side gets to play by them. JFK—the *F* was for "Fornication"—created new rules. His bro Teddy created new rules—and a delicious recipe for a waitress sandwich.[2] Bill Clinton created new rules. And so when the Elite confidently dusted off the old rules to deploy against Donald Trump, they found that the Normals had adopted the new ones.

Do I vote for the guy who lays pipe with supermodels and porn stars, or for the woman who won't let me get a high-paying job laying the Keystone Pipeline because some weather cultists in Palo Alto object?

Tough call.

And there was the undeniable satisfaction that came from watching Donald Trump gleefully fling the monkey poo back at his tormenters. It's hard to underestimate the joy it was for Normals—bereft of a real champion for so long—to see someone finally swinging at the snobs and the schmucks who had trashed them with impunity. The Elite sure as hell was not used to it. The usual Republican was tame, rolling over and displaying various amounts of belly.

Ted Cruz fought, for example, but nicely, using carefully crafted intellectual arguments like those befitting a genius from Harvard Law who had argued in front of the Supreme Court a bunch of times. Liberals pivoted to their usual hate tactics, and Cruz looked like a gentleman—a gentleman who was fighting the good fight but was getting his butt kicked. But then the primary got down to him and Trump, and Trump devoured him like a Big Mac on *Air Force One*.

Trump even insinuated that Cruz's father, Rafael, had helped take out JFK, a bizarre comment that the Elite insisted on treating as an unequivocal statement of fact rather than what Normals saw as good, old-fashioned Queens ball-busting. Cruz fumed, the media wet itself, and, at worst, the Normals thought it was silly while many thought it was hilarious.

Trump knew their weakness. They needed reverence.

That's how the hippies in the sixties had really done their damage—they refused to concede and recognize the status and respect their opponents felt they had earned and deserved. If you spit on a soldier at LAX, you are telling him that the military service he fulfilled means nothing. Now what is he? Just a guy in green clothes with a loogie hanging off his ribbon rack.

Once the Elite had even offered the Normals a slice of reverence. The Elite, though sometimes falsely like the Kennedys, honored and shared the basic bourgeois values of regular Americans. Family, faith, patriotism, hard work. The Elite tipped its bowlers at those values—until people stopped wearing hats. Then those values became a joke that the young Elite giggled about.

Normals' betters thought they were a joke.

The expectation of reverence applied to the senior Elite, too—the sixties can be understood as a civil war within the Elite as the younger generation of the Elite trying to take power from the older generation of the Elite in large part by refusing to revere what they stood for. The sixties were less a rebellion against the Normals than the values the Normals and older Elite shared. But it was the mobilized Normals, in the form of the Silent Majority, who finally crushed the youth movement and forced its members to retreat into the institutions and conduct their Long March toward their current dominance.

Irreverence was akin to ridicule, which Saul Alinsky had pointed out was a devastating weapon. *Laugh-In* socked it to the politicians. It gave them none of the respect they thought they were due—that all the politicians before them had been granted. The fans loved it—they loved seeing the stuffy stodgy Elite battered by the hip, cool, outta sight Elite.

But in 2016, those *Laugh-In* fans from the sixties largely were the politicians, and they were smart enough to pack the cultural institutions to ensure there would be no dangerous irreverence. They now hated irreverence, because reverence is the key to how those with power in the Elite rule. As a practical matter, that meant protecting the Elite's candidate. From *Saturday Night Live* to the interchangeable late-night comics, from movies to music, to the extent the topic of Hillary Clinton came up, it was along the lines of the apocryphal humble job applicant.

My biggest weaknesses? Why, I work too hard. I am a perfectionist. And I care too darn much.

Irreverence was the young Elite's tool back then, but in 2016 those young Elites were the old Elite trying to install Her Hillaryness in the White House. Now, they needed reverence. And they were used to having it. That was a weakness.

Trump was not reverent. He was the anti-reverent. And he knew how to exploit an opponent's weaknesses.

Still, the Elite expected Trump to fold, because all decent folks—that meant all the people who recognized their authority, all the people who were reverent—would join together and help bury this throwback and the agenda he represented. And all reverent folks did. There just weren't enough of them outside of the blue cities to elect the queen.

With everyone against him in the press, and everyone in politics against him, too, Trump's ideology really did not matter, at least not its specifics. It was not about position papers. The Elite allowed him to position himself—a boisterous, pugnacious billionaire who partied with supermodels when he wasn't marrying them—in opposition to everyone who hated the Normals.

They walked right into his ambush. If they had studied some history, if they had understood that the Normals of 2016 were not the Normals of 1964, they might have realized that cranking the contempt up to eleven was not going to have the same effect as it did fifty-two years earlier.

They had options, but it was no longer an Elite that could conceive of them. This Elite had not shared foxholes in the Ardennes with guys from Idaho and Alabama. This Elite was so out of touch it could not conceive of getting back in touch with the Normals. So it could not conceive of how to cut Trump's legs out from under him.

They could have addressed the subjects Trump raised with concern instead of condescension.

They could have talked to the people Trump talked to, out in the small towns he visited.

They could have stopped acting like the people supporting Trump were something to be scraped off the soles of their Manolo Blahniks.

But they couldn't do that.

It never occurred to them.

That would have required the Elite to question their values and norms, and the Elite can't question their values and norms. It's not allowed, because to question the consensus is to question their own status, since being in the Elite is all about agreeing to submit to the consensus. Once you start questioning Elite beliefs, everything falls apart, since you are only Elite because you choose to believe what the Elite believes about itself.

Trump was Trump, a sui generis creature with his own bulging bank account and the unshakeable confidence one needed to truly, deeply not give a flying fig.

Not caring was his Kevlar. Trump didn't need the Elite. If the four prior decades had taught him anything, it was that the Elite needed *him*, or at least the money and exposure he could bestow upon it. Why should he respect people who sniffed around him like stray mongrels hoping for scraps from his table?

The Elite sensed that he refused to respect them, and their hatred grew and grew and grew. And Trump?

He rejected reverence in favor of contempt—the same exchange the Elite had made regarding the Normals when it stopped paying lip service to honoring regular folks and began laughing at them.

Trump laughed at the Elite. He is still laughing. And he fights. To the Elite, that was and remains unforgiveable.

CHAPTER ELEVEN

Never Trump and the Surrender Caucus

The liberal Elite was never going to truly accept Donald Trump. His money, sure. That was always welcome. Remember, the Elite is not necessarily rich, nor the Normals poor. Elite is an attitude. You can be living off kale scraps from the co-op down the street in Brooklyn and be Elite, or flying in your $65 million G6 to your own island in the Caribbean and be Normal—though that's not exactly normal Normality.

But was the liberal Elite ever going to truly accept Donald Trump himself? Oh, hell no. That's crazy talk. They would let him pick up the tab, but he was never going to be one of them. And that bothered him not a bit.

Which raises the question of whether Trump is a Normal. He certainly shares at least a superficial reverence for the values of the Normals. He definitely admires them, both the hardhat types who worked with their hands that he grew up around on work sites as well as the military guys he could never be like after he attended a military high school. He had bone spurs, which disqualify one from service, not that the issue of military service would have ever been a possibility for the vast majority of Elite dorks giggling about his diagnoses. It is difficult to conceive of a better example of hypocrisy than the liberal Elite who spit on our troops returning from Vietnam lashing out at Trump for being medically disqualified from service. But apparently entry into the Elite includes the surgical removal of one's capacity for shame.

Trump was Trump, and he chose to ally with the Normals. This is also true of his partisan leanings. Trump was Trump, but he chose to run as a Republican this time. In fact, he was best understood as a third-party candidate infiltrating the party apparatus and taking it over for his own purposes like some sort of political virus. That's why so many Republicans hated him. They absolutely knew he was not one of them. That was a big part of the genesis of the conservative wing of Never Trump.

But Trump didn't care about them, either.

Some conservatives are Elite. Not all, of course, not by a long shot. But some are. While American Elitism is predominantly liberal in outlook—American liberal, not classical liberal—there is a conservative element within it. Except for specific policies and politics, at least until Trump got elected, their outlook was absolutely Elite. Many lived in the DC region or New York. They fetishized credentials—where you went to school mattered a whole lot.

Harvard, oh yes. Quite so.

Utah State, uh, well how very nice for you. Were you the first in your family to be educated?

And your background was crucial, too.

Oh, you wrote for Foreign Policy? *Bravo. I adored that recent article on the Botswana question. It really deserves more attention.*

Oh, you were in the Marine Corps? That's nice. I believe Great-Grandfather Wellington Fairweather III was in the Coast Guard.

The conservative Elite holds that some people are suited to govern, and others are suited to be governed. Want to guess who deserves to be governed?

Well, it wasn't the people they crossed paths with at *Commentary* mixers and the Alexandria Trader Joe's. They did not spend a lot of time away from the coasts and at restaurants that failed to cater to the gluten intolerant.

You rarely saw these Elite conservatives out in the hinterlands. Instead, they gathered in think tanks in DC or Manhattan writing unread white papers while trying to get their intricate plans for reforming health care or education or whatever published in the marquee conservative magazines.

They were the guys who got the proverbial Georgetown cocktail party invitations. And when you mentioned "Georgetown cocktail party invitations" they would get all huffy and start up with how they never, ever went to cocktail parties, and certainly not in Georgetown. Okay, fine, in Adams Morgan.

The fact is that the people they lived around, talked to, attended their kids' soccer games with, and partied with were other members of the Elite.

And Trump laughed at them all.

Now, there were other conservatives with some pull who were not Elite, not even remotely. They detested the presumption and the snotty attitude of the liberal Elite as much as any other Normal. But they were ideological. Hardcore ideological. They were the kind of people who listened to Hugh Hewitt talk to Hillsdale College president Larry Arnn in excruciating detail about how the Articles of Confederation morphed into the Constitution. And they hated the fact that this is the last thing anyone would imagine Trump doing.

Trump didn't do the ideology thing.

And what's more, he was going off the reservation. He spoke heresy on free trade. Wait, make trade deals work for Normal Americans? But but but Milton Friedman said...

"Screw Milton Friedman," Trump seemed to say. "Tell this Milton Friedman guy to come on out to explain to these guys I just met in Michigan why the light bulbs they used to make in Ypsilanti are now getting made in Peking and shipped back here to be sold to us."

"But but but first, it's 'Beijing,' and second, Milton Friedman is deceased."

"Pipe down, Poindexter, the men are talking."

"What?"

And the guy from Fontana nodded, while Kaden turned even paler.

The real challenge to the Elite occurred when Trump decided to ask some foreign policy questions the experts had neglected to ask. Questions like, "What is in it for us to bomb the hell out of every foreigner who looked at his neighbor cross-eyed?" Sure, Americans were good-to-go on blowing away foreigners who got uppity—oh yeah, if they threaten us then let's get our Genghis Khan on. But spend money and the lives of guys from Nebraska and Ohio to teach seventh-century savages who still wipe their asses with their left paws how to live like Thomas Jefferson and James Madison suggested? Pass.

And NATO? Was that still even a thing? You had America

footing the defense bill for all these European countries who hesitated to pull their own weight, but they never hesitated to give the United States a ration of shit when their socialist rulers got their Euro panties wadded up about the US of A looking out for itself.

If Germany doesn't think Germany is worth German euros and German boys' lives to defend, how the hell is it worth American dollars and American boys' lives?

But but but... *postwar consensus*!

The war was seventy years ago. The Cold War twenty-five years ago. And the Elite, including the conservative Elite, had not bothered to update their consensus. When Trump pointed that out, the Normals nodded.

They got it.

Now, these simply were not traditional conservative views. Plus, there was the whole social conservatism thing. While many evangelicals could tolerate Trump's personal moral choices because they recognized Hillary as an existential threat to their religious liberty, not all of them could. To the extent Trump affirmed conservative social views—like opposition to abortion—they doubted him. To the extent he shrugged when confronted with his colorful past, they hated him.

So, these were the two wings of conservative Never Trump— the conservative Elite who hated him because he wasn't Elite, and the conservative Normals who hated him because they thought he wasn't conservative.

The Elite conservatives are much, much more annoying. After all, they put "Elite" before "conservative." But you can understand, and even sympathize with, the conservative Normals of Never Trump. They were ideological conservatives. They lived and breathed the ideas and the ideology. They cared about policy.

They cared about faith. They took it all seriously. But this guy seemed like he put all sorts of random ideas in a blender and poured out some sort of populist smoothie.

Not wanting to focus on cutting entitlements? What the hell? Paul Ryan had dedicated his life to the cause of entitlement reform.

Think of Paul Ryan, damn it!

But Trump's secret was thinking of—and talking about—what actual voters wanted, thought, and talked about. The conservative movement had a lot of great ideas over the years. It loved its ideas. But those ideas stopped being the ideas of the base and started being the ideas of those inside Conservative, Inc. Elite or not, conservatives were all about free trade because free trade is awesome. But Normals, who were more conservative in temperament and in terms of tradition than ideology, were the ones paying the price of free trade. And they were complaining.

Who was listening?

Not the Elite. And not the conservative activists. Imagine yourself a Normal American, if you aren't. You loved your country and obeyed the laws and paid your taxes and showed up for jury duty, and one day, some guy who you would swear was Mitt Romney's cousin rolls into the factory where you've made forklifts for eighteen years and announces that Acme Forklift is picking up and moving to Tijuana and thanks for the memories. When that happens, you are going to have some questions for the people who are supposed to represent you. And if their answer is, "Well, as Milton Friedman explained, you're inefficient and therefore you and the family you support are expendable," you are probably not going to continue to vote for those people.

As Normal Americans, the base of the Republican Party, were watching their wages stagnate, their jobs depart, their small businesses crushed by big corporations, and their kids slaughtered in wars we refused to win, the Elite and the conservatives did nothing.

Nothing.

Across America, Main Street was a boarded-up wasteland as the kind of small shops and businesses that Normal Republicans founded, built, and operated closed. Yet the conservative Elite could not be bothered. Instead, they catered to the big corporations who pretended to be center right (that is, they positioned themselves as "pro-business") while engaging in policies that seemed more akin to the Elite whims of their CEOs' much younger, liberal second wives.

It's probably wrong to say that the conservative Elite didn't care—they did, in the abstract—but they sure as hell were not going to review their beliefs in light of the current crisis. There were seventeen Republican candidates in 2016, and just one talked about the issues the voters cared about. And he won, which should not be a surprise but still was.

The conservative Normals were the ones who began to rethink the whole Trump question about a year into his presidency when they figured out that this guy was the most conservative president since Ronald Reagan. Some took yes for an answer. Sure, he may spark a media lynch mob with a fiery tweet every seventy-two hours, and he might be a bit, well, Trumpy, but he's actually delivering. At the end of the day, you can't be a conservative and be sad that Neil Gorsuch is on the Supreme Court.

But you can be a member of the conservative Elite. Remember, it's always class first, ideology second.

Take David Brooks of the *New York Times*. He spent a lot of years writing in the various conservative outlets, earning a reputation as . . . one of the guys who writes for the various con-servative outlets. He was hardly a bomb thrower. In fact, the only bombs he was for throwing were at overseas enemies that other people who were not his sons or daughters would go fight. He was the kind of writer about whom no one ever said, "Hey, did you see the David Brooks column today," at least until he got to the *Times* and you wanted to read him out of morbid curiosity. He's the guy who famously deciphered the creases on Barack Obama's slacks and decreed that the Lightbringer would one day be a very good president. Such omen cryptology made him the perfect conserva-tive for the *Times*'s Elite readership—a pliable, agreeable, passive reactionary who wouldn't scare the women or the horses or the liberal men, in that order.

And Brooks has the common touch. He once took a Normal acquaintance out for lunch and wrote about how his sad compan-ion had been baffled by the menu at an upscale sandwich shop. More likely, the Normal was looking for an excuse to duck out on a Bataan Death March meal with that snooty panini-con.[1]

It goes without saying that Brooks was not a Trump fan. Trump just would not do at all. But Jeb!? Oh, now there was a sensible choice—though it probably did not help when Brooks went on *Face the Nation* on November 1, 2015, and recommended Jeb! brand himself the "laxative" candidate.[2]

Still, Jeb! embraced all the Elite positions on all the issues Normals cared about, and above all Jeb! understood that his job was to lose. Losing was his moral obligation, as it was all the conservanerds' moral obligation.

Since Brooks arrived at the *Times*, it is unclear whether he had ever again supported anything conservative except in the most tepid and inoffensive sense. And Brooks's powerful words accomplished exactly what they were meant to accomplish: zip. He's still on that rag's op-ed page.

Or how about Bret Stephens? He came to the *Times* from the *Wall Street Journal*, and he loathed Trump, too. That's called knowing your audience. But he didn't know his audience perfectly. Early on at the Gray Lady, he wrote a piece casting the gentlest of doubts upon the giant, cynical scam that is the climate change hysteria. He didn't deny it—he merely sort of hinted it was a tad overblown. And for that he was blown away in a hurricane of hate from the Elite readers of his new rag.[3]

He learned. His next big splash was when this voice of conservatism came out against the Second Amendment because the Second Amendment is totally not at all important to conservatives.[4]

Let's review. The *New York Times*'s two big conservative commentators are a guy who chooses to make lunch condescending and a guy telling us to turn in our AR-15s. And yet the *New York Times* was stunned when Donald Trump beat the woman their brain trust assured its Elite readership was a shoo-in.

Another pile of smoldering wreckage is George Will, the quintessential bow-tie conservative whose fussy wrath knew no bounds when the Normals dared to defy him. George always liked to flirt with Normality, especially by his tiresome inability to stop yapping about baseball.

"Look at me," he seemed to say. "I am eating a delicacy known as a hot dog. Perhaps I will wash it down with a stout ale like Miller's in the manner of the hearty workingmen who lurk in the bleachers far, far, far from my box seat."

George was the *Washington Post*'s domesticated conservative, and since he received the Pulitzer Prize for commentary in 1977, it was clear the Elite did not consider him a threat but an ally.

He was certainly born to it. Though he grew up in Illinois, his father was a professor of philosophy, and George collected all the credentials that made him Intellectual and Serious and Elite. In 1991, he earned the recognition all conservatives seek by winning whatever the Walter Cronkite Award for Excellence in Journalism is, because every conservative yearns to be spoken of in the same breath as Walter Freaking Cronkite.

Reagan came along and gave George and the rest everything they said they wanted, but what they really wanted was the increased status they would receive within the Elite. It was the effeminacy of the conservanerds like George that rubbed Normals wrong at first, but he seemed to be on the side of the angels even if he was an utter dork, so there was no real problem with him. Live and let live, even if he chose to live as an openly wimpy man.

But for years it had become clear where George's loyalties lay, and those loyalties were not to the Normals. In 2009, for instance, he took on the abomination that is denim in a *Washington Post* column[5] titled "America's Bad Jeans." Get it? Among his insights was: "This is not complicated. For men, sartorial good taste can be reduced to one rule: If Fred Astaire would not have worn it, don't wear it. For women, substitute Grace Kelly." Will confessed to owning one pair of jeans, which he wore once, to former senator John (Will calls him "Jack") Danforth's country music–themed seventieth birthday party. One can imagine Will spending the entire soiree worried that one of other denim-clad partygoers would consume too much Budweiser and decide to give him a wedgie for laughs. Since he never wore his jeans again, it is safe to assume he was not invited back for Danforth's seventy-first.

Will is a man of the people, all right—but only the right people. As always, class trumps ideology. Conservatism was his job, but Elite status was his identity. For all his nattering about baseball, the closest he would ever get to Normality was being passive-aggressively peeved about guys who could do a chin-up.

Imagine George Will venturing outside the Beltway. He'd come back home in tears with his glasses broken and his lunch money taken.

This is a guy who wrote books with titles like *Statecraft as Soulcraft: What Government Does* (New York: Simon & Schuster, 1983). Not only was the title so awesomely pretentious that only someone of his caste might hear it and not burst into laughter, but the concept was deeply, deeply unconservative. Conservatism, the default mode of the Normals, was not about using government to create a race of intellectual *ubermensch* who all worshipped the same fake idols. That was liberalism's jam.

But George's focus was never on the Normals. It was about indoctrinating the Elite in Elite mores and values—soulcrafting, something that would be the job of religion for an actual conservative. Instead, it was a plea for the reproduction and training of the future conservative Elite not to pursue the goals of conservatism, which generally aligned with the goals of Normals, but to perpetuate itself.

It was about making more Elites, and their label would be "conservative." Conservative was who they were in that world, not what they did.

The rise of the Normals horrified George. You could see it in his columns and his increasingly frustrated vibe. Sarah Palin's nomination sent him through the roof—he was horrified that someone from Wasilla, Alaska, who had totally not attended Oxford might be considered for the vice presidency.

He also established himself as a helpful counterrevolutionary, taking on bomb throwers like Newt Gingrich and Ann Coulter apparently because Newt and Ann did not understand that their role should mirror George's—make some statements of alleged principle and lose. But the question really was why he was so very upset about the unseemly nature of the resistance to liberal overreach when he allegedly sought the same ends.

Oh, and did he detest Trump? Of course he did—the rise of Trump devalued the puny, ineffective intellectualism that the conservative Elite had been dining out on for decades.

Trump was crude and vulgar and nailed supermodels, and that bothered conservamonk George. Trump was everything George and his ilk weren't. Most of all, Trump was a man of action—not just with supermodels but in terms of results. George talked and wrote. But Trump *built* things, then slapped his name on them, and then built some more things and slapped his name on those, too. Then he went and had a hit television show. Will wrote books no one between I-5 and I-95 had ever heard of.

Trump never gave a moment's thought to the intellectuals, the theoreticians, the talkers. He was a doer. And he was doing. He was beating all the approved candidates—not just beating them but crushing them. Who the hell was this Queens loudmouth to be on his way to taking the GOP nomination without the permission of people like George Will?

But then, there was that nagging question—what the hell had the conservative Elite actually conserved over the last several decades?

Not much. But then, there is nothing the Elite hates more than accountability and having to answer for their shitty metrics that demonstrate their utter inability to perform. George Will was granted status as one of the intellectual forces within conservatism because he purported to provide some modern intellectual framework for the ideology. But the conservatism of the Normals was instinctive, not something that required an advanced degree. It did not require any George Wills.

And when the Normals embraced their own natural conservatism, out of necessity because intellectual conservatism was leading them to a progressive Hades, they didn't need the George Wills and other True Conservatives of Conservatism anymore.

George Will went from a highly regarded elder statesman of the conservative movement to a guy who couldn't get his calls returned by any of the yahoos ensconced in the White House and Congress. And it grated on him.

Who the hell were they, anyway? What right did they have to...to...to take what was his!

In his December 13, 2017, *Washington Post* column,[6] Will called Trump the worst president ever. "He completed his remarkably swift—it has taken less than 11 months—rescue of the 17th, Andrew Johnson, from the ignominy of ranking as the nation's worst president." Not James Buchanan, either. Not even Jimmy Carter. Trump.

In response to his fuming, the Normals replied, "George Who?"

Which only made it worse. George Will ostentatiously left the Republican Party because it had ceased to meet his exacting standards, which apparently consisted of providing George Will with prestige and reverence while he was sheepishly losing every policy battle. He also signed on to MSNBC as a commentator because Fox dumped him, perhaps to make room for Tomi Lahren.

Fox News always has its finger on the pulse of the people, and what Tomi lacked in advanced degrees and Cronkite Awards she more than made up for by not being a boring, shriveled has-been.

"Boring, shriveled has-been" status became all the rage in the build-up to the Trump election and its aftermath. There were a lot of other big names who had traded on their long-standing sinecures in the conservative Elite for a long time who were suddenly put to a difficult question: "What good are you?"

That's a tough question when you rose in your career focused on climbing the ladder up through the schools and think tanks and government gigs and magazines to the heights of a regular column and a book and maybe some on-camera contributorship and perhaps even a gig where you can rake in some of that sweet, sweet donor conservacash for yourself. Your entire purpose and mandate is to write write write and talk talk talk, and if you do that in a clever and coherent enough way, well, that's sufficient.

That's what you did in Conservative, Inc.—you wrote and you talked and you made a living and got some fame, though it was DC fame, which is to real fame what DC attractive is to real attractive.

But what you never, ever did was have to explain why, despite all your talking and writing and collecting money, nothing ever seemed to get conserved.

What the hell has George Will, who has been writing his column since 1974, ever done for conservatism? This is the cue for the sniffing and the huffing and asking, "How dare you," and then the social justice warrior pivoting back to the questioner, "Well, what have *you* ever done for conservatism?"

But that's a distraction—one of the least attractive tactics of the conservative Elite lately is their copping of the liberal Elite tactic of turning every debate into a referendum on the dissident's personal qualities.

What's the answer?

What did George Will ever do for conservatism and the people it is supposed to serve, the Normals?

Ronald Reagan liked him—he was close to Nancy Reagan especially, providing further evidence that conservative Elitism is about prestige and position. But did Reagan need him? Reagan was instinctively conservative in the way Normals are. That is not to say that the intellectual foundations were foreign to him. They weren't—he read and studied and learned, as many Normals did and do. But he didn't need George Will to explain to him that the damn commies were bad and why giving freeloaders handouts taken from the pockets of people who actually worked for a living was wrong.

Will jumped on George H. W. Bush over the "Read my lips, no new taxes" lie. That was something, though it is unclear whether it was personal animus that motivated it. Will had had a Nelson Rockefeller vibe in the pre-Reagan years, and you might have expected him to harken to President Kinder and Gentler. Maybe they got sideways with each other while sipping spritzers at the club. But again, what was essential about George Will?

There he was during the Clinton years, bemoaning the Clintons and in full ineffectual mode. The guys running up the score against Clinton weren't the pearl-clutchers. They were the insurgents. In the House, Newt Gingrich and his cronies had plotted to outmaneuver both the stale GOP leadership and the Democrats to snatch away the majority for the first time in decades via the Contract with America. The *American Spectator* was using its donors' cash for something constructive for once, investigating the Arkansas Dynamic Duo's antics. Sadly, that gave a start to the career of turncoat David Brock, a weirdo who would go on his knees begging forgiveness from Her Highness Hillary for telling the truth about her and devoting himself to her service in perpetuity via Media Matters.

George Will was there, writing and talking. He wrote and talked during the years of Bush 43, too, and then during the years of Barack Obama. George spent a lot of time trashing John McCain and his running mate, but they did not need his help. They were perfectly capable of losing without him.

Trump was the curtain on his career. Now, age was going to slow him down anyway (he was seventy-five when Trump was inaugurated), but what were the chances he would come back post-Trump even if he was younger? In what world is anyone asking, "Say, where's George Will, because we really need him right now?"

In fact, the fate of George Will is a microcosm of the fate of a whole host of conservative Elite personalities who grew to sort of prominence and then found themselves locked out of influence when Donald Trump swept into office. They did not like that much, to be sure. And these people, deeply affiliated with Conservative, Inc., formed the nucleus of Never Trump.

There was money in Conservative, Inc., once upon a time. Not big money, not real money by the standard of those outside that world, but big and real money to those in it. Of course, money was just one kind of currency. The other was prestige, that amalgamation of position and prestige and influence that was, in many ways, sweeter than cash. It was nice to be able to upgrade your ride from a Honda to an Acura, but if you could get on the round table with Chuck Todd over at *Meet the Press*, well, you were a player.

And these players most definitely did not hate the game.

You could make a career in Conservative, Inc., leaving only for short periods to get another degree or to take a government job when a conservative was in office—one of the useful functions of Conservative, Inc., was to provide a farm team for these kinds of functionaries. In fact, this network of politicians and think tanks and foundations and publications did create a framework that allowed conservatives to develop and, vitally, to communicate to conservatives outside DC and New York City that there was some sort of conservative beachhead in enemy territory.

At its best, Conservative, Inc., provides a brain trust that could both observe and illuminate the activities of the progressive enemy while coming up with ideas and tactics to be implemented when (if) a real conservative should take power. A fine example of Conservative, Inc., providing a useful function is the Federalist Society, which grooms reliably conservative judges for eventual appointment. The imprimatur of the Federalist Society is a near solid guarantee that once he slips on his robe he's not going to morph into David Souter and "grow" and "mature" and become yet another liberal. According to the *Washington Post*,[7] Trump White House counsel Donald F. McGahn II "said it is 'completely false' that the White House has 'outsourced' the selection of federal judges to the organization… 'It's not even necessary,' he said. 'I've been a member of the Federalist Society since law school—still am,' he said. 'So frankly, it seems like it's been in-sourced.'"

Nor is everyone involved with Conservative, Inc., some sort of ineffectual, timeserving striver hack. Conservative, Inc., is the arena—to be an active conservative, you have to be in it. But you can be in it without dedicating yourself to maintaining and increasing your position in it to the exclusion of fighting for conservative progress.

That "conservative progress" can even be a thing demonstrates the necessary change that many old-school conservatives were not ready for. Traditional conservatism eschewed the idea of "progress" as a retreat from traditional, time-proven principles in the pursuit of some sort of inevitably left-wing, arrogant ideology that seeks to disregard human nature and the dictates of God in an effort to recreate Man in the Elite's own image. But that premise assumes there is something left to conserve, that civilization has not yet moved past those time-proven principles and changed into something new and horrible. But it has. Conservatism today is not the ideology of maintaining the status quo that our hack high school civics teachers described.

Conservatism today means change. It means revolution. And a lot of purported conservatives can't get that through their heads.

So, we had a movement that considered itself dedicated to defending the status quo when it had not realized (or would not accept the fact that) the status quo had changed. Then it was further handicapped because a hefty chunk of its members were perfectly comfortable in that status quo—the conservative Elite was allowed to exist within the Elite, only it was denied any real power. But then, if you take the potential for actually doing anything off the table, you can focus on position and prestige.

Conservative, Inc., was subject to all the problems inherent in any human endeavor, the key one being its pursuit of its own unenlightened self-interest in place of the goal it was created to pursue. Conservative, Inc., was rejected—and make no mistake, 2016 was a rejection—because it appeared to everyone outside the DC fishbowl that it was in it for itself.

It used to be about the conservatism. Now it was about making sure John Boehner had some lobbyist to buy him a well-done bone-in rib eye and half dozen Jack and Cokes.

Destroying the Speaker's liver may have been a worthy goal

in the abstract, but it was not the goal of the people who actually sent him and his minions to Washington and who subscribed to the magazines, took the cruises, and wrote the donation checks. The Normals wanted change, and the conservative Elite wanted business as usual. The notion that conservatives were still supposed to conserve in a society where the progressives' long march through the institutions had already changed everything became an all-purpose excuse for avoiding accountability.

Essentially, it went: "You Normals want a revolution, but we are conservatives. We conserve. So stop trying to hold us accountable for not doing anything because the underlying premise of conservatism is that we don't do anything."

Super-convenient—it justified the conservative Elite's utter failure to stop the liberals over recent decades. Except the fundamental premise of the excuse was wrong. The Normals were not seeking a revolution. They were seeking a counterrevolution. They had no intention of creating some new type of leftism-informed New Socialist Human ("Man" being sexist and excluding those who identified in one of the 189,257 brand-new non-cisnormative gender identities).

They wanted things to go back to—wait for it—normal.

And that would take fighters.

People like George Will were not fighters. It's doubtful they were lovers, either, but that's a tangent we need not explore.

Trump was definitely a fighter, and that's what the people wanted. In fact, the people had been making it clear for years and the conservative Elite had responded by shoving their booger hooks into their ear canals and shouting. "LALALALALALALA I CAN'T HEAR YOU!"

The Tea Party was a demand for a counterrevolution, and

Conservative, Inc., tried to have it both ways by attempting to co-opt the energy and the cash to its own purposes while dampening down that terrifyingly implied demand for results. A lot of folks got elected thanks to the Tea Party, not just real insurgents like Mike Lee, Ted Cruz, and Rand Paul (who all knocked off GOP establishment-approved opponents). But once most of them got to DC, they wiped their brows and thought, "Phew, that was a close one—now that the election is done I can get down to business, and my business is being a senator. Summon my pages and have them bring me mutton and ale, for I hunger!"

The troublesome Normals demanding an aggressive response to Obama's hope and change were a real headache. Folks like Boehner and the rest of the Adults in the Smoke-Filled Room had a pretty good idea of what needed to happen. Money had to be squeezed out of the big donors—that was job one. And the way to get the big donors writing checks was to make sure the big donors were kept happy.

Amnesty made them happy, and those peons out in Peonland were harshing that buzz. Letting them all stay would be ideal, but the best that could be done was simply to shrug and moan that Obama would not enforce the law. But maybe they could slip something through while the hicks weren't looking...

And on Obamacare, who really wanted to relieve Obama of that albatross? Now, with the House and then the Senate back in GOP hands, there was nothing stopping the GOP from cutting off the cash. The Congress had the power of the purse, after all, and all the pens and phones at 1600 Pennsylvania Avenue couldn't drum up the dough to keep that abomination alive if the GOP legislature didn't write the check.

But that would take a big, ugly fight, and it might not work out, and it was hard, and really, did we want to give up that evergreen outrage? Every member of the GOP loved to fulminate and thunder about the abomination of Obamacare on the campaign trail.

Nah. Let's keep it. Because conservatism demanded pragmatism, and pragmatism meant whatever is useful for the conservative Elite.

And when the Normals complained, it was just more proof that they didn't understand, that they were just too dumb to actually get the nuances and the stratagems behind a conservative Elite that refused to do what it had promised.

And the Normals fumed.

Their real wages were stagnant at best, and the conservatives they had sent to Washington did not seem to care.

Their culture and religion were under attack, and the people they had sent to Washington did not seem to care.

Their kids were getting killed in wars no one seemed interested in winning, and the people they had sent to Washington did not seem to care.

The people they had sent to Washington did not seem to care about anything important to the Normals. No wonder the Normals were pissed.

But the hell with the Normals. The hell with them, because they were stupid and shortsighted and selfish and refused to see beyond their narrow self-interest to what was truly important— the Elite's self-interest.

They could never be forgiven for betraying their leaders. And many prominent members of the caste attempted to apply the cat-o'-nine-tails to the recalcitrant nobodies.

David Frum started long before most. He was Canadian by birth, giving him the kind of Middle American sensibility the conservative Elite preferred—an absent one. He attended Yale and Harvard, because of course he did. Then he worked at a variety of the kind of jobs any striving Conservative, Inc., functionary would seek out until he joined the Bush 43 administration as a speechwriter. There is some controversy over whether he coined the phrase "Axis of Evil," but there is no doubt he was a big supporter of the Iraq War until it became hard.

Frum, as is customary among his caste, enlisted in the military for no years of service before advocating sending other people's kids off to fight. Then when it went sour, well, oops: "US-UK intervention offered Iraq a better future. Whatever West's mistakes: sectarian war was a choice Iraqis made for themselves."[8]

This Frum guy knows his audience. He left the Bush White House, wrote for and then left *National Review*, and then started some boondoggle called *NewMajority.com*, which was one of those "purple" scams that portray themselves as beyond mere ideology.

Naturally, when someone promotes himself as being "beyond ideology," it means he's trending liberal. Frum was no exception. His big thing was guns. He decided he hated them—oh, not in the hands of soldiers sent off to impose his vision of international order in shitholes across the globe, but in the hands of Normal Americans.

Every time some criminal or leftist or Islamic radical weirdo decided to go on a shooting spree, Frum snatched the Elite's banner and carried it forward. See, the real problem wasn't criminals or leftists or Islamic radical weirdos with guns murdering people, but the folks who were not criminals or leftists or Islamic radical weirdos and who kept guns in large part to protect themselves from criminals or leftists or Islamic radical weirdos.

You have to hand it to Frum—he knows the script. The NRA

is terrible, awful, unspeakable, even though none of these monsters were ever members of it. Why all the hatin'? Probably because it has several million members, and they're pretty much all Normals. And it therefore constitutes a rare institutional power base far outside the control of the liberal Elite.

That is the NRA's real crime, and it is unforgiveable.

Frum hated Trump, and he was one of those True Conservatives of Conservatism warning that Trump would be the death of conservatism. To which most Normals, had they ever heard of David Frum, would have responded, "So what?"

Frum was also one of those intellectuals who never actually made an argument for what he was for, only against people who put his power and prestige at risk. And even then he did not argue. He just declared them bad people, and that was it. That was his argument against Trump—"HE'S HORRIBLE!"—and it has never changed. Facts, schmacts. Trump created the most conservative administration in decades, but that doesn't matter. Trump is so . . . so . . . oh well, I never! That's enough to condemn him.

Frum, and others, were so concerned with Trump's failure to be conservative that he voted for Hillary Clinton in 2016. It's almost as if the priority for the conservative Elite was the Elite, not the conservatism.

Actually, it's precisely that.

The hoary hack cliché about those supporting Donald Trump is that it somehow "reveals" them as terrible people for some reason. You see the conservanerds wag their fingers and cluck their tongues at how Trump support makes clear the conservative apostates, but they never seem to grapple with the conservatism Trump has displayed since his election and how that's exactly what he promised during the election cycle.

They are wrong, as they have been about everything. The truth is that Never Trumpism reveals the truth about its own membership. These members of the conservative Elite were always about the Elitism, with the conservatism just their pose. In fact, Never Trumpism among alleged conservatism always seems to degenerate into outright liberalism—probably as a way for the Elite to let them stay in the club after their usefulness as domesticated conservatives has been so diminished.

Jennifer Rubin writes for the *Washington Post*, and she's billed as one of its resident conservatives. Understand that a conservative writing in a major newspaper is defined as a conservative based not on actually being conservative, but on not claiming to be an outright leftist. But that has not stopped her from trying to go full liberal. In the wake of the Trump movement, she just basically flipped a U-turn on everything she once allegedly believed.

Pre-Trump: Move Israel's capital to Jerusalem!

Post-Trump: Trump moving Israel's capital to Jerusalem is the worst thing ever for some reason!

Ditto the climate change scam. If Normals want it—if they want to back up our ally Israel, if they don't want to be impoverished because of weather paranoia—well, then those things are now wrong because they put a guy in the White House she finds icky.

And of course she now hates guns in the hands of citizens. She sided with the AstroTurf moppet puppets of the March for Our Lives (Except of Babies) because of course a conservative backs up a campaign to eliminate civil rights sponsored by Planned Parenthood and Move On. The headline read, "They came, they marched, they inspired."[9] All true, especially Normals, who were inspired to join the NRA and go get themselves another AR-15 and a few more boxes of 5.56 mm before the aspiring Red Guards that people like Rubin thinks will arrest her last get their American cultural revolution ramped up.

But while Rubin hates Normals, she focuses her unreasoning hate on the Normals' White House avatar. Trump grates at her; he gnaws at her; he drives her into gibbering madness. And most of it is probably because she knows there is no way that he picks up the *Post* and reads her silly column.

So much of Never Trump is status anxiety. But maybe a move to the left can salvage some semblance of prestige...

Maybe she won't get tarred with the Trump brush and be thought of as one of those, those Normals by the smart set...

Maybe, if she holds her breath long enough, he and his Neanderthal followers will go away, and things will come back to normal, and she can again start gently doubting some aspects of the global warming scam...but not too many.

———

But the king of the Never Trumpers has to be Bill Kristol, the guy behind the *Weekly Standard*, the Captain Stubing[10] of conservatism, and another guy who never met a war he didn't like. Trump's doubts about the wisdom of trying to remake the world in our image rubbed Kristol the wrong way, as did Trump's limited subscription to conservative doctrine. In the March 28, 2011, issue of the *Weekly Standard*, he wrote a piece called "You've Come a Long Way, Baby: President Obama's Unapologetic, Freedom-Agenda-Embracing, Not-Shrinking-from-the-Use-of-Force Speech."[11] Three guesses as to who the folks were who were supposed to do the not shrinking from the use of force.

But what really sent him over was Trump's utter lack of

concern about what professional conservatives like Bill Kristol think.

Kristol was a self-made man, if by "self" you mean his father, Irving Kristol, who gave this dull and unimaginative writer a foot in the door to the Elite. The senior, interesting Kristol was one of the original neo-conservatives, before that term was co-opted and rendered meaningless by the slack-jawed morons of the alt-right who tried to attach themselves to the Trump movement like human ticks. The real neo-conservatives were liberals, sometimes even light leftists, who understood the threat of communism and who understood that perhaps the United States was not morally disqualified from fighting for its own interests. They came over from the Democrats but were never entirely comfortable in conservatism. Bill, though, was very comfortable in conservatism—as long as it was Elite conservatism.

He got funders for his magazine and went full Conservative, Inc. He pushed subscriptions and the inevitable cruises and gatherings, with scintillating panels and the opportunity to mingle over plastic cups of second-tier Pinot Grigio with the Monsters of Conservative Lite Rock.

It was a good gig. He had influence on folks like his pal John McCain. Getting along with tiresome maverick John McCain gives you some idea of Bill's dedication to actual conservatism. Still, Bill did push McCain to pick Sarah Palin, proving at least that at one point he was Normal-curious.

But Normals were never his motivation. They were a means to an end, sheep to be sheared, a way to leverage himself more prestige within the Elite. It got him on television, where he mouthed unremarkable things in an unremarkable manner, and it created the impression that he mattered.

Trump demonstrated that he didn't matter.

He unleashed upon Trump and those who supported him with a ferocity he would never deploy against fellow Elitists. At one point, after the election and as the mind-numbing stupidity of the Trump/Russian foolishness was spinning up, he suggested that he would have the liberal pseudo-patriots' "Deep State" rise and cast out the elected president of the United States.[12]

Never Trump was a gateway drug to liberalism, which Kristol confirmed when he discovered that tax cuts were unconservative if they happened with Trump in the Oval Office. Who knew?

The only metamorphosis more astounding, and hilarious, was that of Max Boot. Known foremost as perhaps the world's most stereotypical Caucasian and secondarily as someone who writes about what other people did in the military, Boot breathlessly announced to a waiting world that he had, because of Donald Trump, recently become aware of his "white privilege." He revealed his remarkable epiphany in the pages of the December 27, 2017, edition of *Foreign Policy* magazine.[13]

Those whom Trump would destroy, he makes mad.

CHAPTER TWELVE

Why You Got Trump

The Normals chose Trump. And it was not okay with the Smart Set.

He was no expert, at least not at governing. Now Hillary Clinton—there was an expert! Trained at the finest schools, studying at the side of a master politician, versed in the crafts of domestic governance and foreign policy, she was the Smartest Woman in the World. Plus, it was her turn, damn it!

Her turn!

And then those rednecks chose Trump.

What the folks snickering at that *New Yorker* cartoon about that troublesome, presumptuous, uppity passenger who dared want a say in where he was being taken forgot is that those people who voted against her saw that while she had the credentials that so impressed the Smart Set, Hillary Clinton was terrible at everything she did.

Just terrible.

Her domestic policy legacy was the Clinton health care plan that blew up like the *Hindenburg* without the humanity. In foreign policy, when she wasn't making an idiot of herself by handing reset buttons to baffled Russkies, she was sparking bloodbaths in Libya—and letting our folks get butchered in Benghazi. The Elite hated and resented accountability, and it never saw Their Girl's accountability coming until Michigan flipped into the red column on November 8, 2016.

And there was another thing—Hillary did not know her place, and the Normals knew it. Not her place as a woman—the Elite did what they always did when a liberal woman failed and blamed her rejection on sexism. It was her place as the future president. She did not go into the job search with a sense of humility. She mouthed the right words about working for the People, but no one believed it, not her opponents who distrusted her and not her supporters who never wanted her to work for the People.

She was in it for herself and for her Elite cronies, and everyone could see it. And the Normals were tired of it.

That *New Yorker* cartoon dissing the upstart passenger demanding some input in his ultimate destination—or, more specifically, the attitude behind it—is Why You Got Trump.

Every high school dropout with a zillion-dollar contract and a desire to appear to be more than a goofy clown on a late-night comedy show using his monologue to lecture Normals on why they ought to be thrilled about Obamacare is Why You Got Trump.

Hillary Clinton skipping out on the pokey for her classified materials antics when any Normal who did the same thing in uniform would still be at Fort Leavenworth converting boulders to pebbles is Why You Got Trump.

A silver-spoon doofus tries to exorcise his guilt by shoving illegal aliens down Normals' throats and christening it an act of love—one Ned Beatty would appreciate—is Why You Got Trump.

There are a thousand reasons Why You Got Trump.

The insults.

The attitude.

The nearly unbroken track record of incompetence from the people who presume to be our betters but refuse to be held accountable when they prove again and again and again that they aren't.

The double dealing, double standards, and double crosses. They are all Why You Got Trump.

And what's stunning, and hilarious, is that the Elite did not see it coming.

But why would they? They never cared to look. They were like the courtiers of Louis XVI who had zero idea of what was coming until François looked over the Seine and said, "*Sacre bleu,* Pierre, it looks like the Bastille's on fire! Wonder how that happened? Oh well, back to our cake and Champagne!"

And they still don't get it. Hillary stumbled her way through India in early 2018, and then decided it would be great optics to explain to her foreign hosts that the reason she lost is that half of America is terrible. Her saying out loud what the Elite thinks even shocked the *Washington Post,* which headlined its report on that latest fiasco "Hillary Clinton Takes Her 'Deplorables' Argument for Another Spin."[1]

Clinton offered some rather unvarnished remarks that weekend in India that sound a lot like her "deplorables" commentary from September 2016. She played up the states that supported her as more economically advanced than the states that voted for Trump, calling them "dynamic" and "moving forward." Then she again suggested Trump supporters were motivated by animosity toward women and people of color.

"If you look at the map of the United States, there's all that red in the middle where Trump won," Clinton said. "I win the coast. I win, you know, Illinois and Minnesota—places like that."

She went on: "But what the map doesn't show you is that I won the places that represent two-thirds of America's gross domestic product. So I won the places that are optimistic, diverse, dynamic, moving forward."

Then she turned to Trump's voters: "And his whole campaign— 'Make America Great Again'—was looking backward. You know, you didn't like black people getting rights; you don't like women, you know, getting jobs; you don't want to, you know, see that Indian American succeeding more than you are—you know, whatever your problem is, I'm gonna solve it."

Wow.

The alienation of the Elite from the nation they are supposed to serve is immense, and this kind of thinking should not be a surprise. It has been in effect for a while. Back in the sixties, the young Elite went to cultural war with their Elite parents and differentiated themselves by casting off the older generation's attachment to America's common morals and mores. No, the Elite did not always honor the kind of Main Street values the Normals embraced, but they generally did, and they certainly did not attack those values and seek to overthrow the cultural regime that had made the United States the most powerful nation in the history of the world.

The young Elite of the sixties? Burn, baby, burn.

The young Elite had inherited a utopia—all they had to do was keep on doing what their parents were doing and slip into vacant positions when the older generation got put out to pasture. But they wanted the power right then, and the way to do it was to change the game. It was to play on their own terms—and their own terms did not involve actually tipping their hat to the values the Normals embraced.

They differentiated themselves from the older generation of the Elite by rejecting the values the older generation venerated—values of faith and patriotism, of sexual modesty and self-sacrifice. In fact, they wanted to do more than just differentiate themselves. Barack Obama's pal Bill Ayers advocated a slightly harder line that was repeated in a loving *New York Times* tribute that ran, ironically, on September 11, 2001: "Kill all the rich people. Break up their cars and apartments. Bring the revolution home, kill your parents, that's where it's really at."[2]

So, in the least shocking development ever, the young left alienated themselves from the Normals.

As the older generation of the Elite retired and faded away, the Me Generation slowly slipped into the institutions and began their own long march to conquer the heights of culture and government. They brought with them that profound alienation from those on whose behalf they presumed to rule that they got from listening to Herbert Marcuse and the rest of the poisonous Frankfurt School disciples who spread out through academia. Expressly anti-capitalist, but more than that, anti-bourgeois, the critical theory nonsense these charlatans pushed was irresistible to a generation of young Elitists whose parents' achievements—lifting the world from poverty and ignorance, defeating Nazism—set a standard they could never hope to match. So they embraced a doctrine that excused their meritlessness by providing a plausible-enough moral framework to allow them to justify their own essential worthlessness.

As a practical matter, the psychodrama of an Elite generation that deep down understood it was not actually elite in any mean-ingful sense led to our present predicament, a situation where our Elite has nothing but contempt for those they presume to rule.

Of course, the Elite never saw Trump coming. By the time he rode down that escalator with his Slovenian supermodel wife and started his campaign off by saying exactly what most Americans outside the big, blue cities were thinking about illegal immigrants, the Elite had grown distant from Normals not merely in terms of geography but culturally.

When the Elite traveled, it was to the opposite coast or to Western Europe, where they found people much like themselves, people not limited by some primitive attachment to the idea of nationalism. Instead, they felt more akin to the transnational Elite. They would be citizens of the world, not just their own parochial country. Traditional citizenship? That didn't matter anymore—in fact, it was an obstacle to progress. It complicated the migration that would allow the Elite to import a much more complacent and obedient electorate from the Third World, which was wonderful and beautiful and not at all a bunch of shitholes. Yet it would be a moral outrage to send any aliens back to them.

The Elite was loyal only to itself.

Still, some Normals welcomed their new hipster overlords. The Normals are a diverse lot. But most Normals just got royally pissed off.

The unspoken bargain between the Normals and the Elite was always that if the Elite kept things running smoothly they could have their power and prestige. No Normal ever expected the Elite not to take a little off the top for itself, to do some skimming like a mob boss running a Vegas casino.

But it was a deal the Elite seemed to forget it had made, maybe because it was their dads who made it over previous generations. By 2016, the Elite stopped bothering to even pretend to perform its part of the bargain. It did not even recognize that there was a deal anymore.

Hillary was to be crowned not because of what she could do for the people, but because the people owed it to her.

The Elite became convinced that it ruled not at the sufferance of the Normals and for the masses' benefit, but because of its own righteousness and merit. It ruled by divine right, though of course all that stuff about God was hick bait for the Jesus freaks in Deliveranceland.

And the Elite convinced itself that its own merit derived not from actually doing anything meritorious, but from simply being who they were. They had merit because they were the Elite, not vice versa, and the Elite was open to anyone who chose to harken to its dogma.

So, basically, anyone could be Elite by calling himself, or herself, or xirself, "Elite" and believing in the things the Elite believed in—which mostly boiled down to believing that the Elite was elite and entitled to rule without accountability.

The Normals never signed on to that.

Normals were faced with a bunch of insufferable snobs who thought the rules did not apply to them—though the rules sure as hell applied to the Normals—and who were not constrained by any limitations other than their own desires. And the Normals? When they were a consideration at all, the fact that something made life harder for Normals was a selling point.

Let's take away a lane Normals commute on to work and make

it a bike lane that one guy an hour will use while the suckers sit idling on gridlocked streets.

Wait, the Elite did that in Los Angeles recently, without bothering to ask the Normal victims of its altruism. " 'Change is hard, and people's first reaction to change is the most negative,' said Seleta Reynolds, the Transportation Department's general manager. It helps, she says, if the public is involved in the process.... That was not the case for Vista del Mar, one of the few major streets that bypasses Los Angeles International Airport and connects the South Bay and the Westside. Last month, with little warning, the city narrowed the beachfront street to one lane in each direction in an effort to reduce liability for fatal traffic collisions."[3] Los Angeles backtracked hard when the Normals got up and drew the line.

Let's import a bunch of foreigners to work under the table for half pay.

Who needs Americans? "If we lose the workers who are here illegally, it's hard to see how they'll be replaced, because Americans are reluctant to take these jobs, particularly the ones harvesting crops." So observed a *Washington Post* columnist on March 17, 2017, in an article that does not explore the option of paying Normal Americans a decent wage to do this work.[4] It does, however, recommend paying foreigners more, presumably to obtain the worst of both worlds by creating a more expensive labor force to replace Americans.

Let's make a bunch of movies about how America's soldiers are either psycho killers or guilt-ridden basket cases, and then cry like preteen girls when a rare movie depicts American warriors—Normals, of course—as the badass killers they typically are.

In a *Scientific American* (!) article from February 2, 2015, titled "What War Propaganda Like 'American Sniper' Reveals about Us,"[5] one John Horgan speaks for much of the Elite when he announced that a "real-life 'hero,' Navy SEAL Chris Kyle, was a child killer." It's always good to obtain clarity, and Horgan's disgusting slander of a man whose combat boots he is unfit to lick offers a crystal-clear insight into what a big chunk of the Elite really thinks.

Now, let's shove all of this garbage in the Normals' faces and laugh at how they have to just sit there and take it.

Except the Elite didn't really know Americans very well.

Americans are not a "sit there and take it" kind of people. Hell, even the French eventually stood up for themselves. It should have been no surprise that the American Normals would, and did.

The Elite took Trump as a calculated insult by the people they thought they ruled, and it was hard to imagine any other reasonable conclusion. Trump was a giant walking, talking middle finger to the Elite. And the Elite did everything it could to ensure that the Normals understood that voting for him would create great disappointment among the ruling class. They were a face, aching for a pie.

But why Trump?

He certainly did not embody the values of the Normals, at least on the surface. He was thrice married, with multiple dalliances in between and during them. He lived in a gold-trimmed palace and flew around in his own jet and stuck his name on everything he built.

Maybe that was it—he *built*. He did *something*, something you could see and touch. He built. The Normals built, too, maybe not skyscrapers and casinos, but they sometimes built buildings and sometimes built cars and sometimes they built businesses. Trump, like them, was about the real world even if his personal life seemed more like a fantasy.

In Trump's world, like in the world of the Normals, what you *did* mattered. He was a bottom-line guy for bottom-line people. His talk of winning resonated—you either won, or you lost, and there was no room for participation trophies in the cutthroat real estate jungle of New York just like there were no participation trophies in the real world the Normals called home.

What did you build if you were a journalist? A reputation? What, among other Elites? What did journalists risk? Sure, Dan Rather had some hard times back in 2004 when he decided to run with that manifestly bogus National Guard letter about George W. Bush. He lost his job at CBS—you could almost see them grimace as they cut him loose—but he should not have worried. The Elite came back with a plan to resurrect him. It started with a terrible movie about his unstoppable quest for truth—called *Truth* (2015), of course—that painted him as the victim of a terrifying conspiracy determined to cruelly hold him accountable for taking a giant dump on what was left of the concept of journalistic ethics. And recently, Rather has been running around networks like MSNBC as some sort of journalist emeritus.

Pathetic.

But did Dan Rather ever actually *do* anything? No, he functioned in an environment of theory and shadows, striking the right poses, mouthing the right clichés, and trying to crucify the right enemy. He endured and prospered until he got caught.

And then he endured afterward. Stephanie Ruhle even dragged his wizened countenance on to her MSNBC show to—seriously—opine on journalistic standards with a focus on Fox News.[6] Perhaps for her next guest, she could get some insights into fighting sexism from Clinton friend and noted Democrat donor Harvey Weinstein.

But what happens to Normals who screw up? They face real consequences long before they experience a Rather-level foul-up. And they don't get the entire ruling class to tacitly agree never to bring it up again.

How about an assistant adjunct professor at some law school who pens a tome titled something like *Transgender Issues in Uniform Commercial Code Article 9 Jurisprudence*? Is there any chance, even the slightest possibility, that someone is going to come to him and say, "You know, you contribute nothing to what we are doing here, and you need to go away."

There's *no* chance. It will never happen. Instead he, or she, or whatever pronoun it chooses will have a soft, comfy gig forever.

Trump was about achievement. That's where the whole "winning" meme came from. He did not just fight—and it was great to see him fight—but he competed. He got in the arena and battled and came out on top with an Eastern European hottie and a ton of dough. Even his alleged pre-presidential dalliances demonstrated dominance. How many men were really surprised—or all that concerned—that Trump used to score with Playboy Playmates?

Normals competed, too. They fought hard for what they had. Sure, so did some of the Elite, but decades of watching halfsteppers who never did a damn thing presume to pronounce their judgments upon the lesser mortals out in Normalland left the Normals receptive to a guy who loved to compete and loved to win.

Americans love a winner, General George Patton told his men

in his famous speech to the Third Army that George C. Scott recreated for the 1970 film *Patton*.[7]

> Men, all this stuff you hear about America not wanting to fight, wanting to stay out of the war, is a lot of bullshit. Americans love to fight. All real Americans love the sting and clash of battle. When you were kids, you all admired the champion marble shooter, the fastest runner, the big-league ball players and the toughest boxers. Americans love a winner and will not tolerate a loser. Americans play to win all the time. That's why Americans have never lost and will never lose a war. The very thought of losing is hateful to Americans. Battle is the most significant competition in which a man can indulge. It brings out all that is best, and it removes all that is base.

No, Normal Americans will not tolerate a loser. Truer words were never spoken.

And Trump was a winner going in. And he kept winning even as he refused to compromise. The Elite swarmed like wasps, but they could barely lay a stinger on him. He just kept going, saying things millions of Americans thought but had been taught they were not allowed to say.

He called illegal aliens "illegal aliens" and pointed out that some of them were dirtbags.

You can't say that!

He said guns were cool and that the reason the Constitution talked about them was so that the citizens could resist tyranny.

You can't say that!

He called Hillary corrupt and incompetent, and the whole Elite swamp, too.

You sure as hell can't say that!

But Trump did. And people responded to the one guy who would say what they thought.

They called it the Trump Train, and it's a solid analogy. It just kept chugging along down the track toward its destination. The whole time, the entire Elite sought to derail it. But at every stop, more and more folks hopped aboard.

Especially men. It didn't help that Hillary gave off the vibe that she had a beef with manhood. Her cold, remote father probably started it, and it's reasonable to expect that Bill's shenanigans took a toll on her patience for the unfair sex. But now she was wearing the pantsuit in the Clinton family. Poor Bill had been shuttled off to the gimp box to wait out the election and her inevitable victory.

She was womyn, hear her bore.

It must grate on her to know that if she had actually listened to Bill, who knew Normals and at least was able to fake an affinity for them, she might not be stumbling through the woods of Chappaqua today half-hammered on seven-dollar Trader Joe's Chardonnay.

Men were Trump's secret. He was manly in a way few men in the public eye had been in a long time. If you looked at him on the stage with the 378 other Republicans, he was the only one who really looked like he would get in your face. Well, Chris Christie might, particularly if you had doughnuts.

Who else up there was going to fight? Ted Cruz would, but like a gentleman, with arguments and reason, and of course neither of those applied against the Elite. It's hard to leverage arguments and reason against people who accept an unshakeable liberal dogma on faith.

Trump was alpha, and he did not apologize for it. He embraced it, reveled in it, and promised men that with him in the White House, America was going to be alpha again, too.

The thing is, Normals identify with America. It is part of their identity in a way it can't be to some Davos-loving Elitist goof who considers himself a "citizen of the world." So when he promised to Make America Great Again, what he was promising the Normals was to make *them* great again.

Hillary was promising four to eight years of nagging and hectoring, culminating with her confiscating their guns and their testicles.

Trump promised strength and prosperity. Hillary promised more weakness and more decline.

Not a super-tough choice.

It would be silly to say that every Normal loved Trump, that they all sat in awe of him, that he completed them like some sort of orangey Jerry Maguire.

They didn't.

Many of them actively disliked him. After all, superficially much of what he did and said clashed with the values the Normals celebrated. Faith? He talked about it more and more as the race continued, but he was no born-again holy roller. In some ways, he was closer to an unholy roller. Yet many evangelicals harkened to his call. Why?

Simple. Trump didn't hate them.

The Democrats would sober up Hillary long enough to trot

her out in front of some black church congregation and, in her best What I Imagine Deeply Religious Black Churchwomen Talk Like voice, she would announce, "I don't feel no ways tired."

But you always knew that, once she was done, she would be riding off in the back of her limo on the way to the airport, nursing a Smirnoff and laughing at the marks she had just left cheering in her wake.

Evangelicals knew what she thought of them, even if she would prattle on about her Methodist upbringing. Of course, like most mainline denominations, by 2016 the Methodists had turned so liberal it was doubtful they even had Jesus anymore.

And the working class? Trump at least seemed to know they existed. Who else went out to factories, to farms, to the third- and fourth-tier towns and packed arenas full of people who the Elite would prefer not to know existed—at least until their co-op ran out of arugula and cilantro and they wondered why the bins had not been magically refilled.

The Democrats, the party of the Elite, its vehicle, had abandoned them, and it had done it consciously. The old Democrats were the Party of the Working Man. The new Democrats were the Party of the Soft Hands and the Unworking. White collar? Welcome to the Dems. Lazy? Hey, vote Dem and you'll get your scraps. Outraged that people in Kansas are living the way they see fit? Join the Donkeys.

A guy who turned wrenches had no place in the modern Democrat Party. The wrench part made the Elites uncomfortable, and the turning it made the shiftless welfare cheats uncomfortable.

Another piece of the puzzle were the working minorities. These were Normals, people who loved their families and worked hard and for some insane reason kept buying the bottled bullshit the Elite was selling. There was a huge pull of tradition and habit toward the Democrats, but also a rising sense that those snobs always talked a good game when they needed votes, but little ever changed. According to NBC News, reporting on November 9, 2016, in 2012, Mitt Romney, a guy so white rice once sued him for copyright infringement, got 27 percent of the Hispanic vote. Trump got 29 percent. Trump also received 33.3 percent more of the black vote than Mitt did, but that meant he got 8 percent to Romney's 6 percent.[8]

With the media going 24/7 about how Trump was going to deport everyone who ever met a Latino and how he was going to restart the Klan, too, because of course he was, it was no shock. Still, Trump improved on the numbers. At least there the Democrats could breathe a sigh of relief. They had to go all in on minorities—if the non-Anglo population ever went for any Republican in any significant numbers, it was curtains for the Democrats. There just were not enough Elites out there to win the Electoral College—which suddenly became retroactively racist in 2016—and they needed their minority allies to be competitive since they had driven off the working whites. The Elite felt good and woke doing so, but their wokeness meant they woke up to President Trump on November 9, 2016.

Why Trump?

Why not?

What choice was there?

That shrill harridan who hated everything the Normals stood for, who trashed them as "deplorable" when she wasn't falling over?

Trump made it possible for the Normals to vote for him, but it was Hillary Clinton who made it *necessary* for them to vote for him.

They say luck is opportunity meeting preparation. Hillary

and the decades of misbehavior of her Elite pals provided him the opportunity, and after decades in the public eye he was prepared.

Sure, Trump got lucky. But Hillary Clinton did not get unlucky. She just sucked, and everyone knew it.

But Trump? He would fight for them. And they knew it.

So they elected him.

So what next?

CHAPTER THIRTEEN

The Endgame

If you walk down some streets in some outlying villages in Kosovo—and many Normal Americans have—you can still see ruins even two decades after the civil war. The background of the war goes back hundreds of years, and in the way of the Balkans you can find yourself listening to the locals talk about some terrible crime committed by their neighbors and realize that terrible crime occurred over five hundred years ago. But there is a lesson to be found among those piles of brick and plaster. It's a lesson about what happens when people decide to toss out the rule of law, albeit an imperfect and shaky one, because all that process and all those pesky rights get in the way of their objective, and instead install the rule of power.

The Serbs decided they were not going to be bound by laws and concerns for the rights of the Kosovar Albanians, so they resolved to use their power to drive the K-Albs out of the country. That did not go quite the way the Serbs expected, in large part due to NATO airstrikes, and the Kosovar Albanians ended up taking vengeance upon their tormentors in that way that karma seems to have of turning the tables and then hitting the wrong-doers over the head with one of the chairs. It was the Serbs who ended up being ethnically cleansed once the K-Albs jumped into the driver's seat; many of those ruins are of Serb villages.

There's a lesson there. If you change the rules, just be sure you're good to go with playing by the new rules. Because you may hate the new rules.

Which brings us to the United States of America as the Elite ramps up its campaign to exclude the Normals from power in the wake of their cri de coeur. The Elite, largely because its new progressive ideology taught it to hate the very people it was created to serve, has abandoned the pretense of sympathy for those it leads. The Elite no longer subscribes to the basic principle that those who govern do so only through the consent of the governed. It does not believe that Normals have any right to govern themselves. In fact, it thinks that Normals must not be allowed to do so. And the new rules it is playing by say that the Elite can do whatever it wants to do in pursuit of that goal.

Except this presents a problem, because the Normals internalized all that stuff they were taught in their public schools about citizens having a say in how the country is run. This is especially true among those who actually put on camouflage to go defend the country; they get a little touchy about being told to sit down and shut up.

But that's what the Elite wants them to do—well, not the "sit down" part. You can't work sitting down. The Elite wants—needs—the Normals to keep growing their summer squash and driving it to their Brooklyn co-ops, and pumping their oil to fuel their Priuses (despite the whole Gaia/global warming apocalypse unpleasantness). The Elite wants the Normals to keep doing the dirty work. It just wants them to close their Budweiser holes and do what they are told.

Sure, the Normals can vote. Absolutely they can vote. Voting is a vitally important right of every American, as long as he votes right. They can vote for either of the two approved Elite candidates that the Elite presents them with.

Policy debates, such as they are, are properly conducted between factions of the Elite community. Normals? Butt out, hayseeds.

But the Normals did not get the message. The Normals are militant, thanks to technology stripping the Elite of the ability to completely control the public conversation, a track record of Elite failure, and an Elite that has grown progressively worse at hiding its members' manifest active hatred for Normal Americans.

So, in 2016, after a few pokes at the Elite, they elected Donald Trump, and there are many who see him as the Normals' last chance. If he fails, the Normals fail, forever. But that's not true.

Donald Trump is the Elite's last chance.

It was they who made Donald Trump their hill to die on, an uncomfortable metaphor in light of the trend lines. When you hate someone, and they know it, they tend to hate you back. The Elite's hatred of the Normals has been matched by hatred of the Normals for the Elite.

It's bad when the two main elements of society start hating each other. Really bad.

And it is not just the center-right wing of the Normals, the traditional smaller-town Main Street types, that is pushing back on the Elite. Many left-of-center Normals, who suffered the same economic neglect and contempt as the rest of their caste, tried to be heard by pushing Bernie Sanders. Many of these were real workers (not baristas and other aspiring Elitists) who never saw themselves on the cutting edge of a movement. Though misguided, they just wanted the economy to stop being rigged in favor of the big boys.

But the progressive Elite stole the nomination from Bernie and handed it to the candidate they chose, the candidate of the big boys. Sure, Bernie Sanders is a dictator-fondling fool who embraces an ideology that butchered tens of millions, and his biggest ideological fans (mostly Elite) are morons who think that socialism is totally due for a win since it's failed every single time it's ever been tried. But the Normals who supported Bernie adorably thought that the Elites running the Democrat Party would play by the alleged rules, and that if the people chose him, he would win.

As socialists they are, by definition, suckers, but this was ridiculous.

The fact is that the Elite has systematically stripped away the pretense that it is bound by any rules. Elitist Hillary Clinton skates on her email beef when any Normal would be dodging unwanted attention on the cellblock. Elite media abandons objectivity but demands the respect that comes from objectivity. Elite Wall Street scamsters lose billions and get bailed out, but don't you dare miss a payment on your Jeep Wrangler.

You get the picture. So do the Normals. And they don't like it.

After all, rules that only govern one group of people are not rules at all. They are weapons, tools of control. And the Normals are sick of being controlled.

Tick. Tick. Tick.

The endgame is perilous. History tells us that violence and chaos are not off the table. Rome was a republic once, too, and there once again factions chafed at the obstacles the law and the norms put between them and power. Tradition, the *mos maiorum*, gave way to expedience. And relative peace and order gave way to violence and chaos.

The guys who were not Augustus sure hated the new rules.

At stake here and now is the kind of country the United States will be down the road. Up ahead is a stark choice, two diverging paths.

Will America return to being the kind of representative democracy the Founders envisioned, where the ultimate power rests in the people?

Or will America continue to evolve into an Elite oligarchy that not only oversees the day-to-day operations of the major institutions of American government and society, but that determines the ultimate direction of the nation, all while remaining immune from any accountability to the people it rules?

In many ways, the answer is tied to the fate of Donald Trump, less because he is a leader of the movement to restore power to the Normals than because he is a symbol of it. He has performed much, much better than almost anyone expected as president, but if the Elite can use their rigged system to defeat him, either by tanking his presidency politically or by literally hauling him out of the Oval Office in cuffs, then they believe they will have defeated the Normals. Things can go back to how they were, with the Elite divvying up power and spoils among itself, free of the hassle of answering to farmers in Nebraska and insurance claims adjusters in Georgia.

But that might not be how it goes at all. In fact, the odds are against it. No society has ever purged itself of Normals; the Normals will always be out there, and the Elite will never be able to totally ignore them. The danger is that the Elite, serenely confident of its own invulnerability, will provoke the Normals and spark a conflagration that it cannot control.

Trump might well be the last chance to get out of this mess with the country intact, for the Elite to take a collective personal inventory and start exercising some if its vaunted smarts, and start paying attention to some of the dangers that loom ahead.

If they defeat Trump, how on Earth can they know that whoever the Normals get behind next won't be worse? Not just worse in their fever dreams, but *actually* worse? They call Trump a crook and a dictator and all the rest, but they forget that Trump's own flaws were overlooked by the voters in no small part because the Elite's minions gleefully howled about how George Bush was in on 9/11 and Mitt Romney gave a chick cancer.

The crying wolf thing?

It's a thing.

The Elite could pause to think through the next few years. Trump had, contrary to the expectations of most of the Elite, shepherded through a divided, unpopular Congress a radical (and radically pro-Normal) tax reform bill that immediately started putting money in the wallets of Normal Americans. Notably, it was also probably the first true legislative counterattack against traditionally Elite groups in decades—if you were, say, a lawyer in an expensive coastal blue state, you got schlonged.

The markets were bumpy but also trending up, with unemployment down and consumer confidence growing. ISIS was on the skids because Trump unleashed Secretary Mattis and the military and we stopped playing footsie with these goat-banging seventh-century creeps. Trump's numbers were rising from the murky depths of Gallup and Quinnipiac like some swamp creature bent on taking vengeance upon the fellow swamp dwellers of the Elite.

That would have been a good time to pause and think things through. A rational response on the part of the Elite, because they like logic and profanely love science and so they embrace rationality, might be to look at the facts. The Normals were mad. And, to be fair, they did have some legit beefs. Wars, economic stagnation, illegals. Maybe there was something to that, and as the Elite maybe, just maybe, the response was...suboptimal. But there is a huge—yuge!—appetite out there for a return to normalcy, for a return to calm, to peace, and to prosperity. In some ways, they might assess, Trump is prevailing by doing that.

Maybe we in the Elite could kind of get behind that. Not roll over for him by any means, but instead of making everything no-quarter warfare, cooperate a little. Lower the temperature. Deemphasize the Trump/Russia thing—certainly stop pushing in the whole pot hoping that Robby Mueller's holding a royal flush.

Lull the Normals back to their ideal state—unconscious. Unwoke.

But the Elite will not do that. It cannot do that. It's not just a matter of power and prestige anymore, the traditional motivations behind the Elite. The Elite has gone beyond being a class and has morphed into a cult. It is not just a material choice but a moral one. In the absence of God, they have to worship something, and what they worship is themselves and their own Elite moral vision.

The Elite cannot back down because to do so clashes with the very identity they adopted when they became Elite. They rule because they have a right to rule; the Normals do not rule because they are unworthy of it. Embrace that notion and you are Elite. And you are unable to compromise.

The Elite cannot change its path and cede power back to the Normals because to do so destroys what makes itself the Elite.

So they will continue to #resist. They will continue to fight the devolution of power back to those who rightfully should have it at every step, at every turn. They will fight in the urban community gardens, they will fight in the faculty lounges, they will fight on the Sony Pictures studio lot, they will fight in courts of appeal and in the halls of Congress.

They shall never surrender.

Life is not worth living if they do, because they will no longer be Elite.

So, basically, someone has to lose. The Normals or the Elite.

With the Elite #resisting, the Normals cannot go back to sleep. They cannot simply turn away from politics and go back to their lives, though they would prefer to. This will only make them more militant, because the definition of a Normal is someone who wants to focus on other things besides running the institutions and worrying about whether some teen boy who is pretending to be a girl gets to pee with the ladies in the Billings Montana Unified School District.

And normalcy holds another hazard for the Elite. Its own supporters and activists will become less supportive and active if the vibe of permanent crisis fades.

As long as the Republicans hold the Congress, the political battle will be a rearguard action by Democrats against any legislation that undoes even a thread of the massive web of Elite self-dealing that is the American government today. That is not to say that many of the Republicans in Congress are not Elite, or that they do not sympathize with many of their class's prerogatives. It is just that the Republican voter base is so thoroughly Normal and so thoroughly vindictive to apostates that, with the exception of smarmy posers like Jeff "18 Percent" Flake and Ben "Oh, Well I Never!" Sasse, they will be compelled to go along with Trump's pro-Normal agenda.

No matter what Robert Mueller says or does, the Elite will seethe and demand impeachment, if not burning at the stake. Of course, a couple years of hysterical accusations of "TREASON!" by hyper-partisan liars will not exactly build confidence in the truth of the findings. In the end, impeachment is a political act—you have to get the votes in the House and then in the Senate. And the rules have changed from back when it was Republicans who sealed Nixon's fate. The new rules, enacted during the reign of Clinton I, say that impeachment attempts are partisan maneuvers that have nothing to do with the merits of the charges, even if DNA testing confirms their accuracy.

Bottom line: Good luck with impeachment.

The liberal Elite is going to hate the new rules.

They will fight in the courts, both by blocking Trump's appointments and by mobilizing their own judicial partisans to help. The whole thing about not having to obey the established rules comes in really handy in a judicial setting—when you get rid of that archaic business of relying on precedent and the written text, you are free to follow your heart. And every judge who followed his heart ended up following it as it made a hard left turn.

Until now. Trump is going to appoint up to a third of the federal judiciary before he leaves office. Those darn new rules sure are a pain.

State governments on the coasts will keep firing on Fort Sumter. California recently announced its intention to arrest and prosecute people who cooperate with the federal government's immigration laws, though its jails—which it emptied of real criminals because of compassion and stuff—will soon be filled with waiters busted for handing out unsolicited straws. Sanctuary cities abound. Democrats apparently think that this time they will get secession right.

The media will keep the faux-urgency of #TheResistance alive, because the 24/7 "THIS IS THE WORST THING TRUMP HAS EVER DONE EVER!" mode helps eliminate the possibility of a return to normalcy, and therefore the possibility that the enthusiasm of the Elite's foot soldiers might fade.

The Fredocons and the bowtie boys often fret that Trump provokes this himself, and he occasionally does to great and frequently hilarious effect, but it is ridiculous to accuse him of being solely responsible. Trump was accused of having a White House in crisis, so he moved in John Kelly, and when that chaos stopped, the press simply shifted narrative. When the president tweets, the tweets are the outrage. When he doesn't tweet, something else is the outrage.

CNN will trash Trump for doing nothing if he does nothing, and for doing something if he does something. It does not matter. It will continue, because when you stick a moustache on a guy and call him Hitler, you pretty much have to go all in against him.

The entertainment industry will keep up its political theater/ festivals of Elite onanism with events like the 2018 Grammy Awards, where Gramma Clinton staggered out to read selections of Michael Wolff's silly book to an audience that was down 24 percent from the prior year. Hollywood will churn out more television shows and movies about courageous heroes fighting the threat of a guy who has never arrested anyone for opposing him.

The bureaucracy, even as it undergoes a slow-motion purge through the machinations of time, will keep trying to do what it wants, which means what the liberal wing of the Elite wants, and it will continue to be mortified at the thought that it is answerable to anyone but itself.

Will Trump win this war, meaning "Will the Normals win this war?"

It is too early to tell how Trump will do, though the signs are in his favor—something that could change overnight. Fate will play a part. If that fat weirdo in Pyongyang decides to start a war, that could change the picture completely. If there is an earthquake in Los Angeles and people believe the media when it tries to pin the blame for California's incompetent response on Washington. That could change things, too.

If Trump loses one or both houses of Congress, that becomes a problem. If he does what to date he has not done and betrays the Normals who elected him, that would become a problem, too. But then, betting on the Normals won him a presidency that everyone—certainly everyone in the Elite—told him was unwinnable. At this juncture, you have to see Trump as the favorite for 2020, especially with the kind of panel of nobodies yearning to take him on.

- Kamala Harris? A California lawyer who loves illegal aliens and got her start as the gal pal of a famous Sacramento politician?
- Joaquín and/or Julián Castro of Texas? Two guys who are always the next Great Dem Hope, but who never end up as anything more than Lone Star Martin O'Malleys? And what is it with Democrats choosing candidates with dictators' names?
- Elizabeth Warren? An elderly Harvard Law professor who gamed the affirmative action system by pretending she was a squaw?
- Joe Biden? Really?

These are perfect avatars of the Elite. Except for the Wonder Twins, they come from blue states and adhere rigorously to all the tenets and doctrines of their religion, Elitism. At least Biden can fake it with Normals. If he found himself among a bunch of firemen, you can just hear him begging them to let him sit in the ladder truck's driver's seat with the Dalmatian.

But the rest? Harris wouldn't be caught dead outside a ZIP code where the mean income was under six figures, the Castro Brothers can't even win a statewide office in Texas, and Warren lecturing steelworkers in Michigan about their white privilege would simply be awesome.

The danger, the real and scary danger, is if the Elite starts winning. They will not only ignore the problems that made the Normals militant in the first place, but they will focus on both ensuring that the Normals never again have the ability to interfere in the Elite's affairs while punishing the Normals for their insolence. They will clamp down even as they ensure there is no way for the pressure to vent.

Think of what they would do, if they could—and remember that the rules will not constrain them. The filibuster that is holding up Trump's agenda? That is gone—the liberal Elite is not going to pass up a way to impose its will merely because it has fifty-two senators and some old tradition is in the way. The courts? Look for a succession of leftist loons unconstrained by what they think are old pieces of paper written by dead white guys like a hundred years ago or something.

And we have already seen the unparalleled corruption of the Department of Justice and Federal Bureau of Investigation under Obama. That corruption would get surpassed big time.

After all, if it is okay to fake warrants to spy on Republican campaigns, and A-OK to use the IRS to harass conservative groups, what is the moral argument to stop the Elite from doing much worse to its enemies once it gets back into power? There is none, because the Elite does not consider it wrong to use all its power—or rather, all the power that Normal America lent it to do the job of running the institutions—for its own benefit. And the fact that Normals are evil makes it an affirmative duty.

They will push and push and push.

Taxes? Normals will be paying more, because Normals are merely livestock for the Elite.

Speech? What the government does not ban outright—get ready for a leftist Supreme Court to discover a footnote to the First Amendment containing a "hate speech" exception—Elite companies like Google and Facebook will eagerly censor. Say good-bye to the alternative media and to a free-wheeling social media. Welcome back the gatekeepers, and this time they are making sure the walls stay good and high.

Fossil fuels? Enjoy the bus.

Political correctness? Forget the ideas of colorblindness, gender blindness, and so forth. Get used to being ranked somewhere on the hierarchy of oppression, and if you are Normal accept the idea that you are going to be at the bottom.

Religion? Fine, if you never speak of it or act on it and if the Elite doesn't get around to hassling you about it just for the fun of teaching you your place.

Your guns? Oh, well, that's a twofer. It both insults Normals by demonstrating that they are serfs, not citizens, and eliminates their ultimate veto over tyranny.

To Normals this sounds like a nightmare, but to the Elite this is a to-do list.

Yet there is a complication. And it's one a group of people who have largely never been in a fistfight might not have fully thought through.

Normal Americans do not like being hassled. They get annoyed. They get angry. And they fight back.

The Elite forgets itself, and how it relies on the Normals' sense that obeying the law is the right thing to do. Laws are not enforced by cops waiting to pounce, but by citizens who instinctively obey the law. Watch a stop sign in your neighborhood at three in the morning, when no one is out. Almost everyone stops. Why? Because that's the rule.

But when do the rules lose legitimacy? When the other side is not playing by the rules.

The Constitution contains rules. It contains promises. And the

Elite ignores them at its peril. You unilaterally change the rules about speech, religion, and guns, and you are likely to find the Normals changing the rules about your authority to do anything.

At the end of the day, power is an AR-15 held by a guy willing to die to accomplish his mission. Normals will die for their freedom—military cemeteries are full of Normals who did. But who is willing to die to accomplish the mission of suppressing the Normals for the benefit of the Elite? Are Kaden and his pals going to suit up in Kevlar and start showing those hicks who's boss? Are other Normals going to collaborate?

Nope.

From their coastal vantage points, the Elite has grown accustomed to its authority being respected and its direction taken without question. But what happens when it is not? That is the new rule, isn't it? Elites in California and elsewhere, with their sanctuary declarations, have chosen to defy elected officials holding the positions of power in Washington over policies they dislike. What's to keep the governor of Texas from doing the same when President Elizabeth Warren announces her "commonsense" gun confiscation executive order?

They are really going to hate the new rules. The guys who changed the rules in Kosovo did, too.

How this will be resolved remains unclear, but there is hope for optimism. The Normals outnumber the Elite, and they are voting. But at the end of the day, the Normals have a lot more guns. So, basically, the Normals only lose if the Normals choose to lose.

What is clear is that this cannot go on forever. America cannot survive with an Elite that hates its own people, especially when that hate drives the Elite to wage a cultural war against them.

One side has to win; the other side has to change. Either the

Elite has to morph back into a caste that shares and respects the basic values of those it leads, or the Normals must opt to accept permanent serfdom under the stiletto heel of people who despise them.

If you have ever hung around Normal Americans—and many of the Elite never have—you probably know which one of these options is simply not going to happen.

Normal Americans built this country, powered this country, and defended this country.

They are not about to give up their stake in it without a fight.

We won't give up our country without a fight.

We owe it to that guy from Fontana.

Acknowledgments

It is only fair to share the credit, or the blame, for this book. There are many folks who helped me in some way, whether they know it or not. I'll try to name as many as I can, but please forgive the oversight if I miss someone, which I undoubtedly will.

First, there is hot wife Irina Moises. When I am working, she's working, too. She reads all my work, provides the first and harshest criticism, and deals with me being largely absent (at least mentally) when I am embroiled in the writing. She's the best. Thanks!

Thanks also to my agent, Keith Urbahn, who shepherded this tome through the process. When we first talked, he had to be thinking, *Who the hell is this lunatic?* I'm pretty sure he still wonders about that, and for good reason.

I got plenty of support from my friends Larry O'Connor, Cam Edwards, Cameron Gray, John Cardillo, Tony Katz, Jim Geraghty, David Limbaugh, Arthur Schwartz, Hugh Hewitt, Derek Hunter, Drew Matich, Stephen Kruiser, Robert O'Brien, Owen Brennan, Glenn Reynolds, Salena Zito, Ace, and Kenny Calhoun. They all provided some great suggestions, by which I mean I often borrowed ideas and concepts from them. Shamelessly. Some of them will be all, "What? You were writing a book? When did I suggest something?" Well, you did. Shut up and take the compliment. Sheesh.

Michael Walsh deserves a shout-out for constantly harassing me about my writing, as well as sharing his long experience in the publishing world.

Matthew Betley, who has a number of novels of his own you should check out, shared his Marine Corps wisdom.

I want to give a special thanks to Chris Buskirk. For a while, I have used the term "Conservative, Inc.," to refer to the network of intertwined and often self-dealing think tanks, fundraisers, and publications that did a lot of collecting money in the name of conservatism, but not much conserving, during the pre-Trump era. I intended to use it here. And when researching this book—yeah, I did some research—I discovered that Chris had used a similar term in the title of his book *American Greatness: How Conservatism Inc. Missed the 2016 Election and What the D.C. Establishment Needs to Learn* (Washington, DC: WND Books, 2017). Awkward! Well, I got in touch with Chris, and I told him I had independently coined a similar term, but I would not use it if he wished because he used his first. He graciously told me he had no problem with me using mine. Thanks, man.

I also appreciate the support of the folks at *Townhall.com*, where I have written for the last few years. They are all terrific.

Finally, there's one more guy I need to acknowledge. I always thank Andrew Breitbart whenever I write a book, because I would not be doing this if he hadn't forced me back into conservative writing against my will. I expect he is looking down, smiling and, since it is heaven, drinking a beer.

And, of course, I want to thank all of my Twitter followers for all their #caring!

Notes

One. The Sleeping Giant Awakens

1. "Invasion" (advertisement), January 5, 2016, https://www.youtube.com/watch?v=q-SC1uUiT9s.

Two. Who Are the Normals?

1. "Election 2016: District of Columbia Results," *New York Times*, August 1, 2017, https://www.nytimes.com/elections/results/district-of-columbia.
2. "Election 2016: West Virginia Results," *New York Times*, August 1, 2017, https://www.nytimes.com/elections/results/west-virginia.

Four. A Meritocracy without Merit

1. Matthew Q. Clarida and Nicholas P. Fandos, "Substantiating Fears of Grade Inflation, Dean Says Median Grade at Harvard College Is A–, Most Common Grade Is A," *Harvard Crimson*, December 3, 2013 (updated May 26, 2017), http://www.thecrimson.com/article/2013/12/3/grade-inflation-mode-a.
2. Eric Levenson, "In R-Rated Anti-Trump Rant, Madonna Muses about 'Blowing up White House,'" *CNN Politics*, January 21, 2017, https://www.cnn.com/2017/01/21/politics/madonna-speech-march.

Six. The Expert Scam

1. Neil deGrasse Tyson (@NeilTyson), "To all on the Gregorian Calendar, Happy New Year! A day that's not astronomically significant...in any way...at all...whatsoever," Twitter, January 1, 2017, https://twitter.com/neiltyson/status/815646657194754048.
2. "These smug pilots have lost touch with regular passengers like us. Who thinks I should fly the plane?" *New Yorker*, December 27, 2016, https://www.newyorker.com/cartoon/a20630.

Seven. Institutionalized

1. "Americans' Confidence in Institutions Edges Up," Gallup News, June 26, 2017, http://news.gallup.com/poll/212840/americans-confidence-insti tutions-edges.aspx.
2. Spenser S. Hsu, "FBI Admits Flaws in Hair Analysis over Decades," *Washington Post*, April 18, 2017, https://www.washingtonpost.com/local/ crime/fbi-overstated-forensic-hair-matches-in-nearly-all-criminal-trials -for-decades/2015/04/18/39c8d8c6-e515-11e4-b510-962fcfabc310_story .html.

Eight. Looking Down Their Noses

1. Tim Hains, "Former CIA Official Phil Mudd Warns Trump: 'Think Again' about War with Intel Community, 'We're Going to Win,'" Real Clear Politics, February 4, 2018, https://www.realclearpolitics.com/ video/2018/02/04/phil_mudd_warns_trump_in_war_with_intelligence _community_were_going_to_win.html.

Nine. Pitchforks, Torches, and Conservative, Inc.

1. William F. Buckley, "Our Mission Statement," *National Review*, November 19, 1955, http://www.nationalreview.com/article/223549/our-mission -statement-william-f-buckley-jr.
2. Peter Robinson, "Milton Friedman, Ronald Reagan, and William F. Buckley Jr.," *Forbes*, December 12, 2008, https://www.forbes.com/2008/12/11/ friedman-reagan-buckley-oped-cx_pr_1212robinson.html.
3. David W. Moore, "Bush Job Approval Reflects Record 'Rally' Effect," Gallup News, September 18, 2001, http://news.gallup.com/poll/4912/bush -job-approval-reflects-record-rally-effect.aspx.
4. Chris Isidore, "Buffett Says He's Still Paying Lower Tax Rate than His Secretary," CNN Money, March 3, 2013, http://money.cnn.com/2013/03/04/ news/economy/buffett-secretary-taxes.
5. "Jamiel Shaw Sr: Illegal Who Killed Son Raised 'Like a Rabid Pitbull.'" Fox News Insider, June 29, 2017, http://insider.foxnews.com/2017/06/29/ immigration-illegal-crime-kates-law-congress-mexico-jamiel-shaw.

Ten. "But He Fights!"

1. Stephen A. Camarota, "Welfare Use by Legal and Illegal Immigrant Households: An Analysis of Medicaid, Cash, Food, and Housing Programs"

(report), Center for Immigration Studies, September 2015, https://cis.org/sites/default/files/camarota-welfare-illegals_1.pdf.

2. Michael Kelly, "Ted Kennedy on the Rocks," *GQ*, February 1990, https://www.gq.com/story/kennedy-ted-senator-profile.

Eleven. Never Trump and the Surrender Caucus

1. James Warren, "The Worst Take of the Week? David Brooks Slammed for 'Sandwich Shop' Elitism," *Vanity Fair*, July 12, 2017, https://www.vanityfair.com/news/2017/07/david-brooks-worst-take-of-the-week.

2. Meyer, Jeffrey. "David Brooks: Jeb Should Become the 'Laxative' Candidate," Newsbusters, November 1, 2015, https://www.newsbusters.org/blogs/nb/jeffrey-meyer/2015/11/01/david-brooks-jeb-should-become-laxative-candidate.

3. Liz Spayd, "Bret Stephens Takes on Climate Change. Readers Unleash Their Fury," *New York Times*, May 3, 2017, https://www.nytimes.com/2017/05/03/public-editor/bret-stephens-climate-change-liz-spayd-public-editor.html.

4. Bret Stephens, "Repeal the Second Amendment," *New York Times*, October 1, 2017, https://www.nytimes.com/2017/10/05/opinion/guns-second-amendment-nra.html.

5. George F. Will, "America's Bad Jeans," *Washington Post*, April 16, 2009, http://www.washingtonpost.com/wp-dyn/content/article/2009/04/15/AR2009041502861.html.

6. George F. Will, "Trump's Moore Endorsement Sunk the Presidency to Unplumbed Depths," *Washington Post*, December 13, 2017, https://www.washingtonpost.com/opinions/trumps-moore-endorsement-sunk-the-presidency-to-unplumbed-depths/2017/12/13/3c245482-e036-11e7-bbd0-9dfb2e37492a_story.html.

7. Robert Barnes, "Federalist Society, White House Cooperation on Judges Paying Benefits," *Washington Post*, November 18, 2017, https://www.washingtonpost.com/politics/courts_law/federalist-society-white-house-cooperation-on-judges-paying-benefits/2017/11/18/4b69b4da-cb20-11e7-8321-481fd63f174d_story.html.

8. David Frum (@DavidFrum), "US-UK intervention offered Iraq a better future. Whatever West's mistakes: sectarian war was a choice Iraqis made for themselves," Twitter, July 6, 2016, https://twitter.com/davidfrum/status/750649573245329408.

9. Jennifer Rubin, "They Came, They Marched, They Inspired," *Washington Post*, March 24, 2018, https://www.washingtonpost.com/blogs/right-turn/wp/2018/03/24/they-came-they-marched-they-inspired.

10. *The Love Boat*, ABC Television, 1977–1986.

11. Bill Kristol, "You've Come a Long Way, Baby: President Obama's Unapologetic, Freedom-Agenda-Embracing, Not-Shrinking-from-the-Use-of-Force Speech," *Weekly Standard*, March 28, 2011, http://www.weeklystandard.com/you-ve-come-long-way-baby/article/555622.

12. Bill Kristol (@BillKristol), "Obviously strongly prefer normal democratic and constitutional politics. But if it comes to it, prefer the deep state to the Trump state," Twitter, February 14, 2017, https://twitter.com/billkristol/status/831497364661747712.

13. Max Boot, "2017 Was the Year I Learned about My White Privilege," *Foreign Policy*, December 27, 2017, http://foreignpolicy.com/2017/12/27/2017-was-the-year-i-learned-about-my-white-privilege.

Twelve. Why You Got Trump

1. Aaron Blake, "Hillary Clinton Takes Her 'Deplorables' Argument for Another Spin," *Washington Post*, March 13, 2018, https://www.washingtonpost.com/news/the-fix/wp/2018/03/12/hillary-clinton-takes-her-deplorables-argument-for-another-spin.

2. Dinita Smith, "No Regrets for a Love of Explosives; In a Memoir of Sorts, a War Protester Talks of Life with the Weathermen," *New York Times*, September 11, 2001, https://www.nytimes.com/2001/09/11/books/no-regrets-for-love-explosives-memoir-sorts-war-protester-talks-life-with.html.

3. Laura J. Nelson, "Irate Commuters Threaten a Lawsuit over Narrowed Streets in Playa del Rey," *Los Angeles Times*, June 23, 2017, http://www.latimes.com/local/lanow/la-me-ln-bike-lane-backlash-20170623-story.html.

4. Tamar Haspel, "Illegal Immigrants Help Fuel U.S. Farms. Does Affordable Produce Depend on Them?" *Washington Post*, March 17, 2017, https://www.washingtonpost.com/lifestyle/food/in-an-immigration-crackdown-who-will-pick-our-produce/2017/03/17/cc1c6df4-0a5d-11e7-93dc-00f9bdd74ed1_story.html.

5. John Horgan, "What War Propaganda Like 'American Sniper' Reveals about Us," *Scientific American*, February 2, 2015, https://blogs.scientificamerican.com/cross-check/what-war-propaganda-like-8220-american-sniper-8221-reveals-about-us.

6. Curtis Houck, "MSNBC's Stephanie Ruhle Turns to Dan Rather to Attack Trump's 'Fake News Trophy' Tweet," Newsbusters, November 27, 2017, https://www.newsbusters.org/blogs/nb/curtis-houck/2017/11/27/msnbcs -stephanie-ruhle-turns-dan-rather-attack-trumps-fake-news.

7. F. J. Schaffner, director, *Patton*, 20th Century Fox, 1970.

8. Amanda Sakuma, "Trump Did Better with Blacks, Hispanics than Romney in '12: Exit Polls," *NBC News*, November 9, 2016, Retrieved at https:// www.nbcnews.com/storyline/2016-election-day/trump-did-better-blacks -hispanics-romney-12-exit-polls-n681386.

About the Author

KURT SCHLICHTER is the senior columnist at *Townhall.com*, where his column appears twice a week. He is also a Los Angeles trial lawyer admitted in California, Texas, and Washington, DC, and a retired Army Infantry colonel.

A Twitter activist (@KurtSchlichter) with over 150,000 followers, Kurt was personally recruited by Andrew Breitbart to write for the pre-Bannon-era Brietbart.com. His writings on political and cultural issues have been published in the *New York Post*, *IJ Review*, *The Federalist*, the *Washington Examiner*, the *Los Angeles Times*, the *Boston Globe*, the *Washington Times*, *Army Times*, the *San Francisco Examiner*, and elsewhere.

Kurt serves as an on-screen commentator and guest regarding political, military, and legal issues, and has appeared on Fox News, Fox Business News, CNN, NewsMax, One America Network, The Blaze, *The Hugh Hewitt Show*, *The Dr. Drew Show*, *The Larry Elder Show*, *The Tony Katz Show*, *The John Cardillo Show*, *The Dana Loesch Show*, *The Larry O'Connor Show*, and *The Derek Hunter Show*, among others. Kurt appears weekly on *Cam and Company* with Cam Edwards.

In 2014, his book *Conservative Insurgency: The Struggle to Take America Back 2013–2041* was published by Post Tree Press. His 2016 novel *People's Republic* and its 2017 prequel *Indian Country* reached numbers 1 and 2, respectively, on the Amazon Kindle "Political Thriller" bestseller list.

Kurt is a successful trial lawyer and name partner in a Los Angeles law firm representing companies and individuals in matters ranging from routine business cases to confidential Hollywood disputes and political controversies. A member of the Million Dollar Advocates Forum, which recognizes attorneys who have won trial verdicts in excess of $1 million, his litigation strategy and legal analysis articles have been published in legal publications such as the *Los Angeles Daily Journal* and *California Lawyer.*

He is frequently engaged by noted conservatives in need of legal representation, and he was counsel for political commentator and author Ben Shapiro in the successful defense of the widely publicized "Clock Boy" defamation lawsuit.

Kurt is a 1994 graduate of Loyola Law School, where he was a law review editor. He majored in communications and political science as an undergraduate at the University of California, San Diego, co-editing the conservative student paper *California Review* while also writing a regular column in the student humor paper *The Koala.*

Kurt served as a US Army infantry officer on active duty and in the California Army National Guard, retiring at the rank of full colonel. He wears the silver "jump wings" of a paratrooper and commanded the 1st Squadron, 18th Cavalry Regiment (Reconnaissance-Surveillance-Target Acquisition). A veteran of both the Persian Gulf War and Operation Enduring Freedom (Kosovo), he is a graduate of the Army's Combined Arms and Services Staff School, the Command and General Staff College, and the United States Army War College, where he received a master's degree in Strategic Studies.

He and his wife Irina live in the Los Angeles area with Bitey the Dog.